BABYLON

BABYLON

JAMES G. MACQUEEN

Line drawings by
Sandra Macqueen

FREDERICK A. PRAEGER, *Publishers*
NEW YORK · WASHINGTON

BOOKS THAT MATTER

Published in the United States of America in 1965
by Frederick A. Praeger, Inc., Publishers
111 Fourth Avenue, New York 3, N.Y.

Library of Congress Catalog Card Number: 65 - 15355

PRINTED IN GREAT BRITAIN

CONTENTS

LINE DRAWINGS

7

MAPS

ACKNOWLEDGEMENT

Figures 12 and 14 are reproduced by kind permission of Messrs. Delachaux and Niestlé, of Neuchatel, Switzerland.

PREFACE

The purpose of this book is to give an up-to-date account of what is known of the ancient history of southern Mesopotamia, or at least of its principal city—Babylon. The affairs of neighbouring states are dealt with only when they play a part in the development of this theme, not because I consider them unimportant, but because their inclusion would have made the narrative too cumbersome for a single volume. The detailed history of Assyria, for instance, is better reserved for separate treatment.

If the narrative seems too much concerned with political history, it should not be taken that I am a member of what has been called the "fife-and-drum school" of historians. Good modern accounts of the cultural and economic history of Mesopotamia already exist, and there is little point in duplicating them. Dates, kings and battles, dull though they may sometimes be, are of vital importance for a full understanding of the historical development of an area, and in this field a great deal of information has recently come to light. I feel that there is a place for a detailed account of this to replace older works and provide material for interested non-specialists.

I wish to express my thanks to Mr. B. H. Warmington and Mr. G. Chesterfield for suggesting that such a book might be written, to Mrs. Peter Franklin for her careful preparation of the manuscript, and to my wife, both for her illustrations and for the constant encouragement without which I should never have completed my task.

Bristol,   J.G.M.
February 1963

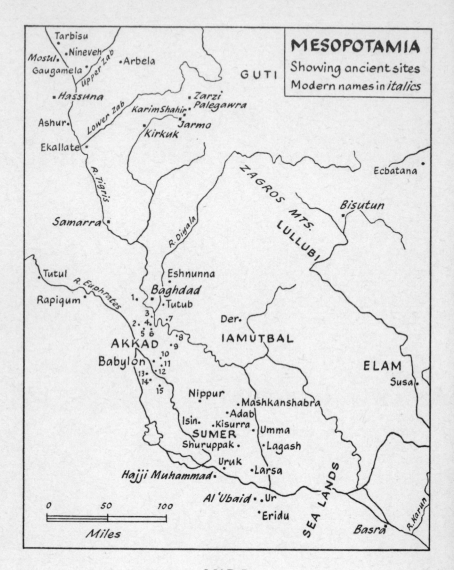

MESOPOTAMIA

Showing ancient sites
Modern names in *italics*

Tarbisu
Mosul. *Nineveh*
Gaugamela· *Upper Zab* ·Arbela
·*Hassuna*
Ashur· *Lower Zab* KarimShahir· Zarzi Palegawra
Ekallate· ·Jarmo
·Kirkuk

GUTI

Ecbatana·

R. Tigris

ZAGROS MTS.
LULLUBI

·Bisutun

Samarra·

·Tutul *R. Euphrates*
Rapiqum· Eshnunna
1· ·Baghdad
·Tutub
3· Der·
2· 4· ·7
5· 6· ·8 IAMUTBAL
AKKAD ·9
10
Babylon· ·11
13· ·12
14· 15 Nippur·
Isin· Mashkanshabra·
·Adab
·Kisurra
SUMER Umma
Shuruppak· ·Lagash
Uruk·
Hajji Muhammad· ·Larsa

R. Diyala

ELAM
Susa·

SEA LANDS

Al 'Ubaid· ·Ur
·Eridu
Basra *R. Karun*

0   50   100
Miles

MAP I

1. Dur Kurigalzu	6. Kutha	11. Akkad
2. Sippar	7. Malgum	12. Kazallu
3. Opis	8. Gudua	13. Borsippa
4. Akshak	9. Jemdet Nasr	14. Dilbat
5. Cunaxa	10. Kish	15. Marad

(1)
The Early History of Babylonia

A CITY cannot exist in isolation. Its history can be understood only by relating it to that of the areas around it. So while the city of Babylon may be taken as a focal point for the study of the civilization which emerged round the lower reaches of the Tigris and Euphrates it is essential to remember that its development and decline were no more than an episode in the larger and more important period which covers the rise and fall of civilization throughout Mesopotamia. The surrender of Babylon to Alexander the Great certainly marks the end of that period, but its beginning lies far beyond the first appearance of the city on the historical scene, and if we are to make a just estimate of Babylon's importance it is impossible to ignore the centuries which preceded its emergence and saw the formation of the environment in which it rose to power.

A great deal of work has recently been done on the earliest periods of Mesopotamian history, and it is clear that the hill-slopes to the east of the Tigris in the region now known as Iraqi Kurdistan were among the first areas to witness the great change from a cave-dwelling, food-gathering economy to one of settled agriculture and stock-breeding. Cave-sites such as Zarzi and Palegawra between Kirkuk and Sulimaniyah, which date from the end of the Old Stone Age (say about 10,000 B.C.), are little different from comparable sites in other parts of the world, and show no signs of the cultivation of crops or the domestication of animals. But a site at Karim Shahir in the same area, which was occupied perhaps a thousand years later, shows changes of great significance for the future. The inhabitants had moved out of their caves into primitive huts of reeds or matting on floors of rough stone. A few sickle-blades and fragments of milling-stones indicate that they supplemented their diet by gathering and preparing the cereal grasses which

grew wild in the area, and an abnormally high proportion of
the bones found belonged to pigs, goats or sheep, a fact which
suggests that these animals were beginning to be tamed or at
least confined near the settlement to ease the problem of
supplying food. The site was occupied only for a short period,
and was probably an interlude in an otherwise nomadic life.
The earliest settled village so far revealed in Mesopotamia is at
Jarmo, a mile or two from Karim Shahir. Here, probably about
7000 B.C., houses were built with walls of pressed mud and floors
of mud laid over reeds, and it is clear that the people who lived
in them were permanently settled farmers and herdsmen who
had no need to do much hunting. Grains of two varieties of
cultivated wheat were found as well as bread ovens and sickles
made of flints set in bitumen and attached to curved wooden
handles. Of the bones discovered all but a tiny minority were
of sheep or goats, and it seems certain that these animals were
kept rather than hunted. In the earliest stages of the settlement
there are no traces of pottery, but in the later levels it begins to
appear, probably introduced from some outside area.

The earliest village so far discovered in the area west of the
Tigris is at Hassuna, some twenty miles south of Mosul. At the
earliest stage Hassuna was a simple camp site like the earlier
Karim Shahir, but by the early part of the fifth millennium it had
become a substantial agricultural community with well-built
houses and a distinctive style of pottery. A later type of painted
pottery, first found at Samarra further down the Tigris, suggests a connection with the Iranian plateau, and in the latter
part of the fifth millennium a third style, common from the area
east of Mosul to the Mediterranean coast and first recognized
at Tell Halaf on the upper Khabur, may also indicate ethnic
movement in the area. It was during this Tell Halaf period that
another important discovery was made, and the first stages of
metal-working began to appear. About the same time settlers
from the Iranian plateau started to move down into the marshlands which lay around the mouths of the two great rivers.

This at least was the picture which until 1952 the archaeological remains seemed to present. Before 4000 B.C., it appeared,
the Persian Gulf stretched much further inland than it does
today, and reached a point some distance north of Baghdad.
But gradually the silt from two great rivers, the Karun from
the Persian hills and the now dry Wadi al-Batin from Arabia,

formed a sand-bar across the Gulf just south of modern Basra, and the silt of the Tigris and Euphrates, instead of being scoured away by the sea-currents, began to fill in the lagoon that had been formed. Slowly the water grew shallower until islands of dry land began to emerge above the surface, and as they appeared they were settled by highland peoples, drawn down by the richness of the alluvial soil. As the dry land increased the settlements grew in size and wealth, and it was in this environ-ment that the later Sumerian culture had its foundations.

Since 1952, however, this picture has not seemed so convinc-ing, for a geographical survey, the results of which were pub-lished in that year, showed that contrary to archaeological opinion the land of southern Mesopotamia was sinking rather than rising, and that the silt of the Tigris and Euphrates was only just managing to keep the land-surface at the same level. In other words the country in 4000 B.C. must have looked pretty much as it does today, the coast-line must have been in more or less the same place, and any archaelogical remains in the area have been steadily disappearing below water-level ever since. There is in fact no certainty at all that the settlers from Iran were the earliest in the region, or that the birth of a neolithic culture took place only in the north. But pending the develop-ment of a technique of underwater excavation it is impossible to guess what may have taken place in earlier periods. For practical purposes, history around the mouths of the rivers begins towards the end of the fifth millennium.

Its earliest known manifestation is at Eridu, traditionally the oldest city in the land and the home of Enki, god of the waters. Here almost from the beginning a shrine was the central feature, and shrines such as this were to remain a dominating influence in later settlements. For the people of southern Mesopotamia, over-awed by their own insignificance in the face of the natural hazards which surrounded them, considered that their lands and their very persons were owned by their nature-deities, and their houses were from the beginning clustered around the homes which they built for their gods. It was this subservience to the divine which in fact proved a decisive factor in the development of Mesopotamian civilization, for in service to the local god there evolved a means of concentrating the wealth of the land and the special skills of its citizens to make possible an expansion into the basic unit which later characterized the area—the city-state. The "Urban Revolution", as it has been called, was brought about by many factors —irrigation and new techniques leading to increased agricultural production and hence to a food surplus which enabled communities to turn to less productive trades such as metalworking and priesthood, and river transport to bring materials such as metal and stone from distant places are among the most important—but it was the religious beliefs of the people which caused the revolution to develop as it did and gave it its characteristically Mesopotamian form. In other areas, such as the valleys of the Indus and the Nile, although conditions and opportunities were in many ways similar, the mental attitude of the inhabitants was very different, and thus the development of civilization varied in each case.

The culture of which we catch the first glimpse at early Eridu was a vigorous one and expanded rapidly, ousting the Tell Halaf culture from the northern parts of the country. In the south settlements grew and multiplied, and as they increased their shrines grew with them. The Al 'Ubaid period, as it is called, saw the beginnings of monumental architecture directed to the glory of the gods. Although in the absence of written texts it is uncertain to what deities these early temples were dedicated, the continuity of the shrines into the historical period strongly suggests that the gods worshipped were the same at the early as at the later date, and that the Al 'Ubaid culture developed directly into the culture of the Sumerian period. A great deal of difficulty has been caused by the loose use of the word "Sumerian" in this connection. "Sumerian" is the name given to the *language* of the written documents which begin to appear about 3500 B.C., and has no necessary connection with any pottery-culture or ethnic movement. People can and do change their language without altering their way of life, and conversely they may change their way of life while retaining the language of their forebears. So an archaeological search for the origins and time of arrival of the speakers of Sumerian will almost certainly yield no definite answer. Several such answers have however been put forward. Naturally none of them is universally accepted. One is that the earliest Al 'Ubaid peoples were already speakers of Sumerian, but every later sign of a foreign "invasion" has its own supporters. For instance the appearance in the first half of the fourth millennium of the plain red or grey pottery which is the characteristic feature of the "Uruk" period has been hailed as the arrival of the "Sumerians", and the introduction of the painted ware of the Jemdet Nasr period (*c.* 3300–3000 B.C.) also has its supporters. Whether the "Sumerians" arrived by land or sea is also a question that remains unsettled, and in the quest for origins there is no help to be found in the study of skeletal remains. The population of Mesopotamia from ancient times to the present day has consisted predominantly of men of the Mediterranean or brown race, with a mixture of broad-headed north-eastern mountaineers, and it is impossible to label either of these types exclusively "Sumerian". The question of the arrival of Sumerian-speakers must in fact remain unanswered until the unlikely event of the discovery of much earlier documents provides linguistic information to supplement archaeological finds.

The Uruk period, whether it may be called Sumerian or not, saw the steady increase of the Mesopotamian townships and the growing wealth of their temples. During the same period the basic forms of Mesopotamian political and economic life were evolved. In considering these it is important to distinguish two completely different but interlocking social institutions the city and the temple-community. Originally these must have been identical—we have seen how the community formed around the shrine of the god who owned it—but as towns grew in size they incorporated the temples and lands of several deities. Thus the political unit—the city—came to be completely different from the economic and religious unit—the temple—although both were based on the same principle of equality under god. Politically this meant government by the decision of all adult freemen, a system which increased in difficulty as the population grew. Day-to-day business was conducted by a council of elders, and in times of emergency the assembly could offer absolute power to one man. For internal crises an *en* or lord was chosen, usually a man of proven administrative ability. For war a vigorous young leader was necessary, and he was known as the *lugal* or great man, a word which is generally translated king. These were temporary offices, and when the crisis was over the *en* or *lugal* returned to private life.

In the sphere of economics and religion the organization was

that of a number of large estates each owned by a god, in which
all citizens had their duties. Each man had his own plot of land
to support him, and he also helped to work the god's land and
keep his canals in order. This meant that large-scale irrigation
was practicable, and indeed it became the basis of all Mesopotamian agriculture. Tools and seeds were supplied by the temple, and the overall control was in the hands of the priestly head
of the temple-community. It must not be imagined that the
priestly class was a purely parasitic one gathering in the profits
of others' work. Like everyone else the priests had their duties,
their rations and their allotments of land, and part at least of
the profit of the temple lands was returned to the people at
feast-days and festivals. But naturally there was corruption in
many cases. Often too the idea of "kingship" was felt to be
ineffective and power was given to the holder of a high office in
the temple-community, normally the *ensi* or chief priest of the
city's most important shrine, a man who would have a lifetime's experience of organization and administration. In other
cities the *en* or *lugal* succeeded in making his position permanent,
and in the city-states of the historic period it was one of these
three who held supreme power.

The growth of city-states and city-temples led to an increased
complexity of organization and accounting, and this in its turn
seems to have been the direct inspiration for the development
of a system of writing. At first it was used only for temple-
business, but later historical and literary texts begin to appear.
The growth of art and architecture in this period will be dealt
with in another chapter. These, too, were intimately connected
with religion, and serve once more to emphasize the close
dependence of Mesopotamian civilization upon the divine.

The Jemdet Nasr period mentioned above, which followed
the Uruk period and formed with the latter part of it an epoch
known as the Protoliterate or Protohistoric, must be regarded
as an interlude rather than a complete break in the Mesopotamian tradition. The sudden introduction of painted pottery
and new burial customs and their equally sudden disappearance
in a series of conflagrations suggests a temporary foreign domination of some sort, perhaps from the Iranian hills. Under their
new masters the peoples of the southern cities continued to
expand. It was in this period that the villages to the immediate
north—Nippur, Kish, Eshnunna and others—began to grow

to city size, and traces of Mesopotamian civilization are to be found in Persia, Syria and Cappadocia. In Egypt too there is strong evidence for considerable Mesopotamian influence on art, architecture and writing in the period immediately preceding the emergence of the First Dynasty there (about 3100 B.C.).

Whatever happened at the end of the Jemdet Nasr period, the only major innovation was the introduction of a new type of building-brick, rectangular in plan, but rounded on top and looking rather like a fruit-cake. The reason for its use during the period known as Early Dynastic is unknown, but it suggests some sort of influence from an area where building in rough stone was the practice. During this period, too, writing, hitherto confined to economic affairs, began to be used for political and religious matters as well, and with this development we enter the realm of history proper. Shadowy as the outlines are at first, new discoveries are constantly adding to our knowledge. Documents concerned with the earliest period show a concentration of cities towards the mouths of the rivers, with outposts of their culture as far upstream as Assur and Mari, and this pattern has been confirmed by excavation. At first the southern cities seem to have been organized in a sort of federal league with a central meeting-place at the holy city of Nippur. There in times of national emergency a regional *en* or *lugal* was elected. This supreme office, like the similar ones within the separate states, was limited to the duration of the emergency, but like them too it contained in itself the seeds of permanence, and from an early period the idea of the supremacy of one city-ruler seems to have been present. About the end of the third millennium a list of kings was drawn up which told how this position had passed from one city to another. The value of this document is lessened but by no means nullified by the fact that in the earliest period reigns are exaggerated into many thousands of years, and that dynasties said to be successive can in fact be proved to be contemporary. Despite these defects, the confirmation given to the list by surviving monuments is sufficient for us to see that it is basically a genuine record. It starts with a series of legendary monarchs of whom nothing is known except that they allegedly ruled for 241,200 years. Then came the Flood. The memory of this catastrophe has been preserved in many sources, of which the best known is the Biblical story of Noah's

Ark, but despite vigorous rivalry in archaeological circles no
single inundation that has left traces in the record can be proved
to be *the* flood of the king-list. The most famous of the floods so
far discovered is that which took place at Ur during the Al
'Ubaid period, but it seems to have been purely local and much
too early to fit the scanty historical facts. Other traces of floods
have been discovered at Kish, Uruk and Shuruppak. Flooding
was, and is, a constant danger in Mesopotamia, and it is likely
that the flood-legend is due to a composite memory of various
disasters in different parts of the country.

After the Flood, kingship descended to earth again. Strangely
enough its first seat was not among the members of the old
southern league but at Kish, one of the newer cities situated
further up the Euphrates. This can be explained only on the
hypothesis that the northern city gained its supremacy not by
the old democratic processes but by force of arms. The fact that
several of its kings have Semitic names attests the power of
another linguistic element in Mesopotamia besides the
Sumerian. A search for the first appearance of the Semites is
as vain as that for the arrival of the Sumerians. It is highly
probable that from the earliest known period Semites were in
the majority in the north and Sumerians in the south, while the
central areas had a population which was linguistically mixed.
Almost nothing is known of the early kings of Kish. One of them,
Etana, was later famous for his ascent to heaven on an eagle's
back, and all of them might be dismissed as legendary were it
not for the unexpected fact that the second last, Enmebaragisi,
is known from other sources to be a historical figure. The discovery of an inscription mentioning him in the Diyala region
suggests that his power extended over a considerable area, and
gives some likelihood to the king-list's statement that he led a
victorious campaign against the Elamites. His reign may be
roughly dated to 2700. B.C.

With the emergence of Kish a new concept of monarchy was
introduced to the south, and the rulers of the older cities were
quick to learn from it. Although kings preserved their traditional functions as defensive leaders and internal administrators, the idea of supremacy by election quickly disappeared,
and was replaced by that of supremacy by force. But territory
won by military power could be held only by the maintenance
of that power, and conquests seldom outlasted a few generations

of the conquering royal house. Then a greater force would appear and another city would exercise an ephemeral supremacy. The truth of this was demonstrated in Kish when Agga, son of Enmebaragisi, came to the throne about 2675, for despite his efforts to placate the south by temple-building at Nippur he found himself involved with Gilgamesh, King of Uruk, a vassal who refused to acknowledge his supremacy. The campaign which followed may well have ended in defeat for Agga, for in the king-list the first dynasty of Kish is succeeded by a dynasty which had its seat at Uruk.

Gilgamesh, the hero of the greatest epic poem of Babylonia, is thus evidently a historical king. The same may well be the case for his predecessors of the throne of Uruk, although they too appear in later literature as heroes and demi-gods, and it is certainly true of his seven successors whose reigns are given normal lengths. By about 2600 the supremacy of Uruk must have been subject to a serious challenge by the rulers of Ur, whose royal graves have provided such sensational discoveries. But the challenge must have temporarily faded, for no mention of Meskalamdug, Akalamdug or any other ruler connected with the royal graves is to be found in the tradition. In the meantime Kish must have regained the leadership for a short period, for about 2550 Mesilim of Kish in his capacity of suzerain was strong enough to act as arbitrator in a boundary-dispute between the cities of Umma and Lagash. About thirty years later the power of Kish was broken by another effort on the part of Ur under Mesannipadda. This king was followed by his sons Meskiagnunna and A-annipadda, in whose reign an attempt was made to defeat the renewed power of Uruk (c. 2490). But the effort proved to be too much for him, and shortly afterwards Ur fell to Urnanshe of Lagash. The hegemony of the country then seems to have passed once more to Uruk, where a second dynasty held power for about forty years without achieving anything of note.

Much more is known of the rulers of Lagash at this time, although they never aspired to national leadership. The oldest known king of the city is Enkhegal, but the only record of his reign which has survived is concerned with the sale of land and provides no historical information. At the time of the arbitration of Mesilim of Kish mentioned above the ruler of Lagash was Lugalshagengur (c. 2550), but he seems to have had no connection with the line begun shortly after by Urnanshe, the son of a commoner, who was specially chosen by a goddess to bring glory to his city. Apart from his defeat of Ur little is known of his conquests, but his impressive building operations suggest that he was a ruler of considerable power. The reign of his son Akurgal probably saw a revival of the first dynasty of Ur under Meskiagnanna, but about 2470 Akurgal was succeeded by his son Eannatum, a ruler of great ambition who early in his reign defeated the armies of Elam and Kish and aspired to the leadership of Sumer. A series of campaigns in the south resulted in the subjugation of Uruk, Ur, and other cities, and then a renewed effort by Umma to alter the boundary fixed almost a century before by Mesilim of Kish was heavily defeated. Ush, the governor of Umma, was killed, and his successor Enakalli was forced to accept humiliating terms. After this Eannatum's conquests seem to have turned against him, and to add to his difficulties there was a destructive raid from the north (c. 2440) led not by his old enemy the King of Kish but by Zuzu of Akshak, Kish's immediate neighbour. Although Eannatum managed to survive these attacks, his power must have been greatly reduced by then. As a final blow he had to deal with an offensive by the distant city of Mari, which under Ilshu gained a temporary hegemony over most of Sumer. It was probably by Ilshu that the first dynasty of Ur was finally ended (c. 2435). Its last two kings, Elulu and Balulu, did little of note, although in the confusion which followed the collapse of Eannatum's conquests Elulu seems to have gained control of Uruk (c. 2445) and installed his son Enshakushanna there. It is not known what caused the army of Mari to retire. Probably Enshakushanna had a hand in it, for shortly afterwards he was campaigning in the north, where he gained a decisive victory over Enbi-Ishtar of Kish and his ally the ruler of Akshak.

In Lagash Eannatum had been succeeded by his brother Enannatum I, and then by his nephew Entemena, under whom the city's power began to increase once more. Umma, the old enemy of Lagash, had in the previous reign renewed her bid for disputed border-lands, but Entemena quickly drove back the invaders, captured their capital and killed their king, Urlumma, son of Enakalla. A governor called Ili was sent from Lagash to govern Umma, and again heavy tribute was demanded. Such was the reputation which this victory gained for Entemena that Uruk, now ruled by Lugalkinishedudu, eagerly proposed a pact of friendship (c. 2420). Under the shadow of Uruk Entemena made himself master of Ur, Eridu and Nippur, constructed a canal system joining the Euphrates to the Tigris, and probably completed a reign of triumph and good fortune.

But under his son Enannatum II fortune rapidly changed. Ur rebelled, but its independence was quickly lost to Lugalkinishedudu of Uruk, who may have come in accordance with his friendship-pact with Entemena. But once he had avenged the son of his friend, the king of Uruk did not hesitate to add Lagash and Umma to his own dominions (c. 2395). As he had inherited Kish and Akshak from Enshakushanna these conquests made him master of Sumer. His son Lugalkisalsi (c. 2390) must have held the same important position, but after him the power of Uruk began to wane. First the northern cities broke away, Akshak under Puzurnirakh, and then Kish under an otherwise unknown barmaid or brothel-keeper Kubaba, who "established the foundation" of her city about 2370. In Lagash power was seized by Enetarzi, who had been priest of the city-god under Entemena, and in Adab just to the north a monarch called Lugalannimundu was powerful enough to defeat a coalition of thirteen hostile princes and secure his position for a long reign. Nothing at all is known of events in Ur. In this shadowy period the greatest power was probably in the hands of Kish under Kubaba and her successors Puzursin and Urzababa, and these rulers must have been able to assert some sort of authority over the princes of the lesser states. The only city on which we have any information is Lagash, where the priestly Enetarzi and his successor Lugalanda (c. 2353–2348) ruled so harshly that the people rose against them and installed Urukagina (c. 2347–2341), a man pledged to restore freedom and the old ways of life in the state. The drive for power under Eannatum and Entemena had meant that the resources of the city had been strained to the utmost. Taxation, appropriation of property and deprivation of personal freedom had been used to supply the men and the rations necessary for a policy of aggression. In wartime such measures had been regarded as unpleasant but necessary, but with the decline of Lagash under weaker rulers they became much less acceptable. Government inspectors and supervisors were everywhere, the palace grew rich at the expense of the common people, and the upper classes and priesthood took advantage of the situation to increase their own fortunes. With the zeal of a true reformer Urukagina set about righting these abuses. The system of government inspection was ended and the seizing of property forbidden. The exorbitant fees which had enriched the governor and the clergy were lowered or abolished, and temple lands used by the governors as private estates were returned to the gods. In all this Urukagina himself was the principal loser, and in other measures too one can see how he sought to serve the interests of those who had given him power. Protection was given to poorer people in their dealings with the rich and powerful, and steps were taken to prevent the victimization of widows and orphans. A drive against crime in the city succeeded in putting a stop to theft, usury and murder, and in his second year Urukagina felt sufficiently secure in his position to claim the title of "king" and refuse to acknowledge the supremacy of Kish. A policy of rebuilding and canal-clearing was begun which, had it been given sufficient time, might have restored the greatness of Lagash, but in concentrating on domestic reforms Urukagina had given too little attention to matters just beyond his boundaries. The ancestral enemy Umma was now in the hands of an active ruler called Lugalzaggisi who about 2340 made a sudden attack on Lagash and completely destroyed it.

The fall of Lagash to Umma might have been merely another incident in a tale of petty state rivalry, but in Lugalzaggisi Umma had a ruler whose ambitions did not stop within a few miles of his own city. The conquest of Lagash was followed by other victories until he had made himself master of the south. In doing so he showed that he did not intend merely to display his strength. A far more grandiose scheme was in his mind—that of reviving the old Sumerian league with himself at its head. His first move in this direction was the transfer of his capital from the unimportant town of Umma to Uruk, the seat of the oldest Sumerian dynasty. More significantly, after the capture of Nippur, the holy city and central meeting-place of the league, he received from the priests there the title of "King of the Lands" and settled down to a studious and seemingly successful attempt to prove himself in his new capacity as federal chief and national arbitrator. In all this he seems to have paid no attention to the claims of Kish, which still under the descendants of Kubaba exercised a nominal suzerainty over the south. It is in fact possible that Lugalzaggisi conquered Kish, although this is nowhere mentioned in the admittedly scanty sources. More probably however his task was simplified by a palace revolt in the northern city during which Urzababa, the king at that time, was overthrown by his cupbearer Sargon (c. 2331). The success of this revolt may well have been due to Lugalzaggisi's encouragement, and it left him free to concentrate on the administration of the south while his new vassal turned to further conquests in the north. Alternatively, if Lugalzaggisi did conquer Kish the fall of Urzababa enabled his cupbearer to set out on a career of conquest for himself. An enigmatic phrase in an inscription of Lugalzaggisi tells of the spread of his influence as far as the Mediterranean coast, but it is difficult to say if this indicates a campaign of conquest or merely that his vassal's conquests were nominally subject to him. At any rate if he did make a northern raid any territory he may have gained was soon taken over by the ambitious Sargon. The early career of this king is lost in the mass of legend with which later generations surrounded him. He was possibly the illegitimate son of a priestess in Kish, and like Moses was laid in a basket and abandoned in the river. Brought up as his own son by the water-carrier who found him, he entered the service of the king and rapidly rose to a position of considerable power. After his successful revolt Sargon decided to found his own city, and work was begun on the building of Akkad. The exact position of this city has not yet been established, but it was certainly somewhere in the neighbourhood of Kish. Meanwhile a programme of rapid expansion was undertaken, for Sargon realized that the unity and prosperity of any conquests he might make would depend largely on the security of his trade-routes to the east, north and west. Early campaigns up the Euphrates resulted in the capture of Tutul (modern Hit) and Mari and penetration as far as the Taurus Mountains and the Mediterranean. It is extremely probable that expeditions were also sent into Asia Minor and across to Cyprus. To the north Assyria was defeated, and in the east the tribes of the mountains were shown that there was to be no easy booty for them in the plain.

Achievements such as this must have appeared somewhat excessive to Lugalzaggisi, who still regarded himself as Sargon's superior, and he marched north, supported by fifty Sumerian governors, with the intention of putting the forward young up-start in his place. At Ugbanda, somewhere in Akkadian terri-tory, the two great armies met, and the result was a decisive victory for Sargon. Sweeping south and carrying the captive Lugalzaggisi with him, he rapidly captured the principal cities of Sumer. Uruk, Ur, Lagash, Umma and Nippur fell almost without a struggle, and Sargon's troops symbolized the com-pletion of their conquest by washing their weapons in the Persian Gulf. In Nippur, Lugalzaggisi was publicly exhibited before the Enlil Gate to demonstrate to all that his power was at an end, and Sargon was crowned legitimate king of the land (c. 2315).

For the rest of his long reign (c. 2331–2276) the Akkadian king was engaged in almost continuous warfare, and at the same time he had to deal with the problems of an empire which stretched from the Persian Gulf to beyond the Taurus, and from eastern Elam to the Mediterranean. This brought about another significant change in the conception of Mesopotamian kingship. The administration of so vast an area by the old federal system was obviously impossible, and the method of rule by force, introduced by the First Dynasty of Kish, could not be used with any prospect of permanent success. This Sargon dis-covered to his cost for, despite the size and power of the garri-sons which were stationed throughout the empire, he and his successors were constantly troubled by revolts. A series of such rebellions in Sumer during the latter part of Sargon's reign had to be dealt with by the strengthening of garrisons, the seizing of hostages, the destruction of city walls and the evolution of a system of central and personal administration. As a northerner and a Semite, Sargon felt no compelling urge to preserve the city-state system of the south. In its place he tried to make use of the personal loyalty which the formerly nomadic Semites naturally felt towards their tribal chief. To satisfy southern feel-ing Nippur was kept as a religious centre, but a civil service of Akkadian citizens was established under personal oath to him-self, and only members of this diplomatic corps were appointed to the control of provinces and other positions of importance. By these measures Sargon sought to bring peace and unity to his empire, and certainly in matters of trade and commerce the period was one of great prosperity. To commemorate the great-

Fig. 1   Bronze head of Sargon of Akkad, now in the Baghdad
Museum

ness of his achievements Sargon chose as his title "King of the Four Quarters of the World", a claim which in fact seems to have been a fairly justified one.

In the reign of Rimush (c. 2275–2267) the younger son and successor of Sargon, the troubles of his father's final years continued, and it was with difficulty that rebellion in the south, in Elam and in the lands along the Tigris was suppressed. When Rimush was murdered in a palace revolution he was succeeded by his elder brother Manishtusu (c. 2266–2252), and again the empire rose in revolt. Once more the army of Akkad proved strong enough to deal with the trouble. The trade routes to the north and north-west were regained, and in the east the rulers of Anshan and Elam were defeated, as well as a coalition of "thirty-two kings of cities beyond the sea", presumably on the south Persian coast. The accession of Naramsin (c. 2251–2215), the grandson of Sargon, was greeted by yet another rebellion, led this time by the cities of Kish and Sippar, but on this occasion, too, the king of Akkad was able to prove his strength, and the revolt was heavily defeated. But Naramsin was not a man to rest content when he had dealt with internal troubles, and almost immediately he began a programme of expansion which was to extend the empire once more to the furthest limits which his grandfather's armies had reached. His first move was an attack on Magan, the source of diorite for statue-making, a land which may have lain in southern Arabia or even on the continent of Africa. In the opposite direction Mari was defeated, and then the king advanced far enough to pacify the area northeast of modern Diyarbakir in Turkish Kurdistan. Further northern campaigns gave him control of the states of Syria and brought the power of Akkad once more to the Mediterranean coast. An invasion of Cappadocia followed which ensured the control of even more distant trading-stations. In the north and east Naramsin also gained a series of victories, but there his campaigns were to safeguard his frontiers rather than to secure trade. Subartu and Elam were firmly suppressed and made effective buffers at either end of the eastern frontier, but between them a dangerous gap existed which Naramsin sought to block by a victorious campaign against the Lullubians of the Zagros Mountains.

In internal administration Naramsin continued the policy of his predecessors by making use of Akkadian officials, often members of his own family, and exercising personal control over them. The system of garrison posts was retained and extended, but at the same time the essential unity of the empire was emphasized by the introduction of a uniform dating system. Unity under Akkadian kingship was stressed still further by Naramsin's deification as the personal protective genius of the empire.

The reign of the great king was however destined to end in a disaster over which he had no control. A period of famine weakened the empire and laid it open to internal strife and to attack by the covetous barbarians who were constantly at the ready in the mountains to the east. The defeat of the Lullubians earlier in Naramsin's reign had postponed this danger, but now the Gutians, a tribe from the hills around the headwaters of the Diyala, began to move down into the plain and close in on Akkad. Naramsin was probably killed in the struggle that followed, and although his successor Sharkalisharri (c. 2214–2190) was able to retain his hold on his capital, the provinces rapidly crumbled away. Elam and Subartu proclaimed their independence, the trade connections to the north-west disappeared, and in the south the Sumerian cities were eager to rid themselves of the hated mastery of Akkad. In the face of all this opposition Sharkalisharri was scarcely able to hold his own, although he did succeed in defeating the Gutians and capturing their King Sharlak. In the end he fell fighting them, and a period of complete confusion followed. Within three years (c. 2189–2187) four kings sat on the throne of Akkad, and one of them, Elulu, was almost certainly a Gutian. Uruk, Ur and other southern cities fell to the barbarians, and the inhabitants were powerless to prevent them from overthrowing altars, sacking temples and spreading destruction throughout the land.

The havoc wrought by the Gutians, coming so soon after the famine of Naramsin's reign, brought a complete economic collapse in Mesopotamia. The loss of the principal trade routes and the neglect of agriculture and irrigation led to stagnation from which it took many years to recover. In Akkad after Elulu had been driven out a degree of stability was regained under Dudu (c. 2186–2166) and Shudurul (c. 2165–2151), but the city had now lost all power and fell an easy victim to a final attack by the Gutians (c. 2151). So thorough was the destruction that the site of Akkad has never been rediscovered.

After their first attacks the Gutians had settled in the northern part of the land and established a loose overall confederacy which seems to have allowed a good deal of freedom to subject-states. The fact that the reigns of twenty-one Gutian kings averaged only about five years each suggests that they were too involved in quarrelling among themselves to pay much attention to the ruling of an empire. On the whole they were content to live on the fat of the land they had won, and gradually they became more and more Akkadianized, using the language of their subjects and making offerings at the shrines which they had formerly desecrated. In the south some cities achieved almost complete independence. After the fall of Akkad a dynasty at Uruk considered itself of sufficient importance to claim the leadership of the country, while at Lagash a line of governors was begun by Urbaba which seems to have been subject to little Gutian control. Eventually the cities decided to free themselves completely from the barbarians. Choosing a moment when the Gutian King Tirigan had been on the throne only a few weeks and had had no time to consolidate his position, the Sumerians rose under Utuhegal of Uruk (c. 2120). A battle at Dubrum resulted in the defeat and capture of Tirigan, and Utuhegal was hailed by all Sumer as a national hero.

Although the extent of Utuhegal's conquests is not certain, they were wide enough for him to claim the title of "King of the Four Quarters of the World" and to have to face the problems of ruling an empire. In doing so he tried to renew the imperial organization which had been evolved by the Akkadian kings. Like them he had his own civil service, and citizens of Uruk were sent out to govern the provinces of the realm. One of these governors, Urnammu by name, was placed in charge of Ur, and although he was at first loyal to his oath and dutifully dedicated new buildings for the life of his lord, he soon grew tired of such restrictions and determined to win the empire for himself. Again our sources fail us, and there are few details of how Uruk was overthrown and Urnammu made himself supreme. His whole reign, in fact (2113–2096), is comparatively unknown. That he was successful in war can be seen from the prisoners depicted on his monuments, but in his titles he confined himself to "King of Sumer and Akkad", so presumably his territory did not stretch beyond Babylonia. The defeat of Lagash seems to have been the greatest military achievement of

his reign. His importance, however, rests not on military conquests but on the rebuilding and social measures which restored
the prosperity of the land after the neglect of the Gutian period.
A code of laws was issued by which thieves and rebels were put
down, the poor were protected from the rich, and a uniform
system of weights and measures was established. The peace and
order which resulted were utilized to re-dig canals and improve
agriculture. As well as all this, Urnammu was an indefatigable
temple-builder, not only in his capital but in Eridu, Uruk, Nippur, Umma and other cities. In this he was followed by his
local governors, the best known of whom is Gudea of Lagash,
a loquacious ruler who has left considerable details of the planning and construction of his public works.

The reign of Urnammu seems to have ended on the battle-
field in some unknown campaign. He was followed by his son
Shulgi (2095–2049), a king who, like his father, was a tireless
builder and restorer of shrines. As well as this he was a considerable warrior, and under his leadership the territory of Ur was
greatly extended. In a series of campaigns he subdued Elam and
Anshan to the east and in the north reduced Assur to the status
of a subject-province. By the end of his reign the land east of the
Tigris between these areas was in his hands, and numerous
victories over the Lullubians and other mountain peoples
ensured that there was no danger from that quarter. To the
north-west no attempt was made to extend the empire beyond
Mesopotamia, but the annexation of Assur meant that Ur
gained control of the many Assyrian merchant-colonies in
Anatolia and northern Syria. Thus the important trade routes
were secured by influence rather than direct conquest, and
since there was no danger on the eastern frontier, conditions
were ideal for the development of a prosperous and peaceful
empire. In ruling this empire Shulgi showed well that he had
learned from the mistakes and misfortunes of the dynasty of
Akkad, for a complete system of central bureaucratic administration was evolved which was designed to prevent the possibility of internal revolt. Provincial governors became entirely
dependent on the king and were regularly moved from one city
to another to prevent them from forming local attachments.
Their main duty was the collection of taxes and their dispatch
to the capital, and all military forces in the provinces were in
the hands of garrison commanders directly responsible to the

king. A regular corps of royal messengers ensured that all news
came swiftly to Ur; and, most important of all, Shulgi founded
just south of Nippur an enormous storehouse to which every
town in the land had to contribute in kind. So it formed a sort
of central exchequer, theoretically the property of Enlil, but in
practice the king's own fund for use in emergencies and for the
payment of his civil service. The revolt of subject cities need no
longer mean that the king lacked finances to oppose them, and
in this system Shulgi found a surer method than force for holding his empire together. So successful was his reign that like
Naramsin he was regarded as the guiding genius of the country
and deified.

The death of Shulgi and the accession of Bursin (2048–2039)
made little difference to the prosperity of the country, for the
new king continued to use the methods of his predecessor. A
campaign against Arbela proved successful, but trouble with
the tribes of the Zagros Mountains was a foretaste of what was
to come. When Bursin was carried off by a disease in his foot, he
was succeeded by Shusin (2038–2030), and this king too had
trouble east of the Tigris, where several outlying provinces
refused to recognize his authority. In the west there were also
signs of danger, and a vast defensive wall was built in the
middle-Euphrates area to counteract it. Behind this fortification
the king of Ur continued his sacral and administrative duties,
and left to his successor Ibbisin (2029–2005) the task of meeting
the dangers which he himself had tried to shut out of his kingdom.

(2)

The First Supremacy of Babylon

SOON after Ibbisin's accession, the dissolution of his empire began. Despite his efforts to hold it together, the provinces one by one began to claim independence. No documents have been found in Eshnunna which are dated by an imperial formula later than Ibbisin's second year, and they stop with year 3 in Susa, year 5 in Lagash, year 6 in Umma and year 7 in Nippur. Later generations retained the memory of rebellion, civil disturbance and disintegration, but it was not merely internal trouble with which Ibbisin had to deal. Invasions from the desert areas proved to be his chief danger, and in fact these nomadic peoples were later to set up independent dynasties ruling over the broken fragments of his empire. The invaders were Semitic in origin, but they belonged to the West-Semitic branch of the family and had entered Mesopotamia originally from the Syrian area. Unlike their modern counterparts, they had no camels, and so were compelled to avoid real desert and cling to the fringes of the civilized areas to find pasture for their sheep and goats. Some of them were to be found in Babylonia as early as the dynasty of Akkad, and after the fall of that dynasty their influence rapidly began to spread. The open plains to the east of the Tigris were the first areas to attract them, and more and more of them passed across to the new territory. To the east they were hemmed in by the mountains, and this forced them south towards and across the Diyala, and so into the area of the empire of Ur. By this time the documents are quite clear about their name; they are the Amorites.

It was these people who provoked the crisis in Ibbisin's reign. He and his predecessors had ringed the land with fortresses to keep them out, but in the event this "Maginot-line mentality" proved useless. One of the fortresses, said to be "facing the mountains", and so presumably to the east, collapsed before the Amorite assault, and the nomads poured into the heart of

31

the country. Ishbi-irra, a civil servant employed by Ibbisin in
his sixth year to buy grain in the areas round Isin and Kazallu,
was so surprised and frightened by the reports of hostile
Amorites in the plains that he withdrew with his grain inside
Isin and sent a report to his master in which he asked to be given
command for the defence of that city and nearby Nippur. His
request was granted, and at the same time the defences of
Nippur and even Ur were strengthened. Most of the cities
managed to hold out, but since the invaders were in complete
control of the countryside, each city was isolated from its
neighbours, and, more important, from its corn supplies, which
fell into enemy hands. Famine and complete economic collapse
followed. Grain rose to sixty times its normal price; offerings to
the gods had to be severely curtailed. Nominally, many of the
local governors remained loyal to Ibbisin, but the Empire of
Ur was at an end. From now on, it was to be a struggle for
domination among princes who rose to power in different parts
of what had once belonged to Ur.

In Isin, for instance, Ishbi-irra, the military commander
appointed by Ibbisin, took advantage of the situation to proclaim his independence. In 2017, five or six years after the
Amorite invasions, he was strong enough to call himself "King
of the Land" and issue his own date-formulae. The only thing
known about his previous career, apart from his grain-buying,
is that he came originally from Mari, a province of the empire
of Ur on the middle Euphrates, and that he brought with him
Dagan, a god worshipped particularly in that area. Nothing is
known of the position of his family in Mari, or of his racial
connections. Although Mari was later ruled by an Amorite
dynasty, there is little to show that Ishbi-irra was himself an
Amorite, as has often been supposed. Under the Third Dynasty
of Ur, Mari was "a thoroughly Akkadian city" with very little
trace of West Semitic elements, and it is possible that Ishbi-irra
began his career as a petty imperial official there before being
transferred to the capital, and sent on the mission which ended in
his kingship. Having achieved this position, he rapidly increased
his power. As well as giving him Isin, Ibbisin had charged him
with the defence of Nippur, the principal sactuary of the area,
and from this basis he began to expand. Isin was strongly
fortified, the Amorites were driven from the border-fortresses
which they had occupied, and allegiance was demanded from

other local rulers, including Puzurnumushda, governor of
Kazallu, a province still loyal to Ur. Then, about 2006,
another enemy appeared. The Elamites from the Persian highlands, who had also regained their independence through the
collapse of Ur, swept down into the river valleys with their allies
the Subarians. By this time Ishbi-irra was strong enough to
defend himself, and he duly records victories over Elam for his
twelfth and thirteenth years. But Ur was now so reduced that
she was easy prey for the mountaineers. In 2005 the city was
captured, the temple of Ningal was destroyed, and King
Ibbisin was carried off into captivity.

When the Elamites retired with their prisoners and booty to
their homeland a garrison was left in Ur. But Elamite strength
was not sufficient to retain conquests in the plain, and within
a year or two tablets from Ur dated by Isin formulae show that
Ishbi-irra had gained some measure of control in his former
master's city. It was several more years, however, before the
Elamite garrison finally surrendered.

Thus Ishbi-irra became master of southern Babylonia. Little
is known of the rest of his reign (2017–1985). His successors
Shuilishu (1984–1975) and Iddindagan (1974–1954) consolidated his work during a period of comparitive peace, and seem to
have concentrated on building and matters of religion rather than
on conquest. Iddindagan however must have undertaken the conquest of Der (modern Badrah on the Persian border of Iraq)
for he installed his son Ishmedagan as governor there, while
between the rivers his authority extended at least as far north
as Sippar. It is clear that after his accession to the throne of
Isin, Ishmedagan (1953–1935) was in control of most of north
and south Babylonia—Der, whose wall he built, Isin, Nippur, Ur,
Eridu, and Uruk, are among the places which acknowledged
him—but he did meet with at least one reverse, when he was
defeated in or around Kish. It is interesting that the memory
of this defeat is preserved in an omen-text from Mari, thus showing that some connection with Ishbi-irra's homeland was still
maintained.

It was from the north too that a raiding party came which
practically destroyed his dominions. The state of Assur on the
upper Tigris, which had also gained its independence after the
fall of the Third Dynasty of Ur, was now attempting to gain control of the trade routes of the north, and this attempt was being

frustrated by Ishmedagan's possession of Der, an important station on the route down from the Iranian mountains. So, marching down the eastern bank of the Tigris, allegedly with the purpose of freeing Akkad from the domination of Isin, the Assyrian King Ilushuma gained the alliance of the unruly nomad sheikhs of the area and crossed into the land between the rivers. Uruk, Umma and other cities were attacked, and Nippur was destroyed; perhaps even Ur in the far south fell to the invaders. But Isin itself survived, and after the Assyrians had gone Ishmedagan was able to restore order. As well as building operations, social reforms were undertaken, mostly concerned with privileges granted to the inhabitants of the holy city of Nippur. This reforming policy culminated in Isin with the law-code issued by Ishmedagan's successor Lipitishtar (1934–1924), which was written in Sumerian and bore in some respects a strong resemblance to the later code of Hammurabi of Babylon. A fuller description of these and other law-codes will be given in a later chapter.

The reign of Lipitishtar was also marked by the rise of another power in the south. During the disturbances at the beginning of the reign of Ibbisin of Ur an Amorite sheikh, Naplanum by name, had managed to infiltrate into Mesopotamia, perhaps from the desert south of the Euphrates, and install himself as ruler of Larsa (2025 B.C.). Situated as it was in the marshlands that lay at the head of the Persian Gulf, Larsa managed to preserve its independence from the new power of Isin while cities like Ur, which lay further from Isin, but on the dry ground west of the Euphrates, fell quickly under her domination.

Little is known of the reigns of Naplanum (2025–2005) and his successors Emisum (2004–1977), Samium (1976–1942) and Zabaya (1941–1933). But under Gungunum (1932–1906) the fortunes of Larsa began to rise. Gungunum's military strength was shown early in his reign by two successful expeditions into the Iranian highlands, after which he concentrated on expansion in the plains. This policy culminated in his capture of Ur from Isin (1926). At this time the two cities must have been in open conflict, and it is tempting to connect the change of dynasty which took place in Isin two years later with the continued success of Larsa. But if this is so, it is surprising to find Gungunum installing Lipitishtar's daughter Enninsunzi as priestess of Nanna in Ur, and her predecessor in that office,

Ishmedagan of Isin's daughter Enannatumma, dedicating a temple "for the life of Gungunum". This evidence seems to favour friendly relations between the cities, and it has been suggested that when Lipitishtar lost his throne in Isin, he and his family fled for protection to Larsa. But although Urninurta (1923–1896), who succeeded to the throne in Isin, was unrelated to the previous royal family, there is no evidence that he did in fact usurp Lipitishtar's position. Whatever did happen, Gungunum took over the title of "King of Sumer and Akkad" which Isin had assumed after the fall of Ur, and Larsa became the dominant power in the area. The conquest of Ur gave her control of trade with Tilmun (modern Bahrein) and other places round the Persian Gulf, and diplomatic relations were established with the Diyala region east of the Tigris, perhaps in connection with the defeat of Malgum, a state which lay on the Tigris south of the Diyala. At home, a vigorous policy of temple-defence- and canal-building was followed, and this policy was continued by Gungunum's successor Abisare (1905–1895), who concentrated especially on the digging and repair of the canals which were an essential part of the country's welfare. Meanwhile at Isin the long but obscure reign of Urninurta was notable only for minor domestic reforms and for a defeat (1898) at the hands of Larsa, which perhaps was the result of an attempt to regain control of Ur. Despite this, Urninurta continued to call himself "King of Sumer and Akkad", but his empty title bore no relation to reality. His death in 1896 may have been by violence, but no details are known.

When Sumuel (1894–1866) succeeded Abisare on the throne of Larsa, he continued the policy of expansion started by Gungunum. In his third year he conducted a campaign in north Babylonia which resulted in the defeat of Kazallu and the capture of Akusum, a small town somewhere in the same area. The capture of Pinaratim followed four years later, and a further campaign in the north led to the defeat of Kish (1885). Not much is known of the history of these northern towns in the years following the fall of Ur. The defeat of Ishmedagan of Isin before Kish has already been mentioned, and an otherwise unknown king of Kish, Ashduniarim by name, records an eight-year struggle with an un-named enemy, perhaps Isin, whom he finally defeated. Halium, another king of Kish, named one of his years "the year in which Urninurta was killed", and if this

is the king of Isin, then presumably Kish was in some way
dependent on Isin at that time (1896). It might be expected
then that when Sumuel of Larsa defeated the army of Kish in
1885, he won the town from the rival dynasty of Isin. But in the
meantime a new power was beginning to exercise its authority
in northern Babylonia, and by 1892 it had gained control of
Kish, which lay only a few miles from its capital, a hitherto
unimportant religious centre called Babylon.

Little is known of the beginnings of Babylon. It is probable
that it was originally a Sumerian foundation, and that the
Sumerian name KA.DINGIR.RA, "Gate of God", was literally
translated as bâb-ili by the Semites who first had contact with
it. This gave rise to Babel, the Biblical form of the name. In
later times the city is referred to as bâb-ilâni, "Gate of the
Gods", which was rendered as Βαβυλών by the Greeks, whence
comes the English Babylon. There is a Babylonian tradition
that when Sargon of Akkad destroyed the town he carried
away some of its earth in order to gain a share of its holiness for
his own capital. Sharkalisharri, a later king of the Dynasty
of Akkad, laid the foundations of a temple in Babylon, and
kings of the Third Dynasty of Ur placed governors there. From
the same period there is mention of Esagila, the temple of
Marduk. It is indeed likely that the original rulers of Babylon
were the high priests of Marduk, and perhaps the city would
have remained a mere place of pilgrimage if it had not been for
the dynasty founded by an Amorite sheikh called Sumuabum,
who in 1894 set himself up as king in the town. Nothing is
known of his origins. He may or may not be connected with a
Sumuabum known from Susa, or with a Sumuabum whose dispatch to Der provides a year-name for a ruler of Eshnunna.
It cannot even be said if he acted at first as a subordinate to
another king, or if he came directly from the desert to capture
Babylon and rule it himself. However he gained control, he
must have had a good eye for a situation that could be developed
to his advantage, for Babylon lay in an ideal position for a city
that was to win control of all Mesopotamia.

Until this time, the centre of power in Babylonia had moved
from one city to another, and at first it seems strange that having
reached Babylon it should have stayed there so long. But it can
be seen from a map of the area how eminently suitable the
city was as a centre of trade and a place of defence. Although

it lay to the north of the country, and thus might not seem ideal
as a central seat of government, its position gave it so many
other advantages that it survived great political and economic
reverses without losing its pre-eminent position. So suitable,
in fact, is the general area for a capital city that almost all
later capitals—Seleuceia, Ctesiphon and Baghdad—were founded
in the same neighbourhood, the only change being a transfer
from the Euphrates to the deeper and more navigable Tigris.
This was inevitable once sea-traffic became more important
and the incorporation of Mesopotamia into the Persian Empire
removed all danger of attack from the east. To the Babylonians,
the Elamites were a constant menace, and it was important
that they should have their capital as far as possible from the
attacks of their foes without taking it across the Euphrates and
thus exposing it to attack from the desert tribes of Arabia.

But it was not mere considerations of defence which made
Babylon powerful. A city's prosperity must depend on trade as
well as war, and as a centre of trade routes Babylon's position
was unrivalled. Situated at the bottle-neck where the Mesopotamian plain is narrowed by the twin rivers to a width of less
than forty miles, it had access to the trade of both these rivers,
as well as being within easy distance of the fertile plains to the
south. The Tigris route led north through Assyria, and so across
the mountains to Anatolia and the Black Sea, while the route
which followed the Euphrates was the natural road to Syria
and the Mediterranean coast. From there it led either through
the Cilician gates to the Anatolian plateau and the west, or
south through Syria and Palestine to Egypt. Another great
route which Babylon controlled was the one which led down
from the highlands of Iran through the gates of Zagros, but
owing to the danger from Elam it was inevitable that Babylon
should concentrate on the north and west. Thus she was able to
take advantage of almost all the commerce of the Mesopotamian world. There is evidence of trade with Syria and
Anatolia even before the kings of Babylon won their supremacy,
and their continued prosperity was based on the maintenance of
these older trade connections.

Such then was the position of the city in which Sumuabum
proclaimed his independence and set about defending it by
building a city wall. Expansion followed rapidly. Fortresses
were built round about the capital, and by his third year Kish

was in his hands. Although Sumuel of Larsa defeated the army
of Kish in 1885, this did not stop the expansion of Babylon. By
that time Sumuabum had already taken and fortified Dilbat,
some twenty miles to the south, and by 1883 he was in full control of Kish once more. In the same year he destroyed Kazallu,
but Larsa struck back, and Sumuel records a victory over
Kazallu in 1874. Babylon's expansion to the south was thus
temporarily blocked by the power of Larsa, and much of the
reign of Sumulael (1880–1845) was taken up with consolidation
of her position and preparation for further advance. Fortresses
and defences were built, and new canals were cut to increase
the city's natural resources. In the meantime Sumuel continued
to gain ground in the south, and by about 1868 he had captured Nippur from the weakened dynasty of Isin. Presumably
as a result of his control of the holy city, he had himself deified,
and for the remainder of his reign concentrated on religious
matters such as the enthronement of his daughter as priestess
of Nanna in Ur.

In the north, Sumulael of Babylon was still having difficulties
with his neighbours. Kish, under its vassal King Iawium, was
a constant danger, and had twice to be taken and destroyed. In
Kazallu another Amorite sheikh called Iahzirel had set himself
up as ruler and had to be driven out in 1864. Further trouble
led to the destruction of the city two years later, but Iahzirel
escaped punishment and had again to be defeated in 1857.
North of Babylon there was more disturbance which led to the
fortification of Gudua, about thirty miles to the north-east of
the capital (1855), and of the vassal state of Sippar (1853). But
by this time fortune had changed in the south. By 1862 Marad,
some thirty miles south of Kish, was in Sumulael's hands, and
he felt sufficiently secure in this direction to build a series of
fortresses in the immediate vicinity of Nippur. Larsa under
Sumuel's successor Nuradad (1865–1850) had been struck by
a great natural disaster when the Euphrates, and perhaps the
Tigris as well, overflowed and destroyed much of Larsa's
territory before finding its way into a new course. Nuradad had
to spend much of his reign resettling people and rebuilding
property, and this policy was followed in the early years of his
reign by his son Sinidinnam (1849–1843). The course of the
Tigris was re-dug, and Larsa, Ur and Eridu were restored.

In the meantime, there was a slight revival in the fortunes

of Isin. After the death of Urninurta (1896), his son Bursin (1895–1874) continued to lay claim to Nippur, Ur, Eridu and Uruk, but of these only Nippur was certainly in his hands. He did, however, succeed in capturing Ur and holding it for a few months. His son and successor Lipitenlil (1873–1869) achieved nothing of importance, and it was probably in his reign that Nippur was lost to Sumuel of Larsa. But Erraimitti (1868–1861) introduced a policy of reform and even expansion. Kisurra and other states in the neighbourhood of Isin were defeated, and Nippur was recovered and restored. Isin's strength, however, was not great enough to stop Sumulael of Babylon fortifying positions in the immediate vicinity of the holy city. According to later legend Erraimitti, having no son to succeed him, appointed his gardener Enlilbani to be his successor, and after a six-month period of disturbance Enlilbani (1860–1837) succeeded in establishing his authority. But as his reign went on that authority grew more and more limited. After Nippur had been once more lost to Larsa under Sinidinnam (1849–1843), Enlilbani's kingdom was reduced to the immediate neighbourhood of Isin, and even Isin itself may have been under Larsa's control for a time. With the conquest of Nippur, Sinidinnam came face to face with the Babylonian forces just to the north, and the battle which followed resulted in a victory for Larsa. With his frontiers secured to the north Sinidinnam now turned eastwards and annexed Ibrat, somewhere east of the lower Tigris, before marching against Eshnunna. The result was once more a complete victory for Larsa, and Eshnunna was destroyed. The small states north of the Diyala and towards the lower Zab acknowledged Sinidinnam's authority, and, with Babylon temporarily neutralized, he could also extend his influence up to Rapiqum on the middle Euphrates. Only to the east was there a hint of trouble, and in his seventh year Sinidinnam had to build the great wall of Mashkanshabra, a fortress facing the area from which danger was expected. But he did not live to see his conquests crumble away, for his reign was brought to an untimely end when a slab of stone descended on him as he was entering the temple of Shamash.

Sineribam (1842–1841), Siniqisham (1840–1836) and Silliadad (1835) followed in rapid succession as rulers of Larsa, while in Isin Enlilbani was succeeded by Zambia (1836–1834). The trouble expected from the east was now coming closer, and although Siniqisham records the capture of Pinaratim and Nasarum and a victory over Zambia of Isin and an Elamite ruler, these were probably much more defensive measures than he cared to admit. As well as proclaiming his victories he was careful to renew the defences of his capital. At the same time, Nippur was lost to Isin, and this began a remarkable period during which the holy city changed hands no less than eighteen times in twenty-four years. During this time Isin under Zambia (1836–1834), Iterpisha (1833–1831), Urdukuga (1830–1828) and Sinmagir (1827–1817) was just strong enough to win Nippur, but never strong enough to hold it, and Larsa was constantly distracted by other events. To begin with, the danger from the east engaged Siniqisham's attention, and he could spare little time or thought for affairs in other directions. The province of Kazallu, which had been won from Babylon, probably by Sinidinnam, was waiting for an opportunity to strike back, and just after the death of Siniqisham (1836), a sudden raid resulted in the capture of Larsa. Siniqisham's successor Silliadad, who ruled for only a few months, became a mere vassal of Kazallu, and no longer called himself "king", but merely "governor" of his city. With Silliadad, the local dynasty came to an end.

The dominance of Kazallu was short-lived. The danger from the east, which the Larsa kings had tried to combat, continued to grow, and Kazallu could do nothing to stop it. Besides, the conduct of the troops of Kazallu in Larsa, especially their desecration of the city's shrines, was so bitterly resented that when Kudurmabuk, the leader of the eastern forces, appeared before the city he was able to enter the city as a liberator rather than a conqueror.

Kudurmabuk's name, and that of his father Simtishilhak, are Elamite, and originally it was taken that his attack was one of the periodic Elamite raids on Babylonia. But Kudurmabuk was ruler of Iamutbal, a country on the eastern bank of the Tigris south of the Diyala in an area which was by this time largely Amorite. His title of *adda*, or father, of Iamutbal seems to alternate with that of *adda* of the Amorites, and if he was a genuine Elamite, it is curious that he gave his sons, Waradsin and Rimsin, names which are pure Akkadian. It is much more likely that an earlier member of Kudurmabuk's family had been an Amorite sheikh in the service of the Elamites, and that as a result of this some members of the family were given Elamite names. In fact, it may have been on Elamite orders that Kudurmabuk attacked Babylonia; but once he had conquered Larsa he set up an independent dynasty, free from Elamite domination, by installing his son Waradsin (1834–1823) as king.

The new king's first action was to punish Kazallu. The city was destroyed, and its leaders who had been captured in Larsa were executed. In this he may have been aided by Sabium of Babylon (1844–1831) the son and successor of Sumulael. This was in fact the only military venture undertaken by Babylonian kings at this period, for Sabium and Apilsin (1830–1813), who followed him on the throne of Babylon, were more concerned with consolidation than with conquest, and concentrated on digging canals and building fortresses and temples. The principal achievement of Sabium's reign was the erection of Esagila, the temple of Marduk in Babylon, while Apilsin strengthened the city wall and placed fortresses at important positions on his frontiers. This activity was confined to northern Babylonia, and left Larsa free to expand in the south. Nippur was recovered, and large-scale building programmes were undertaken in Ur and Larsa. Mashkanshabra, which had belonged to Larsa under Sinidinnam, was recaptured, and a fortress called Karshamash was won from Babylon. It is odd that these military operations were undertaken by Kudurmabuk rather than Waradsin, and in fact there is no indication of what position the adda of Iamutbal held at his son's court. Year-dates and oaths are all in Waradsin's name, but there are details of building operations undertaken by Kudurmabuk, and even a record of his allowance of beer. It is likely that he spent the summer among his semi-nomadic Amorite followers in Iamutbal and retired to the comfort of Larsa only in winter.

Waradsin died after a reign of twelve years. His brother, Rimsin, was still very young, and Kudurmabuk seems to have held the throne of Larsa himself for a few months before deciding that Rimsin was capable of looking after the kingdom. So began a sixty-year reign (1822–1763) which brought Larsa to new heights of prosperity before its final fall. All mid- and south Babylonia was gradually united under a strong and in many ways an enlightened rule. Rimsin concentrated especially on the rivers and canals which were so important for his country,

and throughout his reign he commemmorates the digging of
new waterways or the clearing of old ones. He ranks too as
one of the great temple-builders of the period, not only at
Larsa but also in Ur and other religious centres. The early part
of his reign was, in fact, if we can judge by his date-formulae,
spent largely in building operations. Trade flourished, and his
control of the ports meant that Larsa could tap the rich sources
of copper, ivory and precious stones which came from the
shores and islands of the Persian Gulf and further afield. The
result was that merchants grew prosperous and the private
ownership of property was greatly increased. The old Sumerian
system of economic control by the government and priesthood
seemed to be going rapidly out of date.

As well as securing prosperity at home, Rimsin was engaged
in the constant enlargement of his dominions. No details are
known of his early campaigns, but there is mention of building
operations in places like Zarbilum, on the road to Der, Adab,
north-east of Isin, Mashkanshabra, and, Ennigi between Isin
and Babylon. The struggle with Isin for the possession of Nippur
was still going on, and Rimsin three times gained control of it
only to lose it again. His growing power was beginning to be
recognized as a menace to the other cities, and by 1809 a coalition had been formed against him, consisting of Isin, Babylon,
Uruk, Rapiqum and the Sutians, with Irdameme, king of Uruk,
in command. Uruk, thus called unexpectedly to lead the opposition to Larsa, had until some forty years previously been ruled
by the kings of Isin, but had broken free under Sinkashid, an
intruder who had come perhaps from the area of the middle-
Euphrates. Sinkashid, who built the royal palace and several
temples in Uruk, was followed by Sineribam, who for a time
acknowledged the suzerainty of Larsa, and then by Singamil
and Irdameme. But Uruk's attempt to win the leadership of
the Babylonian states met with no success, for the coalition was
heavily defeated.

The following year Rimsin followed up his victory by capturing Pinaratim and Nasarum, and expansion continued
until in 1803 he destroyed Der in the foothills of the Iranian
highlands. In the same year Kisurra, some twenty miles west of
Isin, was conquered, and the struggle for Isin, and with it the
leadership of southern Babylonia, moved towards a climax.

At the same time Babylon, which under Apilsin had retired

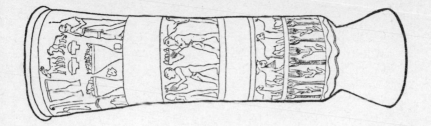

FIG. 2   Alabaster vase from Uruk (after Parrot)

from the contest to nurse her resources, came forward once more under Sinmuballit (1812–1793) in an attempt to assert her supremacy. The coalition with Uruk and the other states which Sinmuballit had entered in the early years of his reign had proved a complete failure. But when Rimsin was engaged in his campaigns in the east, Sinmuballit took advantage of his absence to capture and re-fortify the little town of Ennigi, which lay between Babylon and Isin. This can have had little effect on Larsa, for in 1802 Rimsin turned once more on Uruk, which had temporarily revived under Anam, son of Ilanshemea. The city now became a dependency of Larsa. By this time, too, Rimsin had gained permanent control of Nippur, but his progress to complete domination in the south was halted for a time by the further intervention of Sinmuballit, who inflicted a defeat on him in 1799. Yet this proved to be only a pause, for in the following year Isin fell to Rimsin's forces.

Damiqilishu (1816–1794) who ruled Isin in the final years of her independence, had been careful to renew the fortifications of his city when he saw the danger that was to come, but his defences were of little use against the might of Rimsin. They were just as useless two years later when Sinmuballit descended from the north and seized Isin from Rimsin's forces. The disgruntled king of Larsa could name the year only after the work which had been done on his canal system. The following year he had to deal with trouble on his eastern frontier, but in 1794 he could afford to begin a strong offensive towards Isin. The Babylonian forces in the city managed to withstand his assault, but Dunum, the principal town which remained under Isin's control, fell to Larsa. The following year (1793) another attack was made, and although Sinmuballit did sufficient to claim that he defeated Rimsin's forces, he could not prevent Isin falling into his rival's hands.

So important did Rimsin consider his capture of Isin that it was commemorated in his date-formulae for the remaining thirty years of his reign. Now that it was finally his, he could indeed consider himself "King of Sumer and Akkad", the true successor of the Dynasty of Ur, a living god upon earth. His enemies had been defeated, his country was united and prosperous, and he could now afford to concern himself with social reforms which would consolidate his rule. The prosperity of the merchant classes and their increasing speculation in land and house property seemed to him a danger to his own authority, and besides was contary to the Sumerian practice of his great predecessors, the kings of Ur. More important—for Rimsin was a practical man—his soldiers had fought long and well, and there might be still more fighting to be done. It would be a sensible as well as an economical policy to reward them and at the same time secure their future loyalty at the expense of private citizens rather than the royal treasury. Rimsin did not go so far as to nationalize property and dispossess private owners, but he did make it difficult to buy or own houses and land, and the rich merchant class quickly disappeared. Business documents from the second half of Rimsin's reign are largely concerned with palace transactions, and there is a corresponding increase in the number of civil servants and the documentation so essential to a bureaucracy.

Before going on to describe the fall of the Larsa dynasty, it is necessary to look for a moment at the situation in other parts of what had once been the Empire of Ur. The southern part of that empire was now firmly in the hands of Rimsin, and north of that Babylon was the dominant power. But the kings of Ur had also had control of lands further up the Tigris and Euphrates, and these lands had been among the first to break away in the early part of Ibbisin's reign. At Eshnunna in the Diyala region, for instance, there are no Ur-dates after Ibbisin's second year. The revolt here was led by Ituria, the governor of Eshnunna under the Ur dynasty, and his son Ilushuilia, who became the first independent king of the area, and styled himself "King of the Four Quarters", a title which showed that he considered himself the successor of Ur. The power of Eshnunna was shown almost immediately by expansion towards the north. Ilushuilia's successor Nurahum was successful in a war against Subartu, the general name for north Mesopotamia from the Euphrates to beyond the Tigris, and Kirikiri, who followed him, conducted operations in the same area. His son Bilalama was strong enough to be on friendly terms with Elam (his daughter married the governor of Susa), as well as with Der and even Isin under Shuilishu (1984–1975). Bilalama evolved a novel method of extending his dominions by enlisting the aid of nomad Amorite tribesmen to capture and sack neighbouring cities which he afterwards incorporated into his dominions. Occasionally the Amorites overstepped themselves and had to be dealt with, but on the whole the system seems to have worked very well.

The reign of Isharramashu, Bilalama's successor in Eshnunna, ended in the destruction of the royal palace. This was due to the activities of Annumutabil, king of Der, a state which had also won its independence on the fall of Ur. Annumutabil had just concluded a campaign in the Iranian mountains in which he had defeated Elam and her allies, and now he turned on Elamite supporters in the plain. Eshnunna was burned down and Usurawasu, who had been Annumutabil's ambassador in the city, was set on the throne. Der lost its independence soon afterwards to Iddindagan of Isin (1974–1954), and Eshnunna began to recover her strength. Azuzum, the next king, was on friendly terms with Gungunum of Larsa (1932–1906), and under Urninmar, Urningizzida and Ibiqadad I the palace was rebuilt and extended. A sudden collapse under Abdierah is to be explained by an unsuccessful campaign against Kish which resulted in the capture of the king and the loss of the area around the mouth of the Diyala, where an independent dynasty was set up at Tutub (modern Khafaje). Meanwhile Eshnunna under Shiqlanum and Sharria continued in decline, but a gradual revival began under Sharria's son Belakum and his successor Warassa. Tutub and other former dependencies which had won their freedom were reconquered, and despite the set-back caused by Sinidinnam of Larsa's attack on the city (1844), expansion continued under Ibalpiel I. The city wall was repaired, and the palace again rebuilt. Ibiqadad II, who followed Ibalpiel, called himself "enlarger of Eshnunna" and thought himself sufficiently important to receive deification. About this time the dynasties of the south were much too concerned with their own affairs and the danger from Kudurmabuk to show interest in an area as distant as Eshnunna, while further north Babylon under Sabium (1844–1831) and Apilsin (1830–1813) concentrated on internal strengthening rather than foreign conquests. The result was that Ibiqadad II was able to strike across to the middle Euphrates and capture Rapiqum, a town which had previously been controlled by Sinidinnam of Larsa. This gave him a footing on the trade route up the Euphrates to Syria and Anatolia. Naramsin, the next king, extended the kingdom even further by the capture of Sippar in one direction and Assur in the other. But these conquests did not last

long. Within a few years Rapiqum regained its independence,
Sippar was won back by Babylon, and Assur under a new dynasty rose to dominate the entire northern area of Mesopotamia.
Dadusha, Naramsin's brother, who followed him on the throne
of Eshnunna, attempted to maintain his country's independence
with campaigns to the north and a marriage alliance with the
new ruling family of Rapiqum, but soon after his death about
1785 his successor Ibalpiel II was forced to acknowledge the
supremacy of Assur.

The growing power of Assur had its effect also on another
former province of the Empire of Ur, Mari on the middle
Euphrates. Situated as it was on the old caravan route from
the Persian Gulf to the Mediterranean, Mari had for many
years been an important trading town, and had for a short
time been the leading city of Babylonia. It was included in the
empire of Akkad, and later was ruled by viceroys under the
kings of Ur. Mari was the city in which Ishbi-irra started the
career which was to lead to his kingship in Isin. At some time
after the fall of the Ur dynasty a strong Amorite element moved
in, and an independent dynasty was set up under kings who soon
spread their influence through western Mesopotamia and
northern Syria. Iaggidlim, the first of these kings of whom we
have any knowledge, was a contemporary of Sabium of Babylon
(1844–1831). Almost the only thing known about his reign is
the fact that he quarrelled with one of his neighbours. For
Ilakabkabu, the Amorite ruler of a kingdom somewhere in the
area, perhaps up the River Khabur, claimed that Iaggidlim
had broken an oath made between them, and in protest at this
destroyed his city and seized his son Iahdunlim. But Ilakabkabu's kingdom was in its turn destroyed by Naramsin of
Eshnunna and Assur, and while Iahdunlim recovered the
throne of Mari, Ilakabkabu's son Shamshiadad was driven out
to seek his fortune. Somewhere in Babylonia he gathered a band
of followers strong enough to advance up the Tigris towards
Assur and seize Ekallate, a fortress between the Diyala and the
lower Zab. Erishum II was now ruling in Assur, but his reign
was short, for after a three-year pause in Ekallate Shamshiadad
pushed forward to seize Assur and establish himself as king
there.

Under his rule, Assur rose to a dominant position in northern
Mesopotamia. Her previous history had been one of commercial

prosperity without much political influence. Kings before the dynasty of Akkad are little more than names, and Assur followed the usual pattern of the area by being subject to Sargon of Akkad and then to the dynasty of Ur. After gaining her independence, the city had a wide influence as the centre of a trading system which established merchant colonies far from the upper Tigris, most notably at Kanesh, near modern Kayseri in central Anatolia. This merchant community was probably founded in the reign of Erishum I, son of the Ilushuma whose attempt to secure the trade route through Der to the Iranian plateau by attacking Ishmedagan of Isin (1953–1935) has already been mentioned. As a result of these merchant-ventures Assur remained prosperous throughout the reigns of Ikunu and Sargon I, and it was only towards the end of the reign of Puzurashur, when Naramsin of Eshnunna was beginning to show his strength, that the prosperity of Assur showed a sharp decline. After Naramsin's conquest of the city, Assur under Erishum II had no time to re-establish herself before Shamshiadad appeared from the desert to capture the city and institute revival of its power. Under his vigorous leadership the small kingdom which he had captured was extended to the Mediterranean on one side and the Iranian mountains on the other. In the area with which we are concerned, his first objective was to settle accounts with Mari. By skilful plotting he contrived a palace revolution in which Iahdunlim lost his life, and in the confusion which resulted the Assyrian king was able to move in and install his second son Iasmahadad as governor. Zimrilim, the king of Mari's son, was compelled to flee for asylum to Aleppo. A Syrian campaign followed in which Carchemish, Harran and other states were forced into allegiance with Assur and Iasmahadad was married to the daughter of the king of Qatna on the Orontes. Nearer home, Shamshiadad's elder son Ishmedagan was appointed governor of Ekallate, and the Assyrian king was in control of a strong, well-knit empire which was ready to challenge for the leadership of the Mesopotamian world.

Such was the position of Assyria about the time when Rimsin of Larsa finally conquered Isin. The only power which seemed likely to challenge the supremacy of these two was Eshnunna, which was still in the control of the Diyala region and the area west of it. But in 1793, just after he had lost Isin to Larsa, Sinmuballit of Babylon died, and was succeeded by his son, a vigorous and far-seeing young man whose name was Hammurabi.

In the early years of his reign, Hammurabi was content to follow his predecessors in strengthening his realm and seeking to gain for it the leadership of the south. Social reforms were undertaken which were a prelude to the great legal enactments of his later years, and by 1787 he was ready to move into the attack against Larsa. Isin and Uruk quickly fell into his hands, and the following year Rimsin's homeland of Iamutbal was subdued. But before Hammurabi could strike the final blow against Larsa itself he was forced to turn to meet a danger from another quarter, and the conquest of Larsa had to be postponed for more than twenty years.

In the north it seemed at first that the energetic Dadusha of Eshnunna was more than a match for the might of Assur. Despite Shamshiadad's conquests in Syria and on the Euphrates, Dadusha was able about 1785 to go into the attack against him. The Assyrian army was defeated near Ekallate, where Shamshiadad's elder son was governor, and in a thrust which penetrated almost as far as the Upper Zab several princes of the Assyrian royal house were taken prisoner. But these successes were short-lived. In the following year (1784) Dadusha died, and before his successor Ibalpiel II had time to establish himself firmly, Shamshiadad led a campaign to the south. Ibalpiel succeeded in saving his city, but was powerless to prevent the Assyrian forces from marching down the Tigris and against Malgum, a kingdom situated on the bank of the river south-east of Eshnunna. In the course of this march Shamshiadad must have skirted the boundaries of Babylon, and it was this danger which caused Hammurabi to forego his conquest of Larsa and turn north to meet the menace of Assyria.

One of the main reasons for Hammurabi's greatness was the fact that he could clearly see his own limitations. In later years he was content to wait for his opportunities and play off his opponents against one another. Now, when he saw for himself the size of the Assyrian forces, he realized immediately that for the moment he had no chance against them. Prudently he laid his services at the feet of the Assyrian king. When Malgum was defeated in 1784 it was with the help of Babylonian arms. The following year, when Shamshiadad turned against the kingdom of Rapiqum, Hammurabi again sent a contingent to his aid. About the same time Eshnunna too submitted to Assyria, although no details are known.

Then, about 1781, Shamshiadad died and was succeeded by his son Ishmedagan. Almost immediately the Assyrian conquests began to crumble. Zimrilim, son of the former king of Mari, who was in exile at Aleppo, seized his chance to regain his father's throne. Ibalpiel of Eshnunna was also quick to reassert his independence, and was able to conquer Rapiqum for himself (1777) and even to defeat the army of Assyria. Only Hammurabi made no hostile move. His date-formulae from 1782 to 1776 are concerned with the dedication of thrones and statues of the gods. No doubt he was biding his time and nursing his strength, waiting and watching to see how events would turn out. He was quick to appreciate the fact that with the newly-won independence of Mari he now had on his northern border not one hostile state, but two powers bitterly opposed to each other. An alliance with Mari was the obvious answer, and this was speedily concluded. The conquest of Larsa, which had been abandoned because of Shamshiadad's attack, would be impracticable until affairs in the north were more settled, and so Rimsin was brought into the alliance as well. Thus a few years after he had been a powerless Assyrian vassal, Hammurabi became the leader of a powerful coalition. From 1775 onwards the building of fortresses begins to play a larger part in his date-formulae. Hammurabi was gradually building up his power for a great offensive.

After the breakaway of Eshnunna and Mari, Assyria began to look elsewhere for allies, and turned increasingly to the east. Malgum, Gutium and Elam joined her, and in face of the increasing power of Babylon, Mari, and Larsa, Eshnunna too was eventually forced to throw in her lot with the Assyrian league. Thus all Mesopotamia was split into two rival camps, and for several years an uneasy peace was preserved.

At last in 1764 Hammurabi judged that his time had come. Marching to meet the massive army which had been raised by the north-eastern allies, he inflicted a crushing defeat on it. Well could he claim that he had "re-established the foundations of the Empire of Sumer and Akkad".

After this victory, Hammurabi felt himself secure enough to carry on with the task which the Assyrians had originally

Fig. 3 Steatite head of Hammurabi, now in the Louvre

interrupted. Rimsin of Larsa had now been on the throne for sixty-one years, during the latter part of which he had contented himself with reflecting on his former glories. Long after Isin had fallen into Hammurabi's hands, he continued to date his years by his own capture of that city, and Larsa drifted along in alliance with Babylon without either gaining or contributing much. This was exactly what Hammurabi wanted, for it meant that he could ignore his southern border while his concern was with the north. After the defeat of the Assyrian coalition, Rimsin's usefulness was ended, and Hammurabi, with a promptitude that must have made his more morally-minded subjects blush, besieged and destroyed his city (1763) "and so forced Sumer and Akkad to obey his orders".

Thus Hammurabi became master of all Babylonia. In the north, however, his troubles were by no means over. The year after his conquest of Larsa, the Assyrian coalition made an attempt to re-assert itself. Again it was defeated, and the lands up the Tigris as far as the borders of Assyria were brought under Babylonian rule. Once again Hammurabi felt sufficiently secure from his enemies to turn on his friends. This time it was Zimrilim of Mari who felt the weight of his gratitude, and Mari was defeated and made subject to Babylon. In the same year (1761) Malgum and other Assyrian allies were also defeated, while at home Hammurabi re-dug the canal known as "Hammurabi spells abundance for the people", and so provided a plentiful water supply for Nippur, Eridu, Ur, Larsa, Uruk and Isin. For the next year (1760) no military successes are recorded, but in 1759 Mari and Malgum, which had broken the terms of their peace-treaties, were destroyed. Two years later war broke out yet again with Assyria and her allies, and resulted once more in victory for Hammurabi. In 1756 it was the turn of Eshnunna, for after the city had been badly hit by floods and was in no position to defend herself, by judicious use of what he modestly calls "the wisdom with which Marduk endowed him", Hammurabi moved in and took it over. Finally in 1755 a fourth campaign was conducted against Assyria, and with Assur and Nineveh safe in his hands, Hammurabi could afford to rest. Once again he recognized his limits, and refused to attempt further conquests into the mountains to the east and north or into the desert to the west. His empire was secure, and he could enjoy a few years of peace. The remainder of his reign until his death in 1750 was devoted to law-giving and matters of religion.

Hammurabi has been hailed as one of the great monarchs of antiquity. This judgement was based at first almost entirely on the law code which he issued towards the end of his life, and which was at first thought to be the oldest in the world. More recent excavations have, however, shown that this is by no means the case. Earlier law-codes in both Sumerian and Akkadian have been discovered at Eshnunna, Isin and Ur. These codes tend to show that in many cases Hammurabi merely included in his code the legal customs and precedents which were common throughout the area, rather than creating new and original laws. But the extent and arrangement of the code, and its preservation, under the auspices of Shamash, on stone rather than clay, are the work of Hammurabi himself. Unfortunately for the grandeur of his conception, there is little evidence that his reforms were ever put into general practice, and our knowledge of his code is due solely to the fact that despite the protection of the sun-god the black basalt column on which it was inscribed was later carried away by Elamite raiders to Susa, whence it was recovered by a modern archaeological expedition.

As a conqueror Hammurabi is perhaps more entitled to be considered great. The extent of his dominions, from beyond Nineveh to the Persian Gulf, is perhaps not great enough for him to be considered "King of the Universe", but for a king who started as a powerless vassal of Assyria, the empire he built up was a considerable achievement. The methods by which he built it are perhaps more open to question, especially for a king who boasts of the "righteousness" which he established in the land, but it says much for his diplomacy that despite the activities of many spies at his court he was able for so long to conceal his real purpose from his allies. His policy of biding his time, separating his enemies and attacking them individually certainly paid handsome dividends.

A good deal is known of Hammurabi's administration of his empire, for almost 150 of his letters have been preserved. It can be seen that the king gave his personal attention to all kinds of business connected with the provinces, and gave his own instructions to his governors on matters which many monarchs would have considered beneath their notice. Petty law-suits, the collection of dates and sesame-seed, payment of rent, and sheep-shearing are given as much attention as the care of canals and the collection of taxes. Hammurabi's was in a very real sense a personal empire. He had won it himself and now he ruled it himself. The result of this was inevitably that when he was succeeded by lesser men, his empire began to break up. Exactly the same thing had happened to the Assyrian empire after the death of Shamshiadad, for it too was an intensely personal affair. In fact "empire" is perhaps a wrong word to use in this context, for despite the bureaucratic efforts made by the kings of the Third Dynasty of Ur the conquests in and around Mesopotamia were never fully consolidated and welded into a real political unity. The various cities were naturally in-dependent, and the greater ones had "spheres of influence" rather than empires, which expanded and contracted from year to year without any definite boundaries. This can be seen best in the struggle between Isin and Larsa, when one city could claim the hegemony while the army of the other was only a few miles from its gates. Similarly Rimsin was able to consider himself lord of the world while Hammurabi was attacking Uruk and Isin just to the north. Empires of this type could never have any stability, and it is not surprising that almost immediately after Hammurabi's death Babylon's sphere of influence began rapidly to contract.

In matters of religion Hammurabi had a more lasting in-fluence. He saw that many of the inter-dynastic disputes had been over the possession of Nippur and other religious centres of the land. As long as the principal shrines were in the south—as long, in fact, as there were several shrines over which to quarrel—there would be no possibility of unity under Babylon. Besides this he had to contend with the differing religious be-liefs of the different elements in his population, Sumerian and Semitic. The chthonic nature-religion of the Sumerians did not mix easily with Semitic sun-worship. At one stroke Hammurabi changed all this and succeeded in imposing a religious pattern which long outlasted his dynasty. This he did by the simple method of making Marduk, god of Babylon, into the principal god of the Mesopotamian pantheon. After this, Babylon naturally became the main religious centre, and its god became a unifying link such as had never before existed in the land. At the same time, Hammurabi seized on the gradual disappearance of Sumerian as a spoken language to legitimize his alterations in the order of the gods. To keep them in the language of the people the old legends were having to be translated into Akkadian, which had by this time become the general diplomatic and literary language, and in the course of their translation Hammurabi made sure that they were adapted to his own ends. It was now related that when Anu, the supreme god, was faced by the primeval dragon Tiamat, he did not have the courage to meet her. However Marduk, god of Babylon, succeeding in vanquishing her, and as a result was elected king by all the gods. Thus Marduk was given divine backing for his supreme position. The positions of the other gods were accurately defined, and their shrines were tended with royal favour. So Hammurabi carried out a peaceful reformation which was ultimately of greater importance than his political or military successes.

In other ways too Hammurabi achieved a synthesis of the various elements in his population. His position as king, for instance, managed to combine the Semitic idea of a tribal chief with the Sumerian absolute monarch. As has been pointed out, even his appearance suggests a synthesis, for his short rounded beard, worn without a moustache, is Amorite, while his costume and headgear are Sumerian. In all these and in many other ways Hammurabi succeeded in welding Babylonia into a unity which was to survive many years of foreign domination. It was largely to him that we owe the formation of the civilization and the way of life known as "Babylonian".

(3)
Babylonian Life and Law

LAW-CODES issued by Mesopotamian kings have been mentioned several times in the previous chapters. The fullest and most impressive of these is that of Hammurabi, and it is worth while at this point to consider his code, together with those of his predecessors, before going on to an account of the later history of Babylon. An examination of the codes must necessarily involve a description of the society for which they were intended to legislate, and an especially full picture emerges of life as it was under the Babylonian First Dynasty. But before this description it is necessary to consider the general concept of law in ancient Mesopotamia and the relationship which the codes bear to each other. This entails a return to the period of the formation of the city-states and the development of monarchy.

It has already been seen how in early Mesopotamia the city-state was regarded as the property of the city-god, and the ruler was considered to be god's steward or manager. It was therefore the ruler's duty to see that the state was organized wholly for the comfort of the god who owned it, and that all actions which interfered with this end were firmly repressed. Thus he had to make sure that law and order prevailed in the state, that the weak were fairly treated and not prevented from performing their tasks, and that the rich and powerful did not turn to self-interest rather than the service of god. Gradually a body of law was built up, based on the custom of the area, and it was to this law, unwritten at first, that rulers referred in their judgement of disputes. A king who found on his accession that this customary law was not being observed or who wished to make special provision for specific abuses in his own state might issue a decree emphasizing or adding to the common law, and in fact many kings made a point of "establishing justice in the land" in an early year of their reigns by the issue of just such a decree. The law-codes as we have them are pronouncements of this sort. They are not in fact "codes" at all in the sense of complete codifications of the entire body of law as it existed at that time, but a series of amendments to the law or restatements of particular subjects which seemed to be important to the king of the time. As they are all based on a background of common law the "codes" resemble each other in many ways when dealing with similar subjects, but there is never any hint that one king simply copied from the laws of another. Each group of laws is aimed at a particular situation confronting a particular ruler and is rather a series of variations on common law than a statement of that common law. But sometimes the similarity in the wording of codes is so great that it is virtually certain that there existed not only a common background of customary law but also a common tradition of *written* law handed down in the scribal schools of Mesopotamia. This can be seen especially in the literary form which law codes tend to take. The usual arrangement is first a prologue telling how the ruler was called by the gods to establish justice in the land and bring well-being to the people, then a series of laws suited to the situation as he found it, and finally an epilogue proclaiming the benefits which the laws had brought to the land, calling down blessings on those who respect the king's inscription and heaping curses on those who desecrate it. The normal form taken by a law is "If so-and-so has happened, under these circumstances so-and-so shall be done", and it is clear that each law is a statement of an individual precedent rather than an attempt to cover a general category of crimes. For instance one of Urnammu's laws states "If a man has cut off another man's nose with a *geshpu*-instrument (whatever that may be) he shall pay forty shekels of silver". This is obviously a statement of a single decision. No attempt is made, as far as can be seen, to generalize either on loss of the nose or on assault with or without a *geshpu*, and judges were presumably expected to base their decisions in other cases on the punishment for this particular crime. Doubtless copies of local laws were made so that judges could refer to them, and certainly selections were made for the use of students in the schools. In several cases it is copies such as these that have survived rather than the original royal edicts.

The development of a system of law among the Semitic-speaking communities of Mesopotamia was rather different from the one detailed above, although by the time of the surviving law-codes the two traditions had become inseparably mixed. Among the Semites the father was the head of the family and his word was law. In larger groups the chief held a similar position, generally supported by a council composed of heads of families. In these groups, as in the Sumerian city-states, the basis of law was the custom of the area, and offences within the group were punished according to that custom. When disputes arose between groups no settlement was possible except by means of a blood-feud. If for instance a member of one group was killed by a member of another, then a member of the second group had to be killed to pay for the loss of life. This meant that another member of the first group had to be killed, and so on indefinitely, unless something was done to stop it. So in the interests of sheer self-preservation communities had to lay down the rule that once life had been paid for by life, or limb by limb, the matter must be considered settled and peace be restored once more. Thus there arose the doctrine of "an eye for an eye, a tooth for a tooth", a concept of great importance in ancient law and one which is to a certain extent still with us today. But often enough in ancient as in modern times offenders could pay for their crimes in cash rather than in kind, and scales of fines were evolved to cover all sorts of offences. In this matter the Sumerians seem to have been rather more advanced than the Semites, but this impression may be largely due to a lack of illustrative material.

The first reform code of which we have any record is that of Urukagina of Lagash (c. 2347–2341). This has already been described in Chapter 1. The only record of Urukagina's reforms which has been preserved is on a clay cone commemorating the completion of a new canal, but it is reasonable to suppose that he actually issued an official "code" in the same manner as later rulers. The earliest of these codes which has survived was issued by Urnammu (c. 2113–2096), the founder of the Third Dynasty of Ur. Unfortunately the whole tablet is so badly damaged that only sections of it are intelligible. One of the most important of its provisions has already been quoted. It shows that by Urnammu's time the substitution of a fine for a physical punishment was already the usual practice, and this is borne out by some of the other sections which have survived.

The penalty for cutting off a foot, for instance, is ten shekels of silver, while the fine for breaking bones is sixty shekels of silver.

Urnammu's law-code was written in Sumerian. The next oldest surviving law-code comes from the northern city of Eshnunna and is in the Akkadian language. In a brief preamble mention is made of Bilalama, who ruled in Eshnunna about 1980 B.C., but it can be seen that the laws as we have them are copies made in his reign and that the code itself must have been issued by an earlier ruler. The copies that we possess were probably extracts made for a scribal school and there is no trace of the elaborate prologue or epilogue which doubtless featured in the original composition. The laws, of which fifty-nine are preserved, are often extremely like those of Hammurabi in style, content and language. In fact about three-quarters of them are more or less directly reproduced in Hammurabi's code, and none of the others would look out of place in the same context. The code well illustrates the care and attention to detail with which Mesopotamian monarchs supervised their dominions. It deals not only with criminal offences but also with the control of prices and wages, which were regulated with a firmness that modern Chancellors of the Exchequer find hard to match.

Some fifty years after Bilalama's death Lipitishtar of Isin (c. 1934–1924) issued a reform-code of which considerable fragments have survived. It is written in Sumerian and consisted originally of about one hundred laws, of which only about thirty-five can be read. The prologue tells how Lipitishtar was called by the gods Anu and Enlil "to establish justice in the land, to banish complaints, to turn back enmity and rebellion by force of arms and to bring well-being to the Sumerians and Akkadians". The surviving laws deal with questions of boat-hiring, gardens and palm-groves, slaves, tax on estates, inheritance, marriage, and the hiring of oxen, and again it can be seen that laws are drawn from the same background as those of Hammurabi. An epilogue of the usual type concludes the code.

The code of Hammurabi is a much more elaborate piece of work than any of those mentioned above. Its prologue is a stock composition in an archaic-poetic style which is in complete contrast to the vivid everyday language of the laws themselves. The principal difference from Lipitishtar's prologue is in length, for while the earlier code was that of a city-state, Hammurabi's was that of an empire, and had to be given an elaboration and dignity worthy of its great purpose. So where Lipitishtar contented himself with the description of "the humble shepherd of Nippur, the stalwart farmer of Ur, who abandons not Eridu, the suitable lord of Uruk, king of Isin, king of Sumer and Akkad", Hammurabi hails himself as "the one who makes affluence and plenty abound, who provides in abundance all sorts of things for Nippur, bond of heaven and earth, the devout patron of Ekur, the efficient king, who restored Eridu to its place, who purified the cult of Eabzu, the one who strides through the four quarters of the world, who makes the name of Babylon great, who rejoices the heart of Marduk his lord, who throughout his lifetime stands responsible for Esagila, the descendant of royalty whom Sin begat" and so on through two hundred and fifty lines of text describing the conquest and pacification of his empire. At the end of this elaborate list he comes to the point of his decree. "When Marduk commanded me to give justice to the people of the land and to let them have good governance, I set forth truth and justice throughout the land and prospered the people. At that time I issued the following decrees." Then follow two hundred and eighty-two ordinances by which the great king sought to guide his empire in the paths of justice. An epilogue closes the composition, differing again from Lipitishtar's mainly in length and elaboration. It tells how Hammurabi, after bringing peace to his country, promulgated his laws and set them up in the temple of Marduk in Babylon where the oppressed could read them and find peace of mind. It ends with sixteen lines of blessing for those who uphold his statutes, and two hundred and eighty lines of curses for any man who distorts his words or destroys his monuments. "May the mighty gods of heaven and earth curse him, his descendants, his land, his warriors, his people and his nation with a baleful curse. May Enlil, by his word which cannot be altered, curse him with these curses, and may they quickly overtake him!"

The laws themselves can now be studied in greater detail. It must be stressed again that the code is in essence a series of amendments to a common law which can in most cases only be guessed at, and that there is little hope of gaining a consistent overall picture from it. However, certain aspects of Babylonian life can be well illustrated from the code, and in many cases the background can be filled in from other sources. The code begins with a group of laws dealing with legal procedure in the courts. These are presumably given this prominent position because of their importance in establishing the security of litigants. The first law makes it perfectly clear that if a man brought a capital charge against another and failed to prove it, he would himself be executed. This severe measure was bound to ensure that false charges were not lightly brought to court. The second law deals with a difficulty that must often have arisen in a society that was highly conscious of demons, witches and the supernatural. The situation is the same as in the previous law, except that the charge which the accuser had failed to prove was one of sorcery. In this case there was such fear of witchcraft that despite the lack of proof of his guilt the accused still had to prove his innocence. This he was forced to do by throwing himself into the Euphrates. If he drowned he was guilty and the accuser took his property. If on the other hand he floated he was considered innocent and the accuser was executed. It is interesting to note that the rule here is the exact opposite of the more common one that the guilty float and the innocent drown. Certainly the Babylonian method shows greater consideration for the innocent.

The next two sections of the code deal with perjury. The idea behind them is that anyone who bears false witness in court will suffer the penalty appropriate to the case which is being tried. The next section is designed to ensure the absolute integrity of judges. Any judge who attempted to change a judgement duly given and completed was liable to a fine of twelve times the amount claimed in the case he was trying and to instant dismissal from the bench of judges. By these measures Hammurabi established a firm basis for the rest of his legislation. Given the integrity of prosecutors and witnesses and the impartiality and incorruptibility of judges the citizen of Babylon could be certain that his case would receive a fair hearing and end in a reasonable decision.

Little is known of the composition of Babylonian courts or of the procedure at a trial. Judges generally sat in groups, and trials seem to have been held in the palace or in the temple of Shamash, god of justice. Occasionally too they may have taken place at the city-gate, a favourite place in the Orient for the

administration of justice. There was no police force and no
public prosecutor; only if litigants could not settle a matter
between themselves did they apply to a court for judgement.
Both written and spoken evidence were allowed, and there was
usually no right of appeal to a higher court, although occasionally injured parties were allowed to petition the king as
the highest legal authority. It is clear that the judges were in
origin merely referees employed in settling private disputes,
and even when they became public officials (as they seem to
have been in Hammurabi's day) they had little power to en-
force their decisions. In cases involving property they could
make the losing party renounce his claim in writing, and when
there was a sentence of corporal punishment it was probably
inflicted in some cases at least by the relations of the aggrieved
party in the presence of the judges, who made sure that the
sentence was not exceeded. In other cases this relic of the blood-
feud was superseded by punishment by an officer appointed
by the king. Methods of execution included drowning, burning,
impalement and probably decapitation.

The next sections of the Hammurabi code deal with offences
against property. The great increase in private ownership of
property during the period of the Isin and Larsa dynasties has
already been noted, and its importance is perhaps reflected in
the prominent position given to these sections in the law-code.
The general penalty for theft was death, and the receiver of
stolen goods suffered the same fate. The only exception to this
was the stealing of cattle or boats belonging to the palace or a
temple. In this case a money payment could be substituted, and
it is probable that this was often what happened where private
property was concerned. In cases where there was difficulty in
establishing the real ownership of property an elaborate process
of swearing oaths and producing witnesses was necessary. Any
man who claimed property and then could not prove that it
was his was himself subject to the death penalty. In cases of
this sort a time limit of six months was allowed for the production of witnesses. If a man had sold stolen property but had
died before the case came to court then the property was returned to its owner and the buyer was compensated five-fold
from the dead man's estate.

As a man's children were considered to be part of his private
property the offence of kidnapping is included in this section,

and again the penalty is death. Similarly because a son belonged to his father he was not allowed to sell any of his father's other belongings, and anyone who bought them or accepted them for safe keeping was considered a thief and executed. The same punishment was inflicted on anyone who harboured a runaway slave, and in Eshnunna on any royal official who failed to return within seven days any escaped slave or lost property which he had appropriated in the course of his duty. On the other hand anyone who returned a runaway slave to his owner was entitled to a reward of two shekels of silver. This is in contrast to a similar law in the Lipitishtai code, where the reward is another slave or fifteen shekels of silver.

Burglary, robbery and looting are dealt with in the next sections. The burglar met a particularly unpleasant fate, for after execution his body was hung or impaled before the hole by which he had entered the house. In the absence of windows the common method of entry was obviously by digging through a wall, a comparatively simple task as the usual material was unbaked brick. In the Eshnunna code, though not in that of Hammurabi, a distinction is made between burglary by day, punishable by a fine of ten shekels of silver, and burglary by night, punishable by death. In the Hammurabi code highway robbery, too, incurred the death penalty, and here there is an interesting example of how Hammurabi expected his local governors to be responsible for the maintenance of law and order in their districts. If the robber was not caught the victim of the robbery received compensation from the local authorities for their failure to protect him. The humanity of this provision is in complete contrast to the crudity of the following section, which states that if a man was caught in the act of robbing a house which had caught fire he himself was to be thrown into the fire and burned to death.

The next paragraph of the law-code deals with grants of land to certain officers in the king's service, especially the "runner", a cross between a policeman and a royal courier, and the "fisher", a lesser figure of whose duties very little is known. Plots of land were granted to these officers by virtue of their rank, but their possession of the land was subject to a number of conditions. They had for instance to be willing to be sent on royal missions at any time, and an officer who refused or who sent a substitute was liable to be put to death. But at the same time an officer was provided with a measure of protection if he fell into enemy hands while on royal service. In his absence his son was allowed to keep his land, or, if his son was too young, one-third of it was given to his wife for her support. Even if the land was given to someone else who could look after it properly, it was returned to the officer when he escaped or was ransomed. If on the other hand the officer evaded his duty for two years or more he had no claim over his land, and it was granted to another officer.

Another ruling shows again the responsibility which Hammurabi felt for the safety of his citizens. A captured officer might be found by a Babylonian merchant in a foreign land and ransomed by him. It was the officer's duty to repay the merchant when he reached home, but if he could not afford this the payment of his ransom became the responsibility of the state. Under no circumstances would he have to dispose of his property to find the money.

The code now passes to higher officers in the royal service, the colonel or recruiting-officer and his adjutant. Any of those officers who called up men exempt from military service, or who allowed a runner or fisher to send a substitute in his place, were punishable by death. Similarly any abuse of authority by ill-treating or misusing an inferior officer met with the death penalty. Finally the legislator turns to the restrictions on property owned by royal grant. It could neither be sold nor exchanged nor assigned to a wife or daughter nor used to pay debts. These rules, however, applied only to certain groups of land-holder. Other groups, such as priestesses and merchants, could dispose of their royal grants if they wished, provided that the new owners performed the royal duty that went with the land. The reason for this distinction is not clear.

Agriculture was of primary importance to the Babylonian economy because it provided not only food for the people but also the country's principal materials for export. From the earliest times the maintenance of canals and agricultural land had been one of the state's chief responsibilities, and the next sections of Hammurabi's code are concerned with the preservation and improvement of the country's natural resources. Land which was not cultivated would very quickly return to the natural state, and the farmer had to exercise constant care to see that this did not happen. Land was generally accepted by a farmer on a yearly contract from its owner and in place of rent he paid a proportion of the return from the land. Consequently if he was a bad farmer and failed through negligence to raise a good crop he was compelled to give the owner an amount of corn corresponding to the yield of neighbouring fields which were properly cultivated. If he did nothing at all to cultivate the field and allowed it to become waste land he not only had to provide the owner with the grain it should have yielded but had besides to plough and harrow the land and in general make good his neglect. A farmer who undertook to reclaim waste land was allowed three years in which to perform the task. In the first year he paid no rent at all, in the second just under half the normal rent, and in the third year rent at the full normal rate. Any farmer who failed to produce good agricultural land in three years was compelled by law to plough, hoe and harrow the field before handing it back to its owner, and in addition he was forced to give the owner a year's rent for the land he had neglected.

The laws provided some sort of protection for farmers against damage by storm or flooding. If after the harvest had been gathered and the rent paid any damage was done by the elements to walls and canals, or if any loss of soil was caused by erosion, this had to be made good by the tenant. But if the flooding came before the harvest and as a result the yield was a very poor one then the owner and tenant divided what little there was in the proportions they had previously agreed to and the tenant had no further responsibility. In such a case if the loss was so great that the tenant had not even covered his costs the owner of the land could not refuse him if he wished to cultivate the land for a second year in an effort to recoup his losses. Furthermore if the tenant had borrowed money to buy seed-corn and because of the disaster was unable to pay it back he was excused any payment of interest for that year, although the actual debt was presumably held over until the following year.

The theme of borrowing money for work on the farm is continued in the next sections. Here the loan is made by a merchant, who seems often to have combined his activity as a foreign trader with that of a money-lender at home. The situation seems to be that the farmer, instead of repaying his

5

debt in cash, could hand over a field to the merchant so that
he could cultivate it and keep the crop in payment of the debt.
As this could easily lead to hardship for the farmer, Hammurabi
introduced measures to ensure some protection for him. It
seems that when the merchant took over the field he could
appoint a tenant to cultivate it for him. This remained unchanged under the new legislation, but it was laid down that
when the time of harvest came the original owner of the field
should gather the crop, pay off the debt, the interest and the
cost of cultivation, and then keep any surplus for himself. If the
field given to the merchant was already planted it would need
no tenant to cultivate it. In this case the owner merely paid
debt and interest, with no charge for cultivation. In cases where
the owner could not sell his grain to repay the debt he was
allowed to pay it in corn at the current exchange rate set by
the king. A further eventuality is covered by the next section.
Supposing the tenant appointed by the money-lender failed to
raise a good crop; who was to stand the loss? Clearly by handing over his field the debtor had discharged his obligation, and
although the merchant might be able to sue his tenant he had
no further claim on the owner of the land.

The laws then turn to the question of irrigation. In a country
like Mesopotamia where the life of the community was wholly
dependent on the maintenance of a system of canals and ditches
this was a subject of permanent importance. Royal concern
with the digging and repair of canals has already been mentioned, and in the preservation of the system every citizen had
his part to play. The large canals supplied water to smaller
channels and these in turn fed smaller ones until every acre of
cultivable land had its quota of water. As one channel might
supply water to the land of several owners neglect or carelessness
on the part of one owner could result in considerable damage
to his neighbours' land. So the laws made it clear that every
holder of land had to maintain the bank of any canal that
flowed past his fields, and any failure to do so which resulted in
widespread flooding of neighbouring land was punishable by
having to replace all crops destroyed by the flood. If the mis-
creant was unable to replace the crops he and his goods were
sold and the proceeds were divided among those who had incurred a loss. In cases of less severe damage, for instance when
a man left his sluice-gate open by mistake and thus allowed

water into the next field and destroyed some of its crop, he was obliged to repay a crop corresponding to the one which his neighbour had lost. If the damage was done before the planting of any crops and the water merely ruined his neighbour's ditches and fences, then the wrongdoer had to pay damages to the extent of a year's rent on the field.

Flocks of sheep were another considerable danger to growing crops. It was the custom in ancient Babylonia to let sheep graze on corn-land soon after the appearance of the young shoots in order to stop them running to leaf, but this could be done only by agreement with the owner of the land and any shepherd who let his flock so graze without the owner's consent was liable to a fine of two years' rent for the land, payable in grain. As the crop grew ripe the danger from sheep grew greater, and it is possible that during the critical period before harvest sheep had to be kept penned, at least during the night, to prevent them from doing damage. Any shepherd who let his flock into a field at this time had to guard the field without payment to prevent others committing his offence as well as paying a fine of six years' rent on the field.

Having dealt with grain-crops the laws turn to the other important product of Mesopotamia—the date-palm. It has often been pointed out how vital this was to the Mesopotamian economy. It provided food, wine, vinegar, honey and meal; its fibres were used for baskets and other woven goods; date-stones could be used for fuel or as fodder for animals; finally, its wood was almost the only timber available in the country. The usual method of raising new palms was to plant out cuttings either in reclaimed land or in a field previously used for grain. After four or five years the cuttings began to bear fruit, but until then the cultivator who looked after the plantation had to support himself by growing grain and vegetables in the spaces between the trees. Consequently, for four years he paid no rent to the owner of the plantation but busied himself with building a wall for it, seeing to its irrigation and protecting the young trees from damage. From the fifth year onwards the date-crop was divided equally between owner and cultivator, with the restriction that any portion of the land left unplanted was included in the cultivator's share. Neglect of duty laid the cultivator open to a penalty in the same way as has been seen in the case of corn-land. If the field to be converted to palm-grove was originally arable land then the cultivator who failed to raise palms on it was forced to pay rent for the years of his neglect by providing corn on the basis of the yield of neighbouring fields. In other words he was treated in the same way as he would have been if the land had continued to be used for corn. Similarly if he undertook to reclaim waste land for use as a palm-grove and failed to do so he was treated like the farmer who failed to reclaim land for corn, and was forced to pay a year's rent as well as ploughing, hoeing and harrowing the land at his own expense.

If a man undertook to look after a growing palm-grove his main task was the pollination of the trees, for palm-trees can be of either sex and it is possible by tying male pollen onto female flowers to obtain a large increase in the yield of dates. If a cultivator pollinated his trees satisfactorily he was entitled to one-third of the yield, but if the yield fell he had to bear the loss himself and was not allowed to renew his contract. Finally, the laws make it clear that the owner of a palm-grove might borrow money from a merchant on the security of his grove. If so he was allowed to pick the crop himself and pay the merchant from the proceeds. Again this is similar to the procedure with arable land.

In a country where timber was scarce it was naturally a considerable offence to cut down a tree in someone else's plantation. This was punishable by a fine of thirty shekels of silver per tree destroyed. The same penalty was enforced in Isin, and there too a man caught stealing from an orchard was fined ten shekels.

Laws concerning the sale and letting of property are the next concern of the code. Unfortunately, on the pillar bearing the main text of the laws this section and those that follow it have been erased. This was doubtless done by the Elamite king Shutruknahhunte after his capture of the pillar in order that he might inscribe his own achievements on it, but for some reason, possibly the king's death, this was never done. Some of the gap can be filled in by fragments from other sources, but there is still much that is missing or obscure. The first law which is semi-intelligible is concerned with the sale of a house which is subject to royal service. This is prohibited, but all details are conjectural. Other laws deal with the tenant-landlord relationship and again are too fragmentary to give

FIG. 4

a. Limestone monster, now in the Brooklyn Museum

b. terra-cotta lioness from Aqar Quf

c. granite stele from Uruk

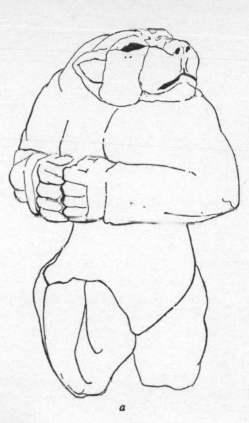

a

b

c

much detail. Apparently a landlord who had accepted a year's
rent in advance from a tenant and then attempted to eject him
before the year was up had to repay the whole of the rent.
Other laws here seem to have dealt with responsibility for the
repair of rented property, and one deals with the case of a man
whose property was in danger due to the neglect of the house
next door. Any householder who felt that burglars could enter
his house from the derelict house of his neighbour could ask
him formally to repair that house. Quite what happened if his
neighbour did not comply has been lost, but a similar law in
the Lipitishtar code lays down the rule that the owner of the
derelict house should restore any of his neighbour's property
which was stolen through his negligence.

From land and property the laws now turn to trade and
commerce, and the first subject to be treated is that of loans
and the interest on them. Rates of interest are laid down as
twenty per cent on loans in silver and probably thirty-three
and a third per cent on loans in corn. A debtor who could not
pay in cash was allowed to pay his interest in corn, although
the original sum had to be returned in money if it had been
borrowed in money. Any money-lender who tried to exact
more than the standard rate of interest was condemned to
forfeit both his interest and the money which he had lent.
Similarly if a money-lender lent corn or silver without witnesses he lost what he had lent, and if he used light weights in
paying out what he lent but heavy weights when he collected
the debt he was also liable to forfeiture of the entire sum.
Various other provisions in the laws were aimed at the protection of the man who borrowed money or grain, but their
interpretation is uncertain owing to the fragmentary state of
the text. One however is clear. It states that if a man had no
grain or silver with which to pay back a debt he could offer any
of his movable possessions and the money-lender was bound
to accept them, provided there were witnesses to make the
transaction legal.

Partnership law is simple and soon dealt with. Two men who
formed a partnership for a business venture had to divide the
profits or losses in the temple of Shamash when the partnership
was dissolved, and the division was in proportion to the amount
of capital each had put into the venture.

The next sections return to the business of the merchant. In this case he is seen not as a money-lender but as one who employs an agent or travelling salesmen to go round the country for him. Such salesmen must have been a common sight on the roads of Babylon. They were paid by results, and so there was every incentive for them to make the largest profit possible. Agents were required to keep details of the profit they made and of the expenses they incurred on their journeys, and on their return the merchant was entitled to any money he had put into the venture together with the interest on it and a share of the profits. Any agent who failed to make a profit was considered to have been negligent and had to repay twice what the merchant had given him. On the other hand if he lost his goods through flooding or other natural hazards he had to repay only the actual sum given to him by the merchant, and if he was attacked by bandits or enemies of the king he was excused from all responsibility.

A merchant could also employ an agent in a town to sell goods such as corn, wool and oil provided by the merchant himself. In this case the agent had to keep a record of all sales and pay some of the money periodically to the merchant. When all the goods had been sold a final reckoning was made and the profits were divided. The laws make it clear that the agent had to take a receipt for any interim payment he made to the merchant, for without one he could not claim at the final reckoning that such payments had actually been made. The importance of correct legal procedure and documentation is also stressed by the following sections, which state that if an agent had taken money from a merchant and then maintained that he had not received it the merchant should be able to produce legal witnesses of the transaction and so prove the agent in the wrong. Any agent found guilty of this offence had to pay the money back threefold. On the other hand if a merchant received his money back from an agent and then claimed that he had not received it the agent should have witnesses ready to swear that he had in fact repaid the debt. In this case the merchant had to pay the agent six times the amount of the debt.

The next subject for consideration is that of taverns. It seems that these had a highly unsavoury reputation and that the women who ran them were brothel-keepers as well as barmaids. Taverns were a natural haunt for undesirable characters, and tavern-keepers were expected to report to the authorities any customers who were plotting with criminal intent. The penalty for failing to do so was death. Women seem to have frequented taverns as well as men, but if a married woman, or a high-priestess who was linked in an indissoluble union with god, attempted to open or even to enter a tavern she was sentenced to death by burning, this being considered the most effective way of cleansing her from contact with the baser side of human life. The principal drinks sold were barley-beer and palm-wine, and grape-wine, imported from the Lebanon, was probably also available. The prices of drinks were regulated by royal decree, but payment for drink was normally made in grain and it is impossible to work out a meaningful price list. One type of cheap liquor mentioned in the law was priced at six measures of liquor for five similar measures of corn, and as there is evidence elsewhere that five measures of corn were sufficient to brew about fifty measures of liquor it can be seen that there was a wide margin of profit. As well as price-regulation there were other measures designed for the protection of the consumer. A tavern-keeper who demanded silver rather than grain for her liquor and then used false measures in weighing out the silver, or who watered down her beer in order to increase her profits, was sentenced to death by drowning, a grim illustration in the latter case of the rule that the punishment should fit the crime.

The next section is concerned with the problems of a trader who wished to send money or goods back to his home town. As there was no postal system he was forced to make use of any traveller he could find who was going in that direction. This must have been a very risky business, for there would be a great temptation to abscond with the valuables rather than deliver them. The penalty for this offence was the repayment of five times the value of the goods which had not been delivered.

A good deal has already been said on the subject of debts and money-lenders. In fact much of Babylonian business and agriculture seems to have been conducted on credit, and no doubt the merchants waxed very fat on the proceeds. If a man failed to pay his debt within the agreed time the merchant was entitled to seize one of his dependants—his wife, his son, his daughter or one of his slaves—and the dependant had to work for the merchant until the debt was paid. Alternatively the debtor could go to another money-lender offering one of his dependants as security and raise sufficient in this way to pay off the first debt. The dependant in this case could either be sold unconditionally to the money-lender or handed over with the right of redemption for a period of three years. After this period elapsed a member of the debtor's family had to be returned to him, but a slave became the absolute property of the money-lender and could be sold by him if he wanted. The only exception to this rule was the slave-girl who had become her former master's concubine and borne him sons. She could be redeemed when her master had raised enough money to buy her back. In Eshnunna a man's house too was not completely at the disposal of a merchant who seized it as the repayment of a debt, for if he later tried to sell it he had to give its former owner the opportunity to buy it back before offering it on the open market.

It can be seen again from the preceding paragraph that a man's wife and children were regarded as his property, and that he had the right to dispose of them as he wished. In fact they were considered of less value to him than his ox or his corn-crop, for these were necessary for his subsistence, and a money-lender who seized them as a payment for what was owed to him was liable to a punishment at law. If he took a man's ox the penalty was twenty shekels of silver, while if he took grain he had to return the amount he had taken and also lost his claim for the repayment of the debt.

Despite her lack of status in her husband's household a wife could protect herself from being sold to pay her husband's debts if at the time of her marriage she had persuaded her husband to draw up a contract of mutual exclusion from responsibility for the other's debts. This meant not only that she could not be sold but also that neither partner was responsible for the other's debts contracted before marriage, and that only joint debts after marriage were a joint responsibility.

A Mesopotamian farmer was often faced with the problem of storing his grain once it was harvested. There were granaries, both public and private, in which he could deposit his crop, and the rate for such deposit was fixed at about three per cent per year. If the owner of the granary helped himself to the farmer's crop or maintained that he had not in fact received it he became liable to pay back double the amount of the corn he had tried to embezzle. The question of the safe deposit of money and valuables is also considered in the laws. Here the difficulty was that there was no such thing as a bank, and a man who wished to find protection for his property while he was away from home could only entrust it to a friend for safe keeping. To ensure that the friend would give him back the goods when he returned it was essential that the transfer should be made before witnesses and a proper contract drawn up. Otherwise the traveller had no claim on his friend if he denied having received the property. But if witnesses of the deposit could be produced the friend had to pay back double what had been deposited. The usual protective clauses were added. For instance if a man's house was burgled and property deposited by a friend was stolen he was liable to pay back only the amount that had been deposited. In Eshnunna the law was even more lenient, for if a man was prepared to swear that his house had been burgled he was considered guiltless and excused all payment. In Babylon, and doubtless in Eshnunna too, a man who tried to make a false claim that his property had been lost was forced to pay double the amount of his false claim.

A long section of the Hammurabi code is devoted to marriage. This was closely regulated and the rights and responsibilities of the partners were clearly defined. The usual way to contract a marriage was for a man (or his father if he was not old enough) to approach the father of his intended bride with an offer of a bridal gift, normally in cash. If the offer was accepted a formal contract was drawn up, the bridal gift was handed over and a marriage-feast was held with foodstuffs provided by the bridegroom. If the couple were old enough to take up residence together they did so immediately, but if they were too young there was a waiting period when the bride, although legally a wife, remained in her father's house and no sexual intercourse took place. During this period she was legally protected from advances by other men, and a law from Eshnunna shows that no one else might have intercourse with her without risking the death penalty. Another feature of the waiting time was that during it either party could withdraw from the contract, although this meant forfeiting the bridal gift or repaying double its value. When the marriage was completed the bride brought a dowry with her from her father's house, and the husband normally settled a share of his property on his wife. This share was intended for the support of the wife under the management of her favourite son in the event of her husband's death, and she was forced to give it up if she divorced him. The dowry on the other hand represented the portion of her father's estate which the bride would have inherited had she continued to live at home, and it remained her property even if she remarried. On her death it passed to her sons, or if she died childless it returned to her father's house.

Another method of arranging a marriage is also mentioned in the laws. By this a father might choose a bride for his son, and on the completion of the contract and the handing over of the bridal gift the girl went to live at her father-in-law's house. There she continued, being treated presumably rather like a daughter, until the son of the house was old enough to marry her, and then the marriage was completed in the normal way. In no case was a marriage considered official without the drawing-up of a legal contract, even if the couple had lived together for a year or more as man and wife.

Chastity in a wife was considered of prime importance, and an extreme view was taken of any wife who associated with another man. If the couple were caught in bed together they were bound in a last grim embrace and thrown into the river. This penalty could be remitted only if the husband was willing to spare his wife, in which case the king issued a special pardon to the adulterer. The next clause is concerned with the case of a bride who was still a child staying at her father's house. Any man who was caught raping such a girl was put to death. As the girl had not consented to the act there was no punishment for her. Even the suspicion of adultery had to be dealt with, and a husband could bring his wife to court although she had not in fact been caught in the act. In this case she had to subject herself to ordeal by oath before god. If she took the oath she was allowed to return to her husband's house, but if she failed to do so she was convicted and drowned. If the accusation of unchastity was made by the neighbours the woman had to submit to ordeal by water like the sorcerer in an earlier section. Here there was no question of execution, for the guilty woman drowned in the course of the ordeal. If the wife was proved innocent she returned to her husband's house while her accuser was flogged and half his hair and beard were shaved off to make him a figure of ridicule.

The obligations of royal and military service in Babylonia often meant that a husband had to be away from home for extended periods, and during his absence his wife would have little news from him. A man was expected to leave sufficient to support his wife and family while he was away, but if he did not do so and his wife was destitute she could marry another man without penalty. When her first husband came back she had to return to him, but any sons born to the second husband stayed with their father. Any wife who married another man when she was not destitute was considered an adulteress and drowned. It is interesting to note that the second husband in this case received no penalty. Presumably he was considered an adulterer only if he seduced a wife who was actually living with her husband. These rules applied only to a man who was absent from his home against his will. If he absconded and thus refused to acknowledge his responsibilities as a husband and a citizen his wife was free to marry again, and if her first husband returned he had no claim to her.

The laws now pass to the question of divorce. This was a male prerogative, and the principal reason for which a man exercised his right was the fact that his wife had not produced sons for him. The actual ceremony seems simply to have been the solemn declaration "you are not my wife", accompanied perhaps by the cutting of the fringe of the woman's robe to indicate the severance of the marriage tie. To prevent a man divorcing his wife without real reason he was required to return her dowry to her and also give her compensation to the value of the bridal gift which he had paid to her father on the occasion of the marriage. If there had been no bridal gift the payment was fixed at sixty shekels of silver.

Barrenness was not the only reason for which a man could obtain a divorce. Even if his wife had given him sons he could get rid of her if he could prove that she was disgracing him by wasting his money, making the neighbours talk, or trying to leave him. In this case she received no money as compensation. If the husband wished to humiliate her still further he could retain her as a household slave, while he himself was free to marry again if he wanted.

A section in the Eshnunna code shows that in that state if a married man fell in love with another woman he could obtain a divorce even if his wife had borne him children. In this case however he had to leave his home and property to his wife and begin life again with the woman he loved.

Although a woman was denied the right of divorce she could force her husband's hand by refusing to have intercourse with him until he took the matter to court. There the case would be examined, and if it was proved that the woman had kept herself chaste and done her duty as a wife whereas the husband was in the habit of living a riotous life and consorting with other women, then the woman could reclaim her dowry and return to her father's house. On the other hand if the examination showed that the woman was spendthrift or unchaste she was condemned as an adulteress and drowned.

The main purpose of Babylonian marriage was the procreation of sons, and anything which interfered with this was sufficient cause for the husband to obtain a divorce. Besides barrenness, mentioned above, there was the possibility that the wife might catch some disease which prevented her from bearing children. The ailment most likely to cause this in Babylonia was malarial fever, and this is probably the disease intended by the laws as a ground for divorce, although the actual meaning of the word in the text is uncertain. A woman divorced through being diseased could not be dismissed from her former husband's household, but was entitled to maintenance there as long as she lived. But if she preferred to leave she could collect her dowry and do so.

The question of crimes connected with marriage is now dealt with. Again the laws deal with a number of isolated instances rather than attempting to evolve general rules. The first law in this group deals with a wife who procured her husband's death because she wanted to marry someone else. The penalty for this was impalement. A man who had intercourse with his daughter was banished from his city and consequently lost all his property and privileges, while anyone who chose a bride for his son and lay with her after the marriage was punished by drowning. However, if a man had intercourse with his son's bride before the couple had consummated the marriage he had merely to pay her thirty shekels of silver and return to her anything which she had brought from her father's house. She was then free to marry anyone she pleased. Finally there is the case of the man who lay with his mother after his father's death. The penalty in that case was that both should be burned. By

Babylonian custom the sons of a family were expected to marry their father's wives after his death, with the exception of their own mother. But by Hammurabi's legislation a man's principal wife who had borne children to him was held to be in a superior position and his sons by other wives were forbidden to marry her or have intercourse with her. The penalty for this offence was that the son should be driven from his home and thus forfeit his inheritance.

Mention has already been made above of how after the marriage arrangements had been concluded there was often a waiting period because the couple were too young or too poor to consummate it in full, and how during this period either partner could break off the marriage at will, subject to certain penalties. Three cases of this sort are mentioned in the laws, the first when the husband decided that he would rather marry someone else. In this case his bride's father kept both the bridal gift and the supplies which the bridegroom had brought for the wedding-feast. If the father refused to hand his daughter over, then he had to double the bridal gift and the provisions for the feast before returning them. Thus in each case the defaulting party lost the value of the gifts. An interesting provision is the one which deals with the case where another suitor, a friend of the bridegroom, slandered his friend to his father-in-law with the object of gaining the bride for himself. The ruling here, as in the previous section, was that the father-in-law should return double the gifts, and in addition the slanderous friend was forbidden to marry the girl. A suitor was similarly protected from his friends in the Lipitishtar code, and in Eshnunna too the marriage laws seem to have been much the same as in Babylon.

The next question dealt with is that of inheritance. The basic unit in all matters of property was the family, and it can be seen that originally everything was owned jointly by all members of it. Even after private ownership by individuals had become the rule traces of the old system remained, for a father did not have absolute control of what happened to his property when he died. The normal rule was that it was divided among all his children, male and female, and, as mentioned above, his wife also had a share which had usually been assigned to her when she became a member of the family on the occasion of their marriage. Daughters who married out of the family were given their shares as dowries, and these passed on to the daughters' children and so out of the family; but there was compensation for this in the property brought to the family by dowries when the sons married. An unmarried daughter shared with her brothers on her father's death, and when she herself died her property, which had remained under the management of her brothers, returned to the other members of the family and was divided among them. If a father died when his children were too young to manage property, the administration was entrusted to his wife (with her second husband if she remarried), and a division was made when the children came of age. This division was made by judges who ensured that there was no favouritism. Sometimes, however, a father could make a special provision for a favourite son by means of a document, legally drawn up, stating that the son should have a certain piece of property as a gift. This was the nearest approximation to a will that the law allowed. Otherwise the division proceeded in the usual way.

It is not clear what happened if a man died without children. In any case this was an unlikely event, for a man who was childless normally adopted children to make up for the deficiency. Those adopted were often his children by an inferior wife, and in this way they were raised to the same status as they would have had if their mother had been his principal wife. In default of these children too a man could adopt a child not of his blood to become his heir and bear his name.

It must be emphasized again that the laws are a list of additions or alterations to customary law rather than a statement of the law itself. They deal rather with special cases than with general principles. So in the section dealing with inheritance there is mention of several problems which presumably needed resolution by Hammurabi. One of these problems is concerned with a woman who died without giving her husband children. Normally her dowry would have returned to her father's house, and her father would have returned the bridal gift which the husband had brought to him when the couple were married, for a childless marriage was regarded as a failure and as far as possible all gifts exchanged were returned to the original owners. In this case, however, the woman's father refused to return the bridal gift, and the ruling was that the husband could deduct its value from the dowry before returning that to the father.

Another case is concerned with a family where the father died before the marriage of his youngest son. Thus the elder sons had received bridal gifts from the estate but the youngest had not. The ruling here was that a bridal gift for the unmarried son was to be set aside for him before the division of the estate into equal shares for all the brothers.

The last of these cases deals with a man who married twice and had children by both wives. On his death the children were required to divide their father's estate equally among them all, but naturally each mother's children divided her dowry among themselves. A similar judgement is recorded in the Lipitishtar code.

A father who did not wish one of his children to inherit any of his property could legally disinherit him, but this could be done only before judges after an investigation of the son's offence, and only if the son was proved to be persistently disobedient and unruly. First offenders were merely warned to amend their ways and returned to their father's keeping.

It was quite permissible for a man to adopt his children by an inferior wife and thus place them on an equal footing with his legitimate children. On the father's death all these children inherited equally, although it is possible that his legitimate children were allowed to choose their portions before his adopted sons. Children by a slave-girl who were not adopted and legitimized by the father during his lifetime were not allowed to share in the division of their father's property, but on the other hand they could not be retained as slaves by the legitimate sons after their father's death. Their mother too had to be released from slavery when the father died.

A widow was entitled to maintenance in her husband's house as long as she lived, and her dowry, together with her portion of her husband's estate, was intended to provide for her upkeep. Any sons who were so lacking in filial piety that they attempted to drive her from her husband's house were subject to a judicial investigation and a penalty which is not specified. On the other hand if the mother wished to leave and marry again she could freely do so, provided she surrendered to her sons the share of the estate which her first husband had settled on her. Her dowry, being her own property, naturally went with her when she left, but if she had no sons by her second husband it returned on her death to her sons by the first.

The Lipitishtar code provides for the case where a man's wife did not provide him with children, but a prostitute from the public square did. If this happened the man had to provide for the prostitute, and her children by him were his heirs. The only restriction was that as long as his wife was alive the prostitute could not live in his house. Similarly even if a man grew tired of his first wife and married another the new wife could not supplant the old as mistress of the household.

Marriage, according to the Hammurabi code, was permissible between a free woman and certain superior classes of slaves, namely slaves of the palace and of certain functionaries connected with it. Although the husband remained a slave the couple could set up house and do business on their own account, and when the husband died his estate was equally divided between his wife and his owner. The wife, of course, retained her dowry if she had brought one, and children of the marriage could not be claimed as slaves by the owner of the father.

The next section is concerned with the protection of the rights of children whose father died when they were still infants. In this case, as mentioned above, the estate was managed by the children's mother, and by her second husband if she married again, until the children came of age. During this time the mother and her husband could not dispose of any of the property, and an inventory was drawn up by the judges to ensure that they did not do so. Any man who was so foolish as to try to buy property thus held in trust was compelled to forfeit the goods as well as the money he had paid for them.

One of the most notable features of Babylonian life was the number of women connected with matters of religion. Often their actual duties are obscure, but it seems to have been a regular practice for a family to devote a daughter to a temple. There were various types of priestess, the highest ranking of whom seems to have been the "bride of god" or "high priestess" of a deity. She was a considerable figure in society and might even be a king's daughter. As she was vowed to chastity any slanderous imputation on her conduct was heavily punished, as in the case of the wife falsely slandered, and the accuser was flogged and half his hair and beard were shaved off. When her term of office was over a high priestess could leave the cloister and go out into the world again. Once outside she might even

6

marry, but so sacred was her person that no one, not even her husband, was allowed to have intercourse with her. It has already been pointed out that the penalty for a high priestess who opened or entered a tavern-brothel was death by burning.

Although chastity was so important in the case of a high priestess, other grades of priestess were less carefully regulated, and some or all of them may in fact have been temple-prostitutes. There was of course no real difference in the motives which lay behind absolute chastity and sacral prostitution. A woman could devote herself to god either by reserving herself solely for him or by giving herself freely for the use and delight of all his servants. Thus it is that women of the next highest grade of the temple hierarchy, who could come from the very best families and whose title is often translated "hierodule" or simply "priestess", considered it no disgrace to be at the disposal of any worshipper who cared to ask. In many ways the priestess was an important figure in the community. She could own, buy and sell private property, and also held land by royal grant which she could sell if she wished. At least some priestesses could leave the cloister after their period of sacral service, and they were then allowed to marry if they wished. The fact that a priestess could not produce children for her husband was probably due to her age when she left the cloister rather than to the existence of any vows of chastity, which would have been a matter of considerable difficulty for an ex-prostitute.

The class of temple-servant known literally as a "woman-man" or "epicene" is one of which little is definitely known. An epicene may have been a sort of temple chamberlain or officer in charge of the women of the temple, and in the laws she is twice classed with the palace chamberlain who was normally a eunuch. The close connection between the two may mean that the epicene, too, was in reality a castrated male used for administrative and disciplinary duties among the women of the temple.

Another class of priestess is known by a title sometimes translated "hierodule" or "temple-prostitute", but there is little definite evidence of her functions except that she was allowed to produce children, though illegitimate ones. The "votaress" also, whatever her religious functions may have been, could not bear legitimate children. Finally the "lay-priestess" could marry and produce children, but apart from the fact that she was inferior to a regular priestess there is little evidence for her religious duties.

The laws deal in some detail with the question of property belonging to the different grades of priestess. Each woman had a right to share in her family property, and just as a girl was given a dowry on her marriage, so a priestess was given one when she entered the cloister. This she would use to maintain herself as long as she was in the service of god, and during this time it was managed for her by her brothers. Sometimes a father granted his daughter who was a high priestess, a priestess or an epicene the authority to appoint a manager of her own choice to run her share of the estate after his death, and in this case the sons had no claim to it while she lived. Sometimes too her brothers mismanaged her share so much that they failed to maintain her from it. If this happened she could again choose her own manager. In either case the property reverted to her family on her death. There must also have been cases when a father failed to give his daughter a dowry when she entered the cloister. If she was a priestess who did not return to outside life, or an epicene, she received a full share in the family estate on her father's death. On the other hand, if she was a priestess who left the cloister in later years, or a hierodule or a votaress, she received only one-third of a normal share when her father died. A priestess of Marduk of Babylon, the most important deity of the empire, received one-third of a share but was excused any duties which might be attached to it. The reason for these distinctions is obscure.

The dowry of a lay-priestess was rather a different case, as she seems invariably to have married. If her father had given her to a husband she would already have received her dowry, and so when her father died she was entitled to no more of his estate. But if he had not given her to a husband before he died it was the duty of her brothers to provide a dowry and find a husband for her.

It has already been pointed out that a retired priestess who married could not produce children. The solution to the husband's problem of finding an heir was that the priestess provided him with a slave-girl to bear children in her place. The children so produced were then legitimized and inherited their father's property. If the priestess provided no slave-girl to meet her husband's need he was entitled to marry a lay-priestess in the hope that she would supply him with sons, but if the priestess had given him a slave-girl he could not marry a lay-priestess as well. Neither the slave-girl nor the lay-priestess who provided sons for a husband was allowed to give herself airs or set herself up as the equal of the priestess who was the principal wife. A slave who did so was degraded to the rank of ordinary slave again, and if she had failed to produce sons she could be sold. No penalty is mentioned for a presumptuous lay-priestess, but the probability is that she was divorced. It is curious that a man who married a priestess or a lay-sister could divorce either at will, even if she had provided him with sons (the lay-sister directly or the priestess through a slave-girl). The only protection that a wife of these classes had was the fact that her husband had to pay her not only her dowry but a half-share in all his property as well. This served to support her and also her sons until they came of age, when they divided the property equally among themselves.

Mention has already been made of the fact that a man could adopt children to carry on his name, and the laws deal with several problems raised by this subject. A man who adopted a child had the responsibility of rearing that child to adulthood and giving him the position of a legitimate son in the household. Any failure to perform this duty gave the child the opportunity to return to his real parents if he wished. An adopted child who pined for his real parents could also return to them, but if the father did his duty and brought the child to adulthood the real parents had no claim on him. A man who adopted a child and then produced children of his own could get rid of the adopted child if he wished, but he had to provide for him by a gift of a third of his inheritance. This could not be paid in family land as the child was no longer a member of the family.

The continuation of the family name was the main but not the only reason for adoption. A childless tradesman would be more interested in adopting a child to carry on the family business. The condition of such adoption was that he trained the adopted son in his trade, and failure to do so meant that the son could return to his parents.

An exception to the usual rules was made in the case of adoption by an epicene or a palace chamberlain. As neither of these could have natural children, they were given an absolute right to retain any child they adopted. If the child refused to acknowledge his new parent his tongue was cut out, and if he ran away to his original home his penalty was the loss of an eye. The severity of the penalties suggests that there was some difficulty in retaining children adopted by a chamberlain or epicene, probably because a child was expected to follow in his parent's footsteps, and in these cases this would mean castration.

Attached to the end of the laws on adoption is a section concerned with wet-nursing. As can be seen from the Eshnunna law-code, this duty lasted for two to three years before weaning, and the wet-nurse, who might well be a slave-girl or a temple-prostitute, received either rations of barley, oil and wool for her keep or a fee of six hundred shekels of silver for the three years. The law in the Hammurabi code is concerned with a case where a wet-nurse allowed a child to die when in her charge. She was then forbidden to enter on any other contract for wet-nursing without revealing to the parents of the new child the fact that she had lost a previous infant. The penalty for disobeying this provision was the loss of her breasts.

From family law the code passes to the question of assault and battery. Here again no attempt is made to evolve a unified system; only isolated instances of individual punishments are given, and all that can be seen from them is that for free men at least the guiding principle was talion—"an eye for an eye, a tooth for a tooth". Both these cases are in fact specifically mentioned in the laws, and similarly a man who broke another's bone had his own bone broken. A son who struck his father was punished more severely, for the hand which had offended was cut off, and the penalty for striking a man superior in rank or position to oneself was also more severe than if the victim was of the striker's own station. For instance a blow on the cheek of a nobleman resulted in sixty stripes with a whip of oxhide, delivered in public as a warning to others. For striking the cheek of an equal, where the principle of talion could scarcely be regarded as a punishment, a fine of sixty shekels of silver was substituted. If a man struck another in a street-brawl he was considered not to be wholly responsible for any injury he caused, and again the principle of talion did not apply. In this case he had to swear that he did not strike the blow deliberately and his only punishment was that he had to pay the fees of any doctor whose services the injured man might require. Even if the victim died the striker was merely fined thirty shekels of silver. The penalties in Eshnunna were on a different scale. There the compensation required for biting a man's nose off or putting out his eye was sixty shekels of silver, for cutting off his finger forty shekels, for knocking out his tooth, damaging his ear or breaking his hand or foot in a fight thirty shekels, and for an accidental blow or a slap on the face ten shekels.

The law of assault for free men was a fairly simple matter, but no single principle can be seen in the treatment of men who were not wholly free. Babylonian society was in fact divided into three classes of which some description must now be given. The free man is the subject of most of the provisions in the code, and in previous sections when a "man" was mentioned it can be assumed that a free man was intended. The status of the slave is also fairly simply defined, but the position of members of the third class is much more difficult, and in fact there is hardly sufficient evidence to come to any definite conclusions. It is clear that a man of this class was considered to be in some way between a free man and a slave. He could marry and divorce in the same way as a free man, although in the latter case the divorce money he had to pay was less than that paid by a free man. He could also own land, houses, and slaves in his own right. The slave of a man of this class appears in fact to have been of a higher rank than a free man's slave, and is several times mentioned in connection with the "slave of the palace", for instance in the case previously mentioned where a slave of the palace or the slave of a member of the third class could marry a free man's daughter. Other instances of a connection between the two types of slave can be seen in the ruling that the penalty for allowing either type to escape from the city was death. A similar penalty was exacted if a man harboured such a slave and did not surrender him at the proclamation of a royal herald. The conclusion seems inescapable that the slave of a member of the third class was in some way connected with the palace, and this probably means that his master too was a palace employee of some sort. This is borne out by a section which classes property stolen from such a man with that stolen from a palace or temple. A recent suggestion that he worked on the royal estates but was free apart from his daily service on them has much to commend it. He may then be called a "villein" by analogy with the medieval English system. An employee of this type could easily rise to a position of considerable importance where he could own slaves and buy or sell land, but despite this he was still not considered of the same class as a free citizen.

A return can now be made to the question of assault. A free man who put out a free man's eye or broke his bone was punished in kind, but the penalty for either assault by a free man on a villein was a payment of sixty shekels of silver, and if the victim was a slave the payment was half his value. The penalty for killing a free man in a brawl, it will be remembered, was a payment of thirty shekels of silver, but twenty shekels were considered sufficient to compensate for the death of a villein in similar circumstances. A villein's tooth knocked out by a free man was valued at twenty shekels of silver, while if one villein slapped another's face the penalty was a payment of ten shekels. If a free man's slave struck his master's cheek he was sentenced to have his ear cut off. Here the rule of talion was replaced by the rule of convenience, for although the natural penalty would have been the loss of the slave's hand a slave without an ear was less of a financial loss to his master.

Assaults on pregnant women are considered as a separate class. A man who struck an expectant mother and caused her to miscarry was forced to pay ten shekels of silver if she was a free man's daughter, five shekels if she was a villein's daughter and two shekels if she was the daughter of a slave. If the woman died the punishment was the killing of the striker's own daughter if the victim was the daughter of a free man, but for other women compensation in cash was considered sufficient, thirty shekels of silver for a villein's daughter and twenty shekels for the daughter of a slave.

The fact that surgeons' fees are considered immediately after penalties for assault can scarcely be taken as a compliment to the Babylonian medical profession. The development of medicine in Babylonia will be described in another chapter; here the laws prescribe the fees for four successful operations and the penalties for failure in two of them. It can be seen that medicine was a profession which involved considerable danger for the man who practised it, and there is a good deal of sound sense in the warning given to students in one textbook that they should have nothing to do with a patient who is likely to die. The first two operations mentioned in the laws are a major operation of some sort on a man's body and an equally dangerous operation on his eye. If a man's life was saved by the first, or his sight by the second, the surgeon was entitled to a fee of ten shekels of silver. If the patient was a villein the fee was five shekels, and if he was a slave it was two shekels. If the operation was unsuccessful and the patient lost his life or his eye then the surgeon was held responsible. If the patient was a free man the surgeon had his hand cut off, and if he was a villein some payment in silver was probably made. If he was a slave, a distinction was made between the operations, for a slave who died had to be replaced by the surgeon, while if he lost his eye his master was compensated by half his value.

The other operations mentioned are setting a broken bone and healing a sprained tendon. For these the fees were five shekels of silver for a free man, three shekels for a villein and two shekels for a slave.

Having embarked on the subject of fees for services rendered the law-giver continues with those of other professions. A veterinary surgeon who successfully performed a major operation on an ox or an ass was entitled to a sixth of a shekel of silver in payment, but if the operation caused the death of the beast the surgeon had to pay a fifth of its value. The profession of barber is the next one mentioned, but it is not as a mere hairdresser that the barber appears in the laws. This was a comparatively harmless means of livelihood and needed little regulation. In Babylonia, however, a barber had other and more dangerous duties, for he had to help in branding slaves with their master's mark of ownership. This process was normally preceded by the shaving of the slave's head, and then the mark was burnt or cut into his cheek or forehead. When a slave changed hands, his slave-mark was presumably changed or effaced, and this too was part of a barber's daily work. A slave who had escaped might well try to persuade a barber to alter his mark, and any barber who succumbed to this temptation lost his hand if the offence was discovered. If the slave was brought to him by a man who claimed to be his owner and after the barber had altered the mark it was discovered that this was not so, but that the man had been trying to steal someone else's slave, then the barber was released on oath as not having known that he was committing a crime, while the thief was put to death and his body hung at the door of his house as a dreadful warning to others.

Builders too were subject to royal regulation. A builder's fee for constructing a house which covered an area about twenty-four feet by twenty was two shekels of silver. As the daily wage of a skilled tradesman was fixed by law at five grains

FIG. 5   Bull's head in copper, now in the City Art Museum, St. Louis

of silver a day and there were one hundred and eighty grains in a shekel, the builder's fee represented seventy-two days' work by a skilled craftsman, and even if he had to provide materials and labour for the job the builder must have had a fair margin of profit. Details of domestic architecture in Babylonia are given elsewhere, but it must be stressed here that houses were normally built simply of sun-dried brick with flat roofs and no windows. As the area of the house normally included a central courtyard this too must have considerably reduced the cost of building.

Jerry-building was frowned on in Babylon, and if the wall of a house began to bulge and became unsafe the builder was expected to strengthen it at his own expense. If the house collapsed and destroyed the furniture and chattels inside then the builder had to replace these as well as rebuild the house without payment. If anyone was killed in the collapse the law of talion followed its course. Thus the builder forfeited his life for the life of the owner, his son's life for the life of the owner's son, and so on. A slave who was killed was regarded as mere property and had to be replaced in kind. A house-owner could be warned by the authorities that his building was unsafe, and in this case he rather than the builder was responsible for its repair. If he failed to do anything about it and the collapse of his wall resulted in the death of a passer-by he was considered to have committed a capital offence.

From builders the law-code passes to sailors. Shipping played an important part in Mesopotamian trade and vessels of varying types and sizes were constantly plying up and down the rivers and larger canals. Perhaps the commonest type was the raft made of wood supported by inflated goat-skins. Steering was by means of a pole or oar at the stern, and otherwise the vessel was completely at the mercy of the current. Naturally it could only sail downstream, but wood was cheap in the north and expensive in the south, so that it was profitable to dismantle a raft at its destination, sell the wood, carry the goat-skins back up the river-bank on donkeys and build a new boat. There were also craft built on a more permanent basis with a framework and planking of wood, the hull being coated with pitch to make it watertight. These heavier boats were propelled by oars sometimes assisted by sails, and so could go up, down or across a river as the captain wished. Small coracle-like craft circular in shape served for local transport. These were made of skins stretched over a framework of reeds and pitched to keep the water out. There were also barge-like vessels for use on canals. These were presumably towed from the bank.

A boatman engaged in river-trade was sometimes the owner of his vessel, but often he hired his ship from someone else and then offered his services and those of the hired ship to a third party who wished transport for his goods. The fee for hiring a boatman was fixed by law, but the code is damaged at this point, and it is impossible to say exactly what it was, or whether it was paid in cash or corn. The laws also give fees for the hiring of boats of different types. A vessel of approximately nine tons burthen cost one-sixth of a shekel of silver per day, a barge one-sixtieth of a shekel and a small boat propelled by oars one-seventy-second of a shekel.

The rivers were crowded with traffic, and accidents must have been frequent. The "rule of the road" was similar to that in use today, for powered craft were expected to give way to vessels propelled by the elements. Thus if a collision occurred between a boat with oars and a drifting raft the captain of the rowed vessel was always held to be responsible, and if the raft was sunk he had to replace it and any goods it contained. Accidents caused by a boatman's carelessness led to similar compensation. A boatman who hired a boat and then sank or wrecked it had to repay with a boat of similar value, and if he was carrying someone else's cargo at the time that too had to be repaid. In addition he probably had to provide the owner of the cargo with another ship in which to complete the transportation of his goods, or with the money to hire one. Should he succeed in raising the ship which he had sunk he had to return it to its owner together with half its value in cash.

Boatmen were concerned with the building and repair of ships as well as with their navigation. Doubtless fees were conventionally fixed for all sorts of repair jobs, but the only one mentioned in the laws is the caulking of a ship of about nine tons burthen. For this a boatman received two shekels of silver. A repair of this nature carried a one-year guarantee, and any defect in the workmanship which appeared during that period had to be made good at the boatman's expense.

From the hiring of boats it is an easy transition to the hiring of oxen. These animals were and are extensively used in Mesopotamia for ploughing and other agricultural purposes. A Babylonian farmer yoked two oxen to his plough, one in front of the other to give a stronger pull than if they were side by side. The heavier beast was given the rear position and the lighter, often a young beast being trained for the work, was harnessed at the front. For a heavy trained beast the rate of

hire was about sixteen bushels of corn a year, and for a lighter
beast the yearly rate was about twelve bushels of corn. A farmer
who hired an ox was expected to return it in the condition in
which he had hired it, and rates of compensation were fixed for
various types of injury. Excessive beating or goading which led
to injury to an ox's back, tail or horn had to be compensated
at the rate of one-fifth of the beast's value. A particularly badly
aimed blow which put out an ox's eye meant that the farmer
had to pay half its value in compensation, while if the beast
was rendered useless by having its leg or the sinews of its neck
broken, or if it died through beating or neglect, he had to repay
ox for ox. There were two exceptions to this ruling. Lions were
an ever-present menace in the country districts, and a farmer
could not be held responsible if a hired ox was seized by one
while in the open fields. In the same way if the ox was "struck
by god", in other words if it simply dropped dead while in his
charge, the farmer swore on oath to that effect and was allowed
to go free. The Isin law-code also contains a few provisions for
damage to hired oxen. The penalties there were a quarter
of the beast's value for a broken horn or damaged tail, a third
for injury to the flesh at the nose-ring and half the value for
damage to the eye.

Other regulations in the Babylonian code were concerned
with the fact that an ox is a dangerous beast, and can quite easily
kill a man. As an ox could turn vicious at any time without
warning no compensation could be expected if it suddenly
broke loose and gored a man to death in the street. But an ox
known to be dangerous had to be kept under control by being
permanently tethered or by having its horns padded. This matter was supervised by the local authorities, who issued a warning
to the owner of a dangerous ox. If the warning was ignored and
the beast gored another man to death compensation was required, thirty shekels of silver for a free man's death and twenty
shekels for that of a slave. The corresponding punishments in
Eshnunna were forty and fifteen shekels respectively, and the
same compensation was demanded for a death caused by a
certified mad dog which its owner allowed to run loose. There
too if one ox gored another and caused its death the two owners
divided between them the price of the live ox and the value of
the one that was killed.

Once embarked on matters of farming the law-giver continues

in the same vein with regulations for workers on the land. The wage of a ploughman is fixed at about thirty-three bushels of corn per year, and that of his mate who went alongside the leading ox at about twenty-five bushels per year. Illegal borrowing of agricultural implements is then considered. A man who appropriated his neighbour's plough or harrow had to pay him three shekels of silver in compensation, and five shekels compensation was required for taking an instrument which may be translated as either a water-wheel or a heavy plough with a seed-sowing funnel attached. One particular case which receives a good deal of attention is that of a man hired to cultivate another's field and entrusted with oxen and their fodder and seed-corn with which to do this. Failure to feed the oxen properly so that they weakened and lost value was punished by the offender having to repay double the amount of grain entrusted to him, while if he was caught stealing the fodder his hand was cut off. He was also punished if he did not fulfil his contract to cultivate the land. If for instance instead of using the oxen entrusted to him for ploughing and harrowing he hired them out to other farmers at a profit, or if he stole the seed-corn instead of planting it, his crime would be revealed at harvest-time when the yield was low or non-existent. In such a case he had to pay for his offence at the rate of double the normal yield of the land. If he was unable to do this he was tied behind a pair of oxen and dragged backwards and forwards like a plough or harrow across the land he had failed to cultivate

The wages of a man hired to look after cattle or sheep were, like those of a ploughman, thirty-three bushels of corn a year. A herdsman entered into a contract with the owner of the animals he looked after. In this contract were specified the number of young and the quantity of milk, hides and so on that the herd might be expected to yield. Any failure to produce the appropriate amount meant that the herdsman had to make up the yield at his own expense. As usual, the terms of employment are accompanied by a list of possible offences. A herdsman who altered the brand on his beasts with a view to selling them had to repay the owner tenfold, and if through carelessness he allowed infection to spread through the herd he had to make good any loss himself. His responsibility for his beasts was only for the time they were out at pasture, and ended when they

were returned to the pens or folds of their owner. So if a sheep
or cow dropped dead in the fold, or was killed by a lion which
had broken in, the loss was borne by the owner and not the
herdsman.

Another subject covered by the laws is the hire of animals
at harvest-time to thresh the corn. This they did simply by
trampling it until the grain was freed from the chaff. The fee
for hiring an ox for this operation was about a quarter of a
bushel of corn, for an ass about an eighth of a bushel, and for
a young beast about one-eightieth of a bushel. The hire of a
farm-cart to transport the corn was fixed at about half a bushel
of corn a day, and if it was hired complete with oxen and driver
the cost for a day was almost two and a half bushels. The
equivalent rate in Eshnunna was about one and a half bushels
of corn or one-third of a shekel of silver.

Skilled tradesmen employed by the palace probably had a
plot of land to support them, and in addition received wages of
one-thirty-fifth of a shekel of silver a day. These tradesmen included carpenters, leatherworkers, clothworkers, reedworkers,
builders, bricklayers, stonecutters, jewellers, smiths and probably potters. Casual labourers on the palace land received one-
thirtieth of a shekel of silver per day in spring and summer when
the work was hardest and the weather hottest. In the cooler
seasons when there was less to do they received one-thirty-fifth
of a shekel a day. In Eshnunna a harvester received one-fifteenth
of a shekel of silver and a winnower one-thirtieth. A worker
hired by the month received one shekel of silver for his work.

The Babylonian code ends with a number of provisions
dealing with the sale and purchase of slaves. Some slaves in
Babylonia were war-captives and others were native Babylonians who had sold themselves or been sold or seized for debt.
Others again were bought in foreign markets by Babylonian
merchants and brought back to be sold at a profit in local markets. A slave thus sold carried a month's guarantee against
epilepsy, and if after the completion of the sale he was claimed
by a third party then the seller had to settle the claim. Slaves
purchased abroad might later be found to have been stolen or
to have run away from another owner in Babylonia. In that
case if the original owner could identify the slave he was entitled
to have him back again, but first he had to repay to the dealer
the price that he had paid for the slave in the foreign market.

If however it could be shown that the dealer ought to have known that the slave was a runaway (if for instance he was a native Babylonian who obviously should not have been a slave in a foreign land) then the dealer had to hand the slave to his original owner without payment. Any slave who denied his master when identified by him was sentenced to the loss of his ear

A man's slaves, male and female, were his absolute property, and one result of this was that he had a free hand in his relations with his slave-girls. A law from Eshnunna however shows that the same freedom was not allowed in dealing with the other people's slaves. Anyone who robbed a neighbour's slave-girl of her virginity had to pay forty shekels of silver and the slave-girl remained with her owner. The children of slaves were of course the property of their parents' owner, and any child who was given, secretly or openly, to someone else to be brought up had to be returned on demand. Children of palace slaves could be adopted by private citizens, but another slave had to be provided in place of the one adopted.

Such in general is the content of the Mesopotamian law-codes. Although no attempt is made in them to give a complete picture of the society for which they were intended, in many cases a fairly clear image does emerge. It is of a society based primarily on trade and agriculture, subject to extensive control from the palace, but in many spheres offering a good deal of scope to private enterprise. But the chief interest of the codes lies in the fact that they deal with the problems which faced the members of communities far removed in space and time from our own, yet which in many cases—prices, for instance, or wages, or marriage, or debt—prove to be little different from those which confront us in our everyday life in the twentieth century.

(4)
Babylon in Eclipse

THE empire of Hammurabi was a personal creation, and it needed the talents of its creator to hold it together. Samsuiluna (1749–1712), who succeeded his father on the throne, seemed at first to be equal to the challenge, and in continuing Hammurabi's policy of close royal supervision of the administration he was for several years able to preserve the peace and unity of the lands he had inherited. A remission of taxation in the first year of his reign helped to secure the allegiance of the subject-peoples, and for the next six years he could concentrate on matters of peace. Canals were dug and dedications made in the temples of the land. Then in 1742 the situation suddenly changed. For many years the prosperous farmers of Mesopotamia had made use of casual labourers from the eastern mountain country to help them in gathering their harvests, and no doubt many of these workers had gone back to their homes with golden tales of the richness of the plains. Such was the attraction of these stories that the Kassites, a people from beyond the upper reaches of the Diyala who had often supplied harvesters in previous years, now decided that a more equitable share of the blessings of civilization could be gained by war than by work and sent down a raiding party to test the resistance of the Babylonians. Although Samsuiluna claims that he defeated them, it is probable that they succeeded in driving his forces back across the Diyala. Assyria was cut off from Babylon and the Kassites were able to set up a kingdom of their own somewhere on the middle reaches of the Tigris.

The success of the Kassite invasion was an inspiration to the other provinces of the empire. In 1741 Iamutbal revolted, abetted by the Elamite province of Idamaraz and led by a Rimsin who was perhaps the son of Hammurabi's enemy. A quick attack on the south resulted in the capture of Uruk, Isin, and Larsa, and Rimsin was acclaimed as king in his father's former capital. On this occasion Samsuiluna's strength was sufficient to meet the threat, and a swift punitive expedition led to the defeat and capture of Rimsin. The following year the Elamites were driven back and the walls of Uruk and Ur were destroyed so that they could not provide refuge for future rebels. By 1739 Samsuiluna could claim that all his enemies had been finally crushed.

But in this he was mistaken. The next year Kisurra rose against him, and in 1737 an un-named usurper incited Akkad to revolt. It is likely that this rebel was Ilumailu, a descendant of the kings of Isin, who had emerged as leader of the south after the defeat of Rimsin. Again Samsuiluna turned south, and the rival armies met on the shore of the great lake south of Ur. The result was almost certainly a victory for Ilumailu, and from that moment Babylon began to lose control of the southern cities. The walls of Isin were strengthened in an attempt to keep out the rebels, but this was not sufficient to stop a steady expansion northwards which drained Babylon's strength and left her open to attack from other quarters. In 1735 the walls of Sippar had to be strengthened against attack from the north-west, and in 1734 the fortresses of Iamutbal were rebuilt to meet danger from Elam and the east. These measures must have been temporarily successful, for in the next two years Samsuiluna could afford to expend his rapidly decreasing finances on the restoration of the temple of Shamash at Sippar and the dedication of two golden thrones to Marduk. In 1731 there was another clash with Ilumailu, and this resulted in a second defeat for the Babylonian king. After this he gave up any idea of regaining his lost territories in the south and devoted himself once again to the renovation of temples and the dedication of thrones. The strengthening of the wall of Kish in 1727 is an indication that danger was coming closer to the capital, but in the following year the only step which Samsuiluna could take towards saving his country was the dedication of a statue of himself striking down his enemies with his mace. Wishful thinking was beginning to take the place of decisive action.

With the loss of the south and the north-east much of Babylon's trade had disappeared. The only route now open was that which ran up the Euphrates to the Lebanon and the Mediterranean coast, and Samsuiluna's greatest achievement for 1725

7

was the transport along this route of a thirty-foot block of black basalt from the Amanus Mountains. Two years later his Mediterranean connections, too, began to slip from his grasp when the area around the middle Euphrates rebelled under Amorite leadership. At the same time panic measures were necessary in the south, where Ilumailu had advanced as far as Nippur. A line of fortresses just south of Babylon which had been built by Sumulae in the early days of the expansion of the kingdom, but had been allowed to fall into ruin as the need for them disappeared, was now rapidly restored and heavily manned. In the north-west Samsuiluna had at first some measure of success and could boast of victory over the Amorite armies, but in 1714 there was another revolt within the land of Akkad. When Samsuiluna died in 1712 the empire of Babylon had been reduced to a very small area around the capital city.

The reign of Abieshu (1711–1684) was apparently notable mainly for pious deeds and dedications. The commemoration of these is a sure sign of lack of military success, and it can be assumed that Abieshu made little headway against his country's enemies. An ambitious scheme to defeat and capture Ilumailu by damming the Tigris and flooding large areas of the plain failed in its purpose, and thereafter Babylonian efforts in the south were limited to the building of a fortress at the point where the river entered enemy territory. Further north a victory over the Kassites was claimed for 1710, but apart from this the king seemed to concentrate more and more on cult-observance and the worship of himself. His successor Ammiditana (1683–1647) also spent much of his reign on the adornment of temples and the dedication of statues of himself in various attitudes of worship, and Babylon must still have been reasonably prosperous to be able to bear the cost of these precious offerings. As well as this Ammiditana seems to have gained some measure of success against the kings of the Sealands in the south. In 1688 he successfully quelled a revolt in the area and from then until the end of his reign his policy was one of steady advance followed by consolidation. Canals were dug in the conquered areas and fortresses placed on them to protect them from sudden attack. In 1649 he destroyed the wall of a fortress built by Damiqilishu, Ilumailu's second successor in the Sealand kingdom, and this perhaps marks the southernmost point of his advance. Further north his works included the building of a palace near Babylon and a cloister in Sippar. On the whole, Babylon seems to have made a remarkable recovery under his leadership, and by recapturing Nippur towards the end of his reign Ammiditana could claim once more the title "King of Sumer and Akkad".

His son Ammizaduga (1646–1626) thus succeeded to a kingdom which was larger than it had been for some time, but there is nothing to suggest that he was able to maintain his father's superiority over the kings of the Sealands. The commemoration of nothing but offerings to the gods for several years is again a sure indication that there were no victories in the field to celebrate. In 1638 Ammizaduga "released the pressure on his land", and in 1637 he claims that he built a fortress at the mouth of the Euphrates, but this is almost certainly an exaggeration to mask a very minor victory. Later in his reign he "brightened his land like the sun-god", but the very vagueness of the phrase indicates that there was little real success of which he could boast. If he succeeded in holding the Sealanders at bay it was probably with the aid of mercenaries hired from the Kassites just to the north. The reign of Samsuditana (1625–1595) was little different from that of his predecessors. He continued to mark his years by the construction of shrines and the dedication of images, and although he claims to have won a certain amount of success, it is difficult to see that the "great strength of Shamash and Marduk" on which he relied had any permanent effect in extending his weakened dominion. But despite his lack of power he still tried to retain his influence along the north-western trade route, and towards the end of his reign he seems to have offered encouragement, if not practical help, to the king of Aleppo when this ruler was faced by the Hittites, a new enemy from beyond the Taurus Mountains. The result was inevitable. After capturing Aleppo and thus winning control of northern Syria the Hittite king Mursilis swept on down the Euphrates to punish those who had dared to help his victims. Samsuditana could offer little resistance to this sudden attack and Babylon was taken and plundered. Thus in 1595 Hammurabi's dynasty came to an inglorious end.

With the fall of Babylon to the Hittites the history of the ancient world entered a new phase. Until this time the principal roles in the development of Mesopotamia had been taken by

speakers of Sumerian or the Semitic languages, but with the
emergence of the Hittites from the Anatolian plateau a new
linguistic element came to the fore. The language spoken by
Mursilis and the other rulers of the Hittite confederation was
an Indo-European one. This great family of languages, which
ultimately spread over most of Europe and large areas of Asia,
seems to have developed somewhere in the plains which stretch
from the Baltic Sea across South Russia to the Caspian Sea,
and by about 3000 B.C. its speakers must have been sufficiently
dispersed to have developed a number of mutually unintelligible
dialects. One of the first groups to break off had by about 1900
B.C. made its way into central Anatolia—the route by which it
did this is still a matter of dispute—and there imposed itself
as a ruling class upon the local people. A series of conquests
within Asia Minor led to the formation of a powerful kingdom
with imperialist ambitions, and the result of these was the
campaign led by Mursilis which had such disastrous results
for Babylon.

The movements of the Indo-European speaking peoples had
other and more permanent effects on Mesopotamia, for after
the breakaway of the group that was later to rule the Hittites,
another group set out on a migration which was to bring it
eventually to north-west India. In the course of this movement
some members of this group made their way across the Caucasus
and, like their cousins in Anatolia, began to impose themselves
on the population of the mountainous areas which bordered
the Mesopotamian plain. In the Zagros Mountains, for instance, they exerted such pressure on the local Kassite tribes
that their presence may have been instrumental in bringing
about the attacks which these tribes began to make on Babylonia from the time of Samsuiluna. Later they began to settle
among the Kassites, and their presence can be seen from the
occurrence of Indo-European elements in some Kassite
names.

Further north the area between the Zagros range and Lake
Van was occupied by a people known as the Hurrians. Since
before the Akkadian period these people had been peacefully
infiltrating into the plains around the Upper and Lower Zab,
and by the time of Hammurabi some of them had spread across
northern Mesopotamia as far as the Mediterranean. With the
increase of Indo-European pressure the trickle became a flood

which rapidly submerged Assyria and swept on through Syria to the coast. Their arrival there had the effect of compressing the Semites of the area, and the result of this may well have been the invasion and conquest of Egypt about 1725 by the predominantly Semitic Hyksos or Shepherd Kings. On their northern flank the Hurrians found themselves faced by the Hittite kingdom in Anatolia, and they probably played a large part in its decline shortly after Mursilis' raid on Babylon in 1595. Despite their numbers and their influence on neighbouring powers the Hurrians do not seem to have formed any large political unit; they simply spread across large areas and were eventually assimilated. In the region around the headwaters of the Khabur, however, they were followed down from their mountain homes by the Indo-Europeans who had driven them out, and before 1500 these new invaders had established themselves as feudal overlords of the district, forming a kingdom known as Mitanni. Their success was due to a new weapon which they introduced and used with deadly effect—the horse-drawn chariot.

So in the century which followed the fall of Babylon the political centre of gravity shifted considerably to the north. Since the earliest period the prosperity of Babylonia had depended largely on its connections with Syria and the Mediterranean. Now these connections were threatened by a vigorous young power which was prepared to challenge not only Babylon but anyone else who dared to interfere with her. Interference was not long delayed. The expulsion of the Hyksos from Egypt about 1567 and the rise to power there of the energetic kings of the Eighteenth Dynasty made it inevitable that Egypt, too, should seek to assert herself in Syria. To the north the power of the Hittites was temporarily in decline, but later Hittite kings and Hittite armies began once more to play a decisive part in international affairs. In all this activity, centred as it was on northern Syria, Babylon played only a peripheral part, but her efforts to assert herself in an area where she had traditionally been dominant, and to mingle as an equal with the other great powers of the time, make it essential to follow at least the outlines of international politics from the sixteenth to the twelfth century. For the internal history of Babylonia our sources are extremely fragmentary and drawn largely from the annals of other countries, but they are sufficient to let us see how the decline of Babylon continued after the Hittite invasion, and how later monarchs attempted without much success to restore it to its former prosperity.

After their sudden descent of the Euphrates in 1595 the Hittites made no effort to retain what they had conquered, but quickly retired towards their homeland carrying their booty and the statues of Marduk and his consort Zarpanit. The territory of Babylon was thus left as a prize for anyone who cared to take it. For several generations the kings of the Sealand had coveted the land on their northern frontier, and Gulkishar, the sixth ruler of the dynasty, almost certainly seized the opportunity which had been so unexpectedly presented to him. However, his control of Babylon did not last long, for he was soon driven out by the Kassites from further north. Since their first martial venture into Babylonia a hundred and fifty years before, these people had built up a state centred probably in the Diyala region but with an influence which had spread at least as far as the area round Mari. Their service as mercenary troops in the armies of Samsuiluna's successors had given them experience of fighting against the Sealanders, and within a few years they had established themselves in firm control of Babylon. The first king who is definitely known to have ruled the city is Agum II, a powerful monarch whose territory extended up the Diyala and into the Zagros Mountains. Of his predecessors on the Kassite throne little is known except their names, and the dates of their reigns are quite uncertain. Gandash, the first known king, may have been the leader of the raid which was defeated by Samsuiluna in 1742, but it is rather more likely that he did not come to the throne until some time after 1700. He was succeeded by Agum I and then by Kashtiliash I, who may have made himself king of Khana on the Euphrates. Abirattash, another Kashtiliash, Urzigurumash, Kharbashikhu and Tiptakzi followed before the kingship descended to Agum II. In his efforts to make his rule legitimate in the eyes of his Babylonian subjects Agum in 1571 brought back from Khana the statues of Marduk and Zarpanit which had been removed by the Hittites twenty-four years before. No explanation has been found for their abandonment there by the Hittites, but when they were returned to the temple which Agum had restored and richly decorated for them the Kassite king was able to "take the hands of Marduk" and establish a dynasty which was to rule Babylon for over four hundred years. After a long rule he was succeeded by Burnanuriash I (*c.* 1530–1500) in whose reign there were signs of trouble from the north. In the confusion of the Hurrian migrations after the reign of Hammurabi the state of Assyria had almost disappeared, and little is known of it except a list of shadowy rulers who were presumably vassals of the Hurrians and their Indo European aristocracy. Towards the end of the sixteenth century Assyrian governors were beginning to re-establish their province and extend it at the expense of their neighbours. So it was that Puzurashur III of Assyria (*c.* 1513–1500) came into conflict with the Kassite kingdom of Babylon. Nothing is known of their dispute except that when an agreement was reached it was in Assyria's favour, a result which must have been a considerable setback for Babylon. Not even the name of the next Kassite king is known. His successor, Kashtiliash III (*c.* 1480–1470), was strong enough to entrust to his brother Ulamburiash the task of crushing the still independent Sealands. Ulamburiash struck while the Sealand king Eagamil was absent on a campaign in Elam and was soon able to win the southern throne for himself. When on his brother's death he succeeded also to the throne of Babylon he became the first king since Samsuiluna to have control of all Babylonia. This did not last long, for on his death about 1460 the Sealands rose again. In a swift campaign of retribution his successor, Agum III (*c.* 1460–1450), captured the rebel stronghold of Dur Ea and destroyed the temple of Ea, its principal shrine. After this defeat resistance in the Sealands disappeared and Kassite control was undisputed.

The reign of Kadashmankharbe I (*c.* 1450–1435) is known only for his struggle with the Sutu, a Bedouin people from the western desert. Despite the difficulties caused by lack of water for his troops Kadashmankharbe succeeded in killing large numbers of the enemy and there was no further trouble from them for the remainder of the Kassite period.

With the accession of Karaindash (*c.* 1434–1418) international politics began to play a larger part in Babylonian affairs. In the early part of the fifteenth century the kingdom of Mitanni had been the dominant power in northern Mesopotamia, and under kings such as Shuttarna I and Saustatar had acquired an empire which stretched from the Syrian coast to the eastern borders of Assyria. An attempt at rebellion by the Assyrian king Ashurrabi I (c. 1473–1453) resulted only in a Mitannian victory and the removal of the treasures of Assur to their capital at Washukkani. A few years later however the Egyptian Pharaoh Tuthmose III succeeded by a series of energetic campaigns in defeating Mitanni and winning all north Syria for himself. A revolt (c. 1442) in the early years of his successor Amenophis II was so firmly suppressed that the rulers of Mitanni, the Hittite kingdom and even Babylon hastened to congratulate him and send their gifts. Yet within a year or two another rebellion, probably prompted by the Hittites, resulted in the expulsion of Egypt, and a period of Hittite domination followed under Tudhaliyas II and his sons Arnuwandas I and Hattusilis II. The danger drew Egypt and Mitanni together, and this potent alliance seemed to offer such rich prospects that Karaindash of Babylon was eager to offer his support. Although his predecessors had reunited southern Mesopotamia, Karaindash found that he had inherited a kingdom which was resting on its reputation rather than on any great material prosperity. With the rise of hostile powers in Syria and the Lebanon Babylon had lost her supplies of timber, metals and other essential commodities. At the same time the series of catastrophes which had followed the death of Hammurabi had led to the neglect of canals and agricultural land in the south, and the little which remained under cultivation had been constantly used for so many centuries that by the Kassite period it had largely silted up. As a result of this many of the ancient cities—Lagash, Umma, Adab, Kisurra and Shuruppak among them—were now deserted, and the country was in a state of chronic poverty from which only liberal doles from some external source could enable it to recover. This was the attraction of an alliance with Egypt, a country with a reputation for the generosity with which she rewarded client powers. At the same time Karaindash felt that there was danger to his land from Assyria, for although this country was still nominally a Mitannian vassal her kings had succeeded in building up a strong and compact kingdom which was ready for further expansion. By a renewal of the boundary arrangements made by Burnaburiash I some eighty years previously, Karaindash succeeded in securing the alliance of Assyria, and Ashurbel-nisheshu, the Assyrian king at the time, was probably glad of his friendship, for it meant that Assyria had an ally for any future action she cared to undertake against Mitanni.

As a result of these alliances the reign of Kurigalzu I (c. 1417–1400) was a period of comparative peace and prosperity for Babylon. Financial support from Egypt enabled him to undertake an ambitious building programme in Nippur, Ur, Eridu, Uruk and other cities, and this was crowned by the foundation of Dur Kurigalzu, about twenty miles west of modern Baghdad, as a new capital city which would serve also as a fortress in case of trouble from the north. A successful campaign against Elam resulted in the capture of Susa, and Kurigalzu considered his achievements so great that he felt justified in hailing himself as "King of the Universe". At the same time he was careful not to offend his more powerful friends. To cement his alliance with Egypt his daughter was dispatched to the harem of Amenophis III (1417–1379), and when he was approached by a group of unruly Canaanite princes who wished to draw Babylon into a plot for the overthrow of Egyptian domination he was firm in stressing his loyalty to Egypt.

Kurigalzu's policy was continued by his son Kadashmanenlil I (c. 1399–1381) who entered into a considerable correspondence with Amenophis complaining of the lack of news from his sister, the need for an Egyptian princess to be his wife, and the smallness of Egyptian gifts. Eventually he was persuaded by the prospect of much gold to send his own daughter to Pharaoh and so was able to continue the building operations which his father had begun.

He was followed by Burnaburiash II (c. 1380–1350), an astute politician who throughout his reign succeeded in manipulating the intricacies of international affairs to his own advantage. His first act was to send off a message of loyalty to Amenophis III, and when Amenophis died about 1379 and was succeeded by his son Akhenaten Burnaburiash was careful to continue the friendship with his "brother" on the Egyptian throne. His letters, like those of his predecessors, are for the most part pretentious appeals for money and yet more money, but they are useful to the historian for the light they throw on the changing international situation. From the start it is clear that Egypt's position in Syria was not what it had been, for it had depended on the power of Egyptian gold, and this gold was no longer forthcoming. Akhenaten in fact was neglecting his empire because he was concentrating on the introduction of a great religious reformation in his homeland, and as he devoted more and more of his time and attention to the worship of the sun-disc as the one true god, and to the building of a new capital where that god might be worshipped without the contamination of the older religion, his Syrian vassals quarrelled among themselves while the other great powers waited to seize what they could. Two letters from Burnaburiash contain complaints that his messengers had been attacked and robbed while passing through the Egyptian province of Canaan, but there is no evidence that any attention was paid by the Egyptian court. Even the acceptance of a Kassite princess in marriage by the Egyptian ruler did not have the effect of restoring Babylonian confidence, and ultimately Burnaburiash turned to operations on his own account. Traces have been found of Kassite interference in the affairs of Byblos and Jerusalem, and these were probably not the only places in which the failing power of Egypt allowed Babylon to assert her strength in the area. But before Burnaburiash had time to indulge in any widespread conquest the picture in northern Syria had changed so completely that he was forced to withdraw to his own land and look around for new allies. The reason for his sudden retreat was the unexpected collapse of Mitanni.

A few years previously the alliance of Egypt and Mitanni had seemed virtually unbreakable. A series of dynastic marriages had linked the northern monarchs firmly to the Egyptian throne, and under Artatama (c. 1425–1420) and Shuttarna II (c. 1420–1390) the country had risen to the status of a first-class world power. The accession of Tushratta (c. 1390–1365) was accompanied by some internal trouble, but despite this there seemed to be no prospect of his country's hold on northern Syria being loosened. About 1380 a strong Hittite raid through the Taurus passes was repulsed with heavy losses, and part of the booty was sent as a gift to the king of Egypt. The accession of Akhenaten in 1379 however meant that Egyptian subsidies were withdrawn, and with the loss of its revenue the Mitannian power quickly collapsed. A renewed effort by the Hittite king Suppiluliumas (c. 1380–1350) brought complete defeat to Tushratta. In his earlier raid Suppiluliumas had found that the concentration of Mitannian forces in the plains at the mouths of the Taurus passes was too great for him to break

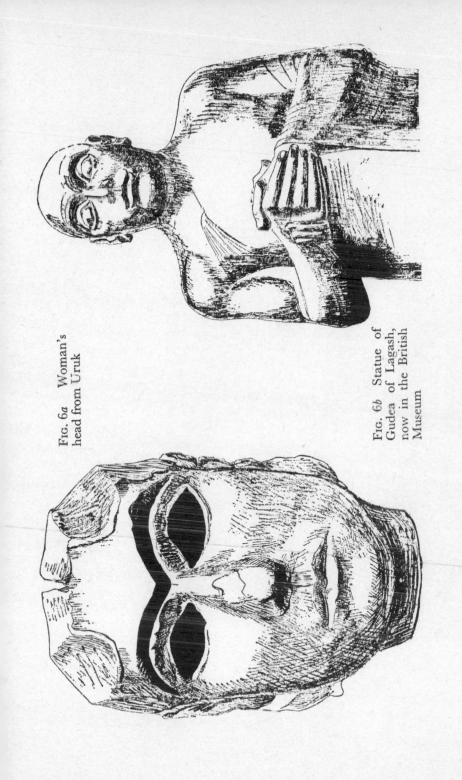

Fig. 6a Woman's head from Uruk

Fig. 6b Statue of Gudea of Lagash, now in the British Museum

through, and so by about 1370 he had evolved an elaborate plan by which he crossed the Euphrates at a point before it descended to the north Syrian plain and then suddenly fell on Mitanni in the rear. Washukkani, Tushratta's capital, was captured and sacked, and quickly most of northern Syria and the Lebanon fell into the Hittite king's hands. Alshe and Assyria, the eastern vassals of Mitanni, took advantage of the situation to break away and proclaim their independence, and of Tushratta's extensive empire only a small district stretching up the Euphrates from the mouth of the Khabur remained in his possession. So weak had he become that about 1365 he was murdered by a rival branch of the royal family, and with the backing of Alshe and Assyria a new line of rulers was established. But the power of Mitanni had been completely broken, and northern Syria lay open for any ruler strong enough to conquer it.

Despite all this confusion in the north, Burnaburiash was powerless to achieve any extension of Babylonian influence. The fall of Mitanni meant only the ever-present danger of a Hittite attack, and Suppiluliumas had already shown what a capable general he was. At the same time there was more immediate danger from the newly revived state of Assyria. Ashuruballit I (c. 1365–1330), the king who had led the Assyrians to independence, was a man of unbounded energy and ambition, and soon he was appealing to Egypt as an equal, demanding gold for the consolidation of his power. This was too much for Burnaburiash, for the Kassites, without any real justification, had always considered Assyria as subject to their own authority. A stiff note was dispatched to Egypt, but when it was completely ignored Burnaburiash began to feel himself isolated. Always at his best in an awkward situation, he succeeded by an adroit piece of political manœuvring in turning about so completely that within a few years he had married Ashuruballit's daughter Muballitatsherua and was on terms of intimate friendship with the Assyrian king.

This marriage of convenience proved almost disastrous for the Kassites. Ashuruballit was not the man to let slip such a glorious opportunity of winning influence at the Babylonian court, and when Burnaburiash died about 1350 the Kassite nobles were dismayed to find that his son Karakhardash II, as befitted a grandson of the great Assyrian king, was wholly pro-Assyrian in his sympathies. So unpopular was this in Babylon that the Kassite army rebelled, killed Karakhardash (*c.* 1348), and placed one of its own number, Nazibugash by name, on the throne. This success was short-lived, for Ashuruballit quickly summoned his army, marched south and heavily defeated the rebels. Nazibugash was captured and killed, and in his place Ashuruballit appointed Kurigalzu II (*c.* 1345–1324), the younger son of Burnaburiash II and again his own grandson. The result was that Babylon under the shadow of Assyria entered another period of prosperity, and Kurigalzu was able to indulge in extensive building operations in Nippur, Ur and other southern cities. He could also build as far afield as Der in the foothills of the Iranian hills. In external affairs his reign is mainly notable for a campaign against Elam. In the confusion which followed the death of Burnaburiash II the Elamites had succeeded in gaining possession of some of southern Babylonia. Kurigalzu now moved against them in force, and after defeating them at a place known as Dur-Shulgi he followed them back into the mountains and captured Susa, their capital city. Elam became a Kassite province and Kurigalzu assumed the title of "King of the Universe".

In the north the Babylonians had to act with greater circumspection. The Mitannian kingdom established after the murder of Tushratta existed only through the support of Assyria, and quick action might have meant great success for anyone who had the strength to oppose Ashuruballit. But when Tushratta's son Mattiwaza approached Babylon with an appeal for help he was driven off and forced to turn to the Hittite king, Suppiluliumas, the conqueror of his father. Suppiluliumas had no desire to see the Mitannian supremacy replaced by that of Assyria, so about 1340 he returned to Syria and soon succeeded in placing Mattiwaza on his father's throne and making Mitanni a mere buffer-state between himself and Assyria. Thus Babylon's opportunity was lost and for the next ten years Kurigalzu was the obedient servant of Ashuruballit. On the Assyrian monarch's death about 1330, however, he refused to admit his subservience to the new king Enlilnirari (1329–1320) and proceeded to renew the fortifications of Dur Kurigalzu in preparation for a struggle. A battle fought at Sugagi, somewhere on the Tigris, resulted in a victory for Babylon, but when the armies met again Kurigalzu was defeated and probably killed.

A new boundary-agreement was made and the two kingdoms
settled down to a period of uneasy peace. This lasted through
most of the reign of Kurigalzu's son and successor Nazimaruttash (c. 1323-1298) and it gave that king the opportunity
to go on a successful campaign in the mountainous region of
Namri. Unfortunately the Assyrian monarch Adadnirari I was
campaigning in the eastern hills at the same time in an effort
to protect his boundaries, and when the rivals met at the hill-
town of Karishtar the result was a defeat for Nazimaruttash.
Again the border between the two countries was adjusted in
Assyria's favour, and the province of Elam took advantage of
Babylon's discomfiture to break away and regain its independence. Thus the Kassite dominions were reduced once more to
the confines of Babylonia.

While Babylon and Assyria were quarrelling over the
mountainous districts east of the Tigris, in Syria the international situation was changing yet again. In Egypt a new
dynasty had risen which was eager to regain the power and
prestige which had been lost under Akhenaten. Sethos I (c.
1318-1305) was able to reach the River Orontes and force the
Hittites to make peace with him, but in the years that followed
the Hittite king Muwatallis (c. 1321-1297) was able to build
up an enormous force of allied and mercenary troops with
which he hoped to drive the Egyptians back to their borders
again. On the accession of Rameses II to the Egyptian throne
about 1304 open hostility began again, and in 1299 the two
great powers met at Kadesh. Despite the boastful account of the
battle given by Rameses there is little doubt that the result
was a decisive victory for the Hittites, and Syria remained firmly
in their hands.

In Babylon Nazimaruttash was succeeded by his son
Kadashmanturgu (c. 1297-1280) shortly after the Battle of
Kadesh. This emphatic assertion of Hittite power, coming as it
did so soon after his father's humiliation by Assyria, was sufficient for Kadashmanturgu to send overtures of friendship to
the Hittite capital. By about 1285 he was on sufficiently good
terms with Hattusilis III (c. 1288-1260), the new Hittite king,
to offer him military support for a campaign against Egypt.
But by now Egypt was no longer the main danger. In the years
following the Battle of Kadesh, Adadnirari of Assyria had built
up his strength to the point where he could strike through Syria

and capture Carchemish on the Euphrates. The success of this campaign caused such alarm that by 1283 the Hittites and Egyptians had hastily made up their differences and concluded a treaty of friendship. It was obviously to Babylon's advantage to join this powerful alliance, and Kadashmanturgu was careful to remind the Hittites of his previous services. In fact so involved did he become with Hattusilis that when he died (c. 1280) the Hittite king, eager to secure the succession of Kadashmanturgu's infant son Kadashmanenlil II (c. 1279–1265), wrote in rather peremptory terms to the Babylonian prime minister Ittimardukbalatu saying that unless the young prince was crowned immediately he would break off diplomatic relations. Needless to say his letter was not well received at the Babylonian court, and for some time there was a certain lack of cordiality between the powers. Yet so great was the menace of Assyria that each needed the friendship of the other, and within a few years relations were back to normal. In fact Hattusilis was so alarmed at Assyrian expansion that he was almost too anxious to please his Babylonian allies. In a long letter he was careful to show that he had meant no harm in interfering with the Babylonian succession, and to stress that he would punish his Syrian subjects who had murdered a group of Babylonian merchants. The purpose of his letter is made clear by a final appeal for help in attacking Assyria, and in fact he may have been successful in winning Babylonian support for this venture. If so, it met with no success.

The next thirty years were quiet ones for Babylon. Virtually no information has survived from the reigns of Kudurenlil (c. 1264–1256) or Shagaraktishuriash (c. 1255–1243), but it is clear that Shalmaneser of Assyria was too concerned with wars in Syria, the eastern hills and the area towards Lake Van to trouble himself with his southern neighbour. The accession of Tukultininurta I (c. 1244–1208) in Assyria seemed at first to make little difference to Babylon, and most of the reign of Kashtiliash IV (c. 1242–1235) was as quiet as that of his predecessors. Then in 1235 Kashtiliash conducted a campaign in the eastern hill-country which must somehow have conflicted with the interests of Assyria. Probably he was trying to retain a hold on the trade route from Iran to compensate for the fact that the Tigris and Euphrates routes were now in Assyrian hands. At any rate Tukultininurta decided that the time had come to deal firmly and finally with Babylon. The first battle between the powers produced no decisive result. Kashtiliash retreated towards Babylon, but Tukultininurta quickly followed him and succeeded in inflicting a crushing defeat. Kashtiliash was captured and carried off to Assur, and with him went all the treasures of Babylon, including the great cult-statue of Marduk without whose approval no future pretender could rightfully claim the kingship. Many Babylonian citizens were killed while the city was being plundered, and finally the Assyrians dismantled the fortifications to make certain that Babylon could never again be a centre of resistance to their power. Then Tukultininurta left a governor in charge of the city and set out on a campaign which dealt with both the Bedouin tribes to the west and the Elamites to the east. By the end of this it seemed that Babylonia had become merely a subservient buffer-state on Assyria's southern border.

Despite his success in quelling Babylon's resistance and pacifying its neighbours, Tukultininurta failed to win any support for Assyria or Assyrian policies. On the contrary the rule of a foreign power succeeded only in waking the long dormant nationalism of the native Babylonians. The Kassites had been in the land for more than three hundred and fifty years and had by now been largely assimilated. The arrival of the Assyrian armies drew Kassites and Babylonians even closer together, and when after seven years of Assyrian rule (c. 1234–1228) the southern cities rose in revolt it was the combined action of Kassites and Babylonians which won them final success. By 1227 the rebels had captured the holy city of Nippur, and Enlil-nadinshumi, a Babylonian, was crowned king. But before they could advance further against the Assyrians holding Babylon a new danger appeared from the east, for Kidinkhutran king of Elam took the opportunity offered by the disturbances to descend on Babylonia. The border-town of Der was sacked and Enlil-nadinshumi was captured. He was succeeded as chief of the rebel forces by a Kassite called Kadashmankharbe (c. 1226–1225) who was defeated by the Elamites but succeeded in saving Nippur. After a rule of eighteen months Kadashman-kharbe died or was killed, but before this he had probably driven the Elamites back to the hills. His successor, Adad-shumiddin (c. 1224–1219), carried on the struggle against Assyria until his reign was ended by another attack from Elam which resulted in the capture of Isin. Yet although the Elamites probably managed to retain their hold on southern Babylonia for two or three years the combined Kassite-Babylonian forces were able to drive out the Assyrians and regain Babylon. Once established there they placed Adadshumusur (c. 1218–1189) on the throne. He was the son of Kashtiliash IV, whom Tukul-tininurta had carried into captivity, and so the old Kassite royal family returned to power.

During the reign of Adadshumusur the international situation once more underwent a great change. The old enmity between the Hittites and Assyria had long ago been settled and their border fixed on the line of the Euphrates. As a result of this, trade between the two powers vastly increased, and much of the raw material which was essential for Assyrian greatness came from the mountains of Asia Minor. But now the Hittite empire was beginning to break up. The trouble was centred in the western provinces of Asia Minor and the destruction was completed about 1200 by a great invasion which swept through Anatolia and Syria and was stopped only on the borders of Egypt. The precise composition of the "peoples of the sea" who caused this great destruction is at present unknown, but with their arrival the Hittite empire disappeared and Assyrian trading contacts with Asia Minor were irretrievably lost. Cut off thus from the sources of their raw materials the Assyrian kings were unable to hold their conquests, and inevitably the successes of the early part of Tukultininurta's reign were followed by a period of decline. In Adadshumusur the Babylonians had a king who was quite prepared to take advantage of this, and the result was a complete reversal of fortunes in Mesopotamia. Perhaps Tukul-tininurta himself was partly to blame for this, for despite his destruction of Babylon he had introduced the cult of Marduk to his own capital, and this act must have caused a good deal of Assyrian resentment. Finally about 1208 he was murdered by his son. The assassination was almost certainly at the instigation of Babylon, for his successors Ashurnadinapli (c. 1207–1204) and Ashurnirari III (c. 1203–1198) were little more than vassals of Adadshumusur. Enraged by this subservience the nationalist party in Assyria elevated Enlilkudurusur (c. 1197–1193) to the throne with the express object of freeing themselves from Babylonian influence. At the same time Ninurta-apilekur, an Assyrian pretender distantly related to the royal line, fled to Babylon for protection, and Adadshumusur gathered an army to put him on the Assyrian throne. In the battle which followed (1193) a fire broke out in the Babylonian camp, and this forced Adadshumusur to retire to his own country. Ninurta-apilekur however was able to seize the Assyrian capital in the absence of its king. Once he was established, however, he refused to acknowledge his subservience to Babylon and decisively defeated an expedition which was sent to eject him. The territory of the Kassites was once more limited to Babylonia.

Little is known of the reigns of the next two Kassite kings, Melishikhu (c. 1188–1174) and Mardukapaliddina (c. 1173–1161). Although the latter called himself "King of the Four Quarters of the World" there is no indication that he was able to expand beyond the boundaries of Babylonia. Fortunately for Babylon Assyria at the time was in a similar state of weakness and for a time neither side was capable of attacking the other. The accession of Zababashumiddin to the Babylonian throne in 1160 gave the rising Ashurdan of Assyria (c. 1179–1135) his chance. A swift attack by the traditional route down the eastern bank of the Tigris led to the capture of Zaban on the Lower Zab and several other towns. Although Zababashumiddin managed to repel the attack he was so weakened by it that he was quite unable to resist another sudden incursion, this time by the Elamite king Shutruknahhunte. Eshnunna, Sippar, Kish, and eventually the whole country fell to the invaders, who gathered the ancient monuments of the land as they advanced and sent them back as trophies to their capital. Among the objects which went to Susa at this time were the stele of the Akkadian King Naramsin's victory over the Lullubians and the stone pillar on which the laws of Hammurabi were engraved. Shutruknahhunte then demanded tribute, imposed heavy taxes, and left his son Kudurnahhunte to see that they were collected. The Elamite prince's first action was to appoint Enlilnadinahhe (1159–1157) as puppet king of Babylonia, but soon the puppet turned against his master. This so enraged Kudurnahhunte that he viciously ravaged the country. Babylon and other cult-centres were transformed to ruins and the cult-statue of Marduk was carried off to Susa. Enlilnadinahhe was also taken as a prisoner of war, and with his capture (c. 1157) the Kassite line came to an inglorious end.

Despite their defeat of the Kassites the Elamites do not seem to have gained any real control of Babylonia. The capture of Enlil-nadinahhe meant the end of a dynasty at Babylon, but further south resistance still went on. The centre of this resistance was Isin, where nationalist feeling seems to have been strongest, and in the eyes of the historians of Babylon the Kassite Dynasty was directly succeeded by an Isin Dynasty without an interval of Elamite supremacy. This presumably means that it was not long until the nationalists seized Nippur and so established themselves as legal rulers of Babylonia. Gradually Marduk-kabitahheshu (c. 1156–1139), the first king of the new dynasty, and his successor Ittimardukbalatu (1138–1131) succeeded in ousting the Elamites, and a final victory near Babylon gave the new dynasty complete control of Babylonia. The rise of Babylonian power coincided with a period of civil disturbance in Assyria, and when Ashurdan died in 1135 his successor Ninurtatukultiashur was forced to flee for refuge to the southern capital. So complete was the reversal of positions that Ittimar-dukbalatu was able to restore the Assyrian king and demand allegiance from him, an act which was symbolized by the return of the statue of Marduk removed by Tukultininurta a hundred years before.

Nothing is known of the short reign of Ninurtanadinshum (c. 1130–1125), but the king who followed him on the Babylonian throne was undoubtedly the greatest figure of his dynasty. The country had been freed from the Elamites by the vigorous action of his predecessors, but Nebuchadnezzar I (c. 1124–1103) determined to exact full vengeance by an invasion of the Elamite homeland. A damaged tablet tells of an initial reverse, but it is not clear if this was in fact sustained by Nebuchadnezzar or one of the earlier kings. An advance into Elam met with no success, and the outbreak of some disease in his camp caused the Babylonian king to retreat hastily to Durapilsin. Even there he was not safe, and was compelled by an Elamite advance to retire yet again. So desperate was the situation that only the gods could save it; and by some miracle, the precise nature of which is unknown, the Babylonian king succeeded in defeating the Elamites and retrieving his position. Soon after Nebuchadnezzar was able to advance from Der into Elamite territory. The district of Namar was captured and the Elamites were finally brought to bay on the banks of the River

Ulai, not far from Susa. There they were utterly routed and all Elam was captured and plundered. Further north, victories over the Lullubians and the homeland of the Kassites gave Nebuchadnezzar overall control of the eastern mountains.

Encouraged by these successes the Babylonian king turned to the west and succeeded in defeating the desert tribes of the middle Euphrates. His next aim was the conquest of Assyria, which under Ashurreshishi (*c.* 1133–1115) had succeeded in reasserting its independence and was again interfering with Babylonian interests in the eastern hills. Heavy siege-engines were moved up against the border-fortress of Zanqu, and Nebuchadnezzar settled down to a protracted siege. To counteract this, Ashurreshishi sent out a highly mobile chariot-force which so terrified the Babylonian king that he was forced to retire at speed, burning his siege-engines to prevent them falling into enemy hands. His next expedition was less encumbered by heavy equipment, but his infantry and chariots were quite unable to cope with the strength of the Assyrian army. The Babylonians were forced to retreat again with the loss of forty chariots, all their baggage train and their general Karashtu, who was carried off as a prisoner to Assur.

This defeat brought a temporary end to Babylonian aspirations in the north, and while Tiglathpileser I of Assyria (*c.* 1114–1076) was engaged in a series of mighty campaigns to the east, north and west of his homeland, in the south Babylonia seems to have remained in a state of complete inaction. The latter part of Nebuchadnezzar's reign and the whole of that of Enlilnadinapli (1102–1099) were passed in complete obscurity. A grant of land by the governor of the Sealands is the only document which can be definitely assigned to the period. But the continued absence of Tiglathpilescr on distant campaigns gave Babylon a sense of false security, and Marduk-nadinahhe (*c.* 1098–1081) gained some success by a sudden attack on the Assyrian town of Ekallate, in the course of which he seized the cult-statues of Adad and Shala and carried them back to Babylon.

Such conduct could not go unpunished, and soon the great conqueror descended from the north to avenge the insult. Again the Assyrians chose the route east of the Tigris, and in a two-year campaign they forced their way across the Lower Zab and down into Babylonia. Despite ineffective attempts at

resistance by Marduknadinahhe the Assyrians marched on and
seized Dur Kurigalzu, Sippar, Opis and finally Babylon itself.
The captured statues were hastily removed to the Sealands for
safety, and Tiglathpileser probably did not bother to follow
them, for having added control of the southern trade routes to
his earlier conquests he was now indisputable master of all the
sources of the wealth of Mesopotamia. Yet his reign was destined
to end in a disaster so complete that it was to end any possibility of Assyrian or Babylonian recovery for almost two hundred years. The cause of this disaster was the irresistible pressure of the Aramaeans, yet another wave of Semitic nomads
from the western desert.

The expansion of the Aramaeans began, like all other Semitic
migrations, in the deserts of central Arabia. There was no
sudden invasion; a gradual accumulation of these nomadic
peoples around the fringes of civilization had been going on
since before the time of Hammurabi. At first it proved simple
enough to beat them off—mention has already been made of
Kadashmankharbe's defeat of the Sutu, an Aramaean group,
about 1450—but inevitably the pressure built up until the
sheer weight of their numbers overwhelmed the surrounding
areas. By the beginning of the eleventh century they had
established themselves firmly in northern Mesopotamia and
even crossed between Assyria and Babylonia to the plains east
of the Tigris. At about the same time the Kaldu or Chaldaeans,
another group related to the Aramaeans, were moving into
the Sealands along the Persian Gulf. At first Tiglathpileser was
strong enough to deal vigorously with these nomads and keep
them firmly in check, but towards the end of his reign the
Assyrians found themselves engaged in a desperate struggle for
their existence. The immediate reason was a famine which
proved so severe that the inhabitants were reduced to canni-
balism. This gave Aramacans their opportunity. Quickly they
moved in and seized the weakened land, and the Assyrians were
driven before them into the northern mountains. Then the
situation grew even worse. The famine was followed by rain-
storms of unprecedented severity and this led to an outbreak
of plague which destroyed many Aramaeans as well as
Assyrians. Further south similar circumstances drove Marduk-
nadinahhe from the throne of Babylon (c. 1081) and he disappeared for ever. Mardukshapikzeri (c. 1080–1068) had soon to

face a vast coalition of Aramaean princes who so threatened
his land that he was forced to go to Assyria to appeal for help.
Ashurbelkala (*c.* 1073–1057), the new king of Assyria, was himself in such desperate straits that he was glad of friendship from
any quarter, but although strong protestations of friendship
were exchanged there is no evidence that Assyria was able to
send any material help. Mardukshapikzeri returned empty-
handed to his country, but when he reached Sippar he found
that he could advance no further. In his absence an Aramaean
chief called Adadaplaiddina had seized Babylon and set himself up as king there.

The accession of Adadaplaiddina (*c.* 1067–1046) is the beginning of the darkest period of Babylonian history. By this time
many of the Aramaeans had settled down and formed small
states throughout Mesopotamia, and although they were never
able to organize themselves into a political unit their possession
of all the trade routes gave them a complete stranglehold on
the Babylonian economy. Despite the fact that the new
Babylonian king was himself an Aramaean he had cut himself
off from his people by settling down in one of the older centres
of civilization, and so he soon had to defend himself against
further attack by his desert brethren. Again Babylon turned
to Assyria for help and again there were protestations of eternal
friendship, strengthened this time by the marriage of
Adadaplaiddina's daughter to the Assyrian king. Yet although
the Babylonian king was able to drive out an Assyrian usurper
in 1054 and put Shamshiadad IV, the youngest son of Tiglathpileser, on his father's throne, the alliance proved quite powerless to check the advance of the Aramaeans. The circumstances
of Adadaplaiddina's death are quite unknown, and not even
the names of his successors on the Babylonian throne are
certainly known. The next king was probably called Mar-
dukahhe-eriba (*c.* 1045), and he was followed by another
monarch whose name began with Marduk, and whose reign
lasted from about 1044 to about 1033. The last king of the Isin
Dynasty was Nabushumilibur (*c.* 1032–1025), a ruler vain-
glorious enough to consider himself "King of the Universe".
The one thing certain about his reign is that this title in no
way corresponded to the facts of the period.

The dynasty of Isin was followed by a short-lived line of
rulers from the Sealands. The first of these, Simmashshihu

(*c.* 1024–1007), is notable only for restoration work on the temple of Shamash at Sippar, and his reign ended in another period of violence when he was assassinated by Eamukinshumi. A few months later Eamukinshumi was replaced by Kashunadin-ahhe (*c.* 1006–1004), and with his death the dynasty came to an end. The same conditions of poverty and civil disturbance continued during the reigns of the next three kings, known collectively as the House of Bazi, but apart from their names and the lengths of their reigns nothing is known of them. They were Eulmashshakinshumi (*c.* 1003–987), Ninurtakudurusur (*c.* 986–984) and Shiriqtushuqamuna (three months *c.* 984). The next king, Marbitiapalusur (*c.* 983–978), is said to have been of Elamite origin, although his name is Babylonian, and again nothing is known of him. The accession of Nabumukinapli (*c.* 977–942) marks the beginning of a period of greater dynastic continuity, but the state of the country was not immediately improved by this. The Aramaeans were in fact able to operate so close to Babylon that they could control the river-crossing between the capital and Borsippa. This meant that several times during Nabumukinapli's reign Nabu, the god of Borsippa, could not be brought to Babylon, and so the great New Year Festival could not be held. Thus Babylon struggled on, her trade cut off and her most important ceremonials disrupted, through the reigns of several more shadowy kings. Ninurtaku-durusur II ruled for nine months about 941 and he was followed by Marbitahheiddin and Shamashmudammiq, the lengths of whose reigns are uncertain. It was in Shamashmudammiq's reign that the first signs of a revival in the north were seen.

For over a hundred and fifty years Assyria had only just managed to maintain a precarious position as a small state around the upper reaches of the Tigris. The foundations of her recovery were laid by Ashurdan II (934–912), who built up an army strong enough to win some success in the mountains to the north and north-east. His successor Adadnirari II (911–891) continued the process of expansion, and his campaigns in the eastern mountains quickly brought him into the Babylonian sphere of influence. By this time pressure from the Aramaeans must have begun to die down, for Shamashmudammiq was able to gather an army and march to face the new enemy. Near Mount Ialman, south of the Lower Zab, he was decisively defeated and forced to cede to Assyria a strip of territory east

of the Tigris and stretching as far south as Der. Shortly afterwards he was murdered by Nabushumishkun, but the new king
fared no better in his attempt to stop the advance of Assyria.
Again the Babylonian army was defeated and Nabushumishkun
was forced to accept a line south of Sippar and Dur Kurigalzu
as his northern border. But Adadnirari had no desire to treat
Babylon as a conquered province, for he had dreams of wider
conquest in the west and so found it expedient to adopt a
policy of pacification and friendship in the south. A new boundary-treaty was made and sealed by an exchange of matri-
monial alliances, and this left Adadnirari free to concentrate
on the defeat of the Aramaeans and of Hanigalbat and other
western states. When Tukultininurta II (890–884) succeeded
to the Assyrian throne Babylonia was so friendly that he was
able to go on what seems to have been a peaceful expedition
down the Tigris and up the Euphrates in the course of which he
spent a night at both Dur Kurigalzu and Sippar. He was
succeeded by Ashurnasirpal II, (883–859) while in Babylon
Nabushumishkun was followed by Nabuapaliddin (c. 881–
851).

From the beginning of his long reign the Assyrian king
followed a vigorous policy of war and conquest to the east,
north and especially the west, while to the south the policy
of friendship with Babylon was continued. The arrival of
Assyrian troops in northern Syria, however, was not something
on which Babylonians could look with any enthusiasm. Grateful
as they were to Assyria for the way in which she had destroyed
the power of the Aramaeans, they had no desire to see control
of the rich trade route to the Mediterranean fall into the hands
of Ashurnasirpal. Since he was powerless to make a direct attack
on Assyria, Nabuapaliddin attempted to hinder the progress
of her armies by allying himself with Shadudu, prince of
Sukhi at the mouth of the River Khabur. Three thousand
troops were despatched under the command of the king's
brother Zabdanu, but despite the assistance of a prophet who
accompanied them they succeeded only in falling into Assyrian
hands. Realizing the futility of resistance to Assyria Nabuapaliddin hastened to re-establish friendly relations, and for the
rest of his reign he concentrated on the restoration and re-
endowment of the temple of Shamash at Sippar and other
buildings damaged by the Aramaean raids.

The death of Ashurnasirpal in 859 and the accession of Shalmaneser III (858–824) were marked by a renewal of the Assyro-Babylonian peace-treaty, and it was in accordance with this that Mardukzakirshumi, who came to the Babylonian throne about 851, appealed for Assyrian help when he was faced by the revolt of his younger brother Mardukbelusate. Immediately Shalmaneser advanced into Akkad and stormed the city of Meturnat. He then moved on to the rebel stronghold of Gannanate, and when Mardukbelusate dared to come out against him he drove him back inside the town and ravaged the country round about. The following year (850) the Assyrian king marched south again. The city of Lahiru was stormed and plundered, and then Gannanate fell, but Mardukbelusate escaped into the hills and shut himself up in Arman This town too quickly fell to Shalmaneser's troops and Mardukbelusate was killed in the fighting. At the conclusion of the campaign the Assyrian king descended into the plains again and made a triumphal progress round the principal shrines of Babylonia. Kutha, Babylon and Borsippa were honoured with sacrifices and rich gifts. Then Shalmaneser turned on the Chaldaean tribes of the Sealands. Bakani and Enradi fell, and their king, Adinu, was forced to offer tribute. The Assyrians advanced to the shores of the Persian Gulf, and there Iakinu, king of the Sealands, met them with rich offerings of gold, silver, lead, copper and elephants' hides and tusks. All Mesopotamia was again united under one ruler.

Unity however did not last long. Before the end of Shalmaneser's reign there was a widespread revolt in the Assyrian provinces, and when Shamshiadad V (823–811) came to the throne he was faced with the problem of restoring order. So desperate was the situation that he was forced to appeal to Babylon for help, and Mardukzakirshumi, the Babylonian king who had so recently been an Assyrian vassal, did not hesitate to impose the most humiliating terms. The treaty which he drew up was careful to mention Akkad before Assur and refused the very title of king to Shamshiadad. Then a Babylonian army marched up the Tigris and within a year had reconquered Assur and restored Shamshiadad to his throne.

Once he was firmly established, however, the Assyrian king followed the usual pattern in refusing to acknowledge his

overlord. Mardukbalatsuiqbi (c. 821–814) was now ruler of
Babylon, and in 815 he found himself faced by a hostile
Assyrian force descending from the eastern hills. So sudden was
the attack that before he could muster his forces the inhabitants of the north-eastern districts had been driven in
panic into the fortress of Dur Papsukal, which lay on an island
in the Diyala. The capture of this town resulted in a vast loss
of Babylonian life and equipment. Too late Mardukbalatsuiqbi
mustered a large force which included Elamites, Chaldaeans
and other allies and advanced to do battle. The two armies met
near Dur Papsukal and the result was a decisive victory for
Assyria. Five thousand Babylonians were killed and two thousand captured, while the booty included even the Babylonian
king's tent and camp-bed. The following year (814) Shamshiadad crossed the Lower Zab again and marched on Gannanate. This time Mardukbalatsuiqhi did not dare to face him
but fled south for his life. He was overtaken near the town of
Nimittisharri and captured in the course of a fierce encounter.
Shamshiadad advanced as far south as Der but was unable to
break Babylonian resistance, now organized by Baba-ahi-iddin
(814–813). The next year, however, a third expedition succeeded in capturing the new king, and all Babylonian territory
east of the Tigris fell into Assyrian hands. Crossing into Babylonia proper Shamshiadad marched in triumph through
Kutha, Babylon and Borsippa, making offerings to the gods of
each in order to make public display of his position as lord of
the land. Then he turned towards the Persian Gulf and received the tribute of the Chaldaean kings of the Sealands.
Finally a new boundary-treaty was drawn up and once again
Babylon seemed firmly in Assyrian hands.

The years that followed Shamshiadad's conquests are an
obscure period in Babylonian history. Between 812 and 803
a series of rulers maintained southern resistance to Assyrian
rule, but their actions and in several cases even their names are
unknown. Nabumukinzeri, Mardukbelzeri, and Mardukapaliddina II are among those who must be fitted into this period.
In Assyria Shamshiadad died in 811, and from then until 806
the government was in the hands of his wife Sammuramat, a
Babylonian princess of remarkable strength of character who
became famous in Greek and modern legend as the mighty
queen Semiramis. Under her rule the worship of Nabu, the

Babylonian god of Borsippa, was introduced to Assyria, but there is little evidence of political supremacy in the south.

In 806 Sammuramat's son Adadnirari III came of age and took over the government. A reference to a campaign against the Sealand in 803 may indicate the final subjugation of the rebel dynasty of Babylonia, and it was about this time that a Chaldaean called Eribamarduk (c. 802–763) founded a new dynasty which at first owed its stability to Assyrian support. Babylonian captives were returned to their homes and the peoples of Assyria and Babylon lived together in peace. While Adadnirari of Assyria indulged in campaigns in Syria and the north-eastern hills Eribamarduk of Babylon was left to clear his country of the Aramaeans who still infested the fields and gardens around the major towns of his realm. Although he met with some success in this it is probable that his authority did not extend far beyond the immediate vicinity of his capital and that most of Babylonia under other Chaldaean chieftains achieved almost complete independence. Assyrian attacks on Der in 796 and 795 show that the alliance between the countries had already collapsed, but Assyria was now beginning to face new problems in the north and was unable to devote time or military forces to large-scale campaigns in Babylonia. When Adadnirari died in 783 he was followed by his son Shalmaneser IV (782–773), in whose reign Assyrian power was greatly limited by the rise to prominence of Urartu, a Hurrian power centred around Lake Van. The reign of his successor Ashurdan III (772–755) saw the continuation of this decline, and under Ashurnirari V (754–745) Assyria was reduced to complete impotence.

In the meantime Babylon continued in a state of mediocrity. Eribamarduk was able to ward off a minor Assyrian attack in 770 and again in 766, but when he died in 763 his successor Nabushumishkun (762–748) was too concerned with insurrection in his own country to take advantage of the Assyrian decline. Even in Borsippa, a few miles from Babylon, there was anarchy and civil war which was quite outside the control of the Babylonian king.

Faced by these conditions Nabunasir (747–734) was forced to look round for external aid, and his first thought was of Assyria, where a revolt had just succeeded in placing a successful general on the throne as Tiglathpileser III (744–727).

The Assyrian, eager to restore the military glories of his country as well as to secure his rear for future campaigns in the north, was quick to answer the appeal. His first campaign was directed down the eastern bank of the Tigris against the Aramaean tribes of Babylonia, and it was immediately obvious that he was adopting a new policy of administration in the area. After the subjugation of the tribes and the capture of Dur Kurigalzu, Sippar and other centres of resistance Tiglathpileser built two entirely new Assyrian foundations, Kar Assur and Dur Tukultiapalesharra, as garrison-stations and residences for himself and the governors he appointed. Central and eastern Babylonia as far south as the Persian Gulf became Assyrian provinces paying Assyrian taxes, and many of the inhabitants were deported and replaced by subject-peoples from other areas. Only the districts immediately surrounding Babylon were left to Nabunasir, and it must have been obvious to him that his turn too would come. Yet he was powerless to do anything to save his city, for even when the Assyrian king was heavily involved in other quarters Nabunasir was unable to retain his influence in a town as close to Babylon as Borsippa. In 734 he was succeeded by his son Nabunadinzeri, but Babylon was now in such chaos that after a reign of only two years (733–732) the new king was assassinated by a provincial governor called Nabushumukin. A month later he too was killed by an Aramaean chief called Nabumukinzer and Babylonia was completely in the hands of the most unruly element of its population.

The news of the accession of an Aramaean soon brought Tiglathpileser to the scene once more. It was now evident that his previous settlement had not been firm enough, and in the next few years he followed a policy of systematic destruction of cities and deportation of peoples in the hope that no such assertion of independence could take place again. By 729 Nabumukinzer was confined to the fortress of Sapia, somewhere south of Babylon, and in the course of the siege he was killed. Overawed by the might of Assyria Mardukapaliddina, king of the Sealands, came to offer his gifts at Tiglathpileser's feet. Then the conqueror returned to Babylon where in 728 he took the hands of Marduk and under the name of Pulu became the legitimate king of the land.

The death of Tiglathpileser in 727 made little immediate difference to Babylon. His successor Shalmaneser V (726–722) ascended the Babylonian throne as Ululai, and the system of administration continued as before. But Shalmaneser was not a warrior of the same calibre as his father, and gradually Mardukapaliddina, the vassal king of the Sealands, was able to extend his influence northwards. In 722 Shalmaneser was murdered by the usurper Sargon (721–705), and in the confusion following his death Mardukapaliddina succeeded in gaining control of Babylon. In this revolt against Assyrian rule he was joined by Khumbanigash, king of Elam, who moved down into the Babylonian plain to support his ally. Hastily Sargon mustered his forces to quell the rebellion, but when the armies met before Der the Assyrians were driven from the field and Mardukapaliddina was left in possession of Babylon. There he confirmed his position by restoring lands confiscated by the Assyrians and by other measures calculated to gain popular approval, while Sargon was forced to turn to the quelling of further rebellion in Syria and Palestine, and after that to the conquest of Urartu. By 710 however the Assyrian king was free to turn on Babylon once more. Mardukapaliddina, anticipating this, had tried to form an anti-Assyrian coalition and had even attempted without success to win the support of Hezekiah, the king of Judah at the time. He had also taken care to reinforce his army and strengthen his defences, but these measures proved useless against the veteran warriors of Assyria. Sargon advanced rapidly south from Der, driving a wedge between Elam and Babylon, and when he had overcome all resistance as far as the Persian Gulf he crossed the Euphrates and continued his triumphant progress up the western bank. Mardukapaliddina fled from Babylon in a vain attempt to regain Elamite support, and with his departure the citizens of Babylon and Borsippa opened their gates to the king of Assyria. Amid great rejoicing (or so Sargon would have us believe) he made sacrifice to the gods of the land and redug the ancient Borsippa canal so that Nabu could come in state to Babylon. There on New Years Day Sargon took the hands of Marduk as the new king of Babylon.

In the months following his coronation Sargon continued his operations against the Chaldaeans. The Hamaranu, a tribe who supported Mardukapaliddina, had retired to Sippar, and there they were defeated and destroyed. Mardukapaliddina himself had concentrated his forces and retired to Dur Iakina,

a fortress in the marshes at the head of the Persian Gulf. Here
in a desperate attempt to strengthen his defences he had torn
down bridges, destroyed dams and allowed the Euphrates to
inundate the fields around the town. Despite these precautions
he could not hold out against the Assyrian assault, but although
he was wounded in the arm he managed to escape to Elam before his city was stormed and plundered. Sargon did not bother
to follow him. He ordered the release of the hostages whom
Mardukapaliddina had taken from Sippar, Nippur, Babylon
and Borsippa, and restored their lands to them. Then he re-
established the freedom of Ur, Uruk, Eridu, Larsa and other
southern cities which had been under Chaldaean control and
returned their gods to their shrines. Finally he cleared the
country as far as the Elamite border and built defences there
to prevent further trouble. Even the king of distant Tilmun in
the Persian Gulf sent his tribute.

From 709 to 705 Sargon ruled as governor of Babylon. On
his death there was widespread rebellion which ended with his
son Sennacherib (704–681) being proclaimed king of Assyria.
In 704 and 703 Sennacherib was regarded also as the rightful
king of Babylon, although the actual administration was probably in the hands of his younger brother. In 703, however,
there came the first of the Babylonian troubles which were to
haunt Sennacherib throughout his reign. The throne was seized
first by Mardukzakirshum II, a former lieutenant of Mardukapaliddina, but only a month later Mardukapaliddina
himself reappeared with an Elamite army and easily replaced
his ex-subordinate. All Babylonia quickly rallied behind him
and Sennacherib hastened south to retrieve the situation for
Assyria. Mardukapaliddina had for some reason split his army
into two groups, one of which was stationed in Kutha and the
other slightly further south at Kish. One Assyrian force was
therefore sent against Kish while the other, commanded by the
king himself, moved more slowly against Kutha. The first
assault on Kish was a complete failure and the Assyrian commander was forced to send back an appeal for help. This
angered Sennacherib, and he quickly stormed Kutha and
moved south to the aid of the troops round Kish. The siege was
immediately successful, but Mardukapaliddina again managed
to escape with his life. Babylon fell to Sennacherib without
further fighting and its treasures were removed as booty. For

FIG. 7 Stele of Naramsin, now in the Louvre

five days Assyrian soldiers searched the marshes, but no trace of Mardukapaliddina could be found. Eighty-eight walled towns and eight hundred and twenty villages of Chaldaea were occupied, and then Sennacherib settled down to find a solution to the Babylonian problem. His answer on this occasion was to appoint as king Belibni (702–700), a Babylonian prince who had been educated at the Assyrian court. He thus hoped to appease Babylonian nationalism and at the same time safeguard the interests of Assyria. But the scheme proved to be a dismal failure. As soon as Sennacherib's back was turned Belibni joined forces with the still hopeful Mardukapaliddina and another Chaldaean called Mushezibmarduk. The return of Sennacherib resulted in a quick defeat for the coalition at Bittutu (700). Mushezibmarduk fled into the marshes, Belibni was sent back to Assyria, and Mardukapaliddina, accompanied by the images of his country's gods, was forced to seek refuge across the sea on the Elamite coast. Again the towns of the Sealands were ravaged, and again Sennacherib had to consider how he could keep Babylon secure. This time his solution was the appointment of his eldest son Ashurnadinshum to the throne of the conquered city.

For six years (699–694) there was peace around Babylon, and in the meantime Sennacherib made every effort to ensure that she would have no more support in future risings. First he dealt with the hill-tribes east of the Tigris, and then he prepared a sea-force to attack the Chaldaean remnants on the Elamite coast. The expedition was a successful one—more damage was done to his ships by the tide than by the opposing forces—and after the defeat of the Chaldaeans several Elamite towns were destroyed. This however had the unfortunate effect of making the king of Elam invade Babylonia behind Sennacherib's back. Sippar was plundered and Ashurnadinshum was taken to Elam as a prisoner of war. Then Babylon fell (694) and Nergalushezib was placed on the throne. By 693 all northern Babylonia was in the hands of the rebels and Sennacherib's army was cut off from Assyria. Then fortune changed in favour of Assyria. First the Elamite army was defeated, and then a fast-moving column succeeded in capturing Uruk. On their return journey the Assyrians had even better luck, for they encountered a small force led by Nergalushezib. In the resultant scuffle the Babylonian king was betrayed by his friends and led in chains before Sennacherib, and when the Assyrians reached home he was publicly exhibited as a mark of final degradation.

The loss of their king did not end Babylonian resistance. Mushezibmarduk, the Chaldaean who had joined in the rebellion of Belibni eight years previously, now returned with Elamite assistance and seized the throne for himself (692–689). Sennacherib tried to strike back by a winter campaign far into the mountains of Elam, but although he succeeded in defeating the Elamite army the weather finally drove him back to the plains. When spring came a motley host of Elamites and their allies descended into Babylonia to help Mushezibmarduk to expel the Assyrians from his land. Sennacherib made a stand at Halule on the eastern bank of the Tigris, and despite his grandiose description of his own prowess in the course of a great victory it is clear that he suffered a crushing defeat. Mushezibmarduk was left in complete control of Babylonia and Sennacherib retired to his magnificent new capital at Nineveh to plot reprisals. His opportunity came on the sudden death of the king of Elam in 689. This left Babylon in isolation, and quickly Sennacherib struck. The city was stormed and Mushezibmarduk was taken in chains to Assyria. Then his city was systematically destroyed. Houses, temples and defences were pulled down and set on fire, and the rubble was thrown into a canal which passed through the town. Then the banks of the Euphrates were breached and the whole site was flooded and turned to a swamp. Sennacherib was confident that he had completely eliminated Babylon, and that its very position would be forgotten for ever.

For the next eight years (688–681) Sennacherib was nominally king of Babylon. Although the city had ceased to exist the country round about still required administration, and this task was entrusted to the king's son Esarhaddon. Much as he may have hated Babylon when he first arrived, Esarhaddon soon realized that his father's destruction had done nothing to suppress the resistance of the Babylonian people. This was brought home to him immediately after his succession to the throne of Assyria in 680, for he found himself opposed in the south by Nabuzerkittilishir, king of the Sealands, who supported a rival Assyrian candidate and tried to capture Uruk in his name. Finally he was driven off and forced to flee to

Elam, where he was put to death; but the support that he had
gained in Babylonia was sufficient to show Esarhaddon the
weakness of his father's policy. During his governorship of the
south the Assyrian king had married a Babylonian wife and he
and his mother had adopted the worship of Marduk, Nabu and
other Babylonian gods, so now personal feeling and political
expediency were combined in a policy of reconciliation. The
gods, the stars and the planets, it was declared, were now
favourable for the rebuilding of Babylon. On an auspicious
day in 680 carpenters, stone-masons and metal-workers were
dispatched to begin the work, but as soon as they reached the
site they ran into difficulties. After the devastation wrought by
Sennacherib a local tribe called the Dakkuru had moved into
the deserted fields and gardens, and now they claimed them as
their own. Their formal protest to Esarhaddon was rejected,
and the insurrection which naturally followed had to be crushed
before building could begin in earnest. Temples and defences
were renewed on an even larger scale than before, and the
image of Ea, though for some reason not that of Marduk, was
returned to its shrine. The rights and privileges of the citizens
of Babylon were restored to them, and it seemed that the days
of the city's greatness had returned.

When Esarhaddon considered that he had done sufficient
for the Babylonians to ensure that they would not attack him
in the rear, he departed to the west in an attempt to fulfil a
long-standing Assyrian ambition—the conquest of Egypt. His
first attack was a dismal failure, and when the news of it reached
Babylonia it was sufficient to induce the Elamites to make
another attack. Sippar was captured with great slaughter, but
owing to dynastic difficulties no attempt was made by the
Elamites to follow up their success, and soon under a new ruler
they made peace with Assyria once more. About this time too
Esarhaddon's wife fell ill and the royal couple took up residence
in Uruk so that the queen might visit the shrines of the local
deities. However despite Esarhaddon's liberal gifts to the gods
of Babylonia his wife died in 671. A second expedition to
Egypt followed, and this proved more successful than the first.
But Esarhaddon's conquests crumbled as soon as he left the
country, and he had to make preparations for a third attack.
Before he left he made arrangements for the future of his kingdom. The throne of Assyria, he had already decided, was to go

to his son Ashurbanipal, but now he formally installed another son Shamashshumukin as crown prince of Babylon and indicated that after his own death Shamashshumukin was to be an independent king, inferior in rank only to his brother in Assyria.

On the way back to Egypt in 669 Esarhaddon died, and Ashurbanipal (668–631) became king of Assyria. Immediately after his accession he confirmed his brother's position as king of Babylon, and soon Marduk's statue was replaced amid rejoicing in his newly redecorated shrine. Yet despite the theoretical equality of the two kings it was obvious that the system would never work. Although he was careful to mention his brother's name in building-inscriptions in Babylon, Ashurbanipal made certain that real power was in his own hands. Shamashshumukin was allowed to rule only the area in the immediate vicinity of his capital, and even there his independence was curtailed by officials who reported directly to Assyria. The maintenance of an Assyrian garrison at Nippur was a further check on his movements, and although the Assyrian king sent horses, chariots, soldiers and other gifts to Babylon these were obviously meant to appease his brother rather than give him any real military strength.

For seventeen humiliating years Babylon remained quiet. The countries round about were not so subservient, and several times Elamite raids had to be suppressed. In Babylonia itself the Aramaean elements of the population never ceased to give trouble, and to the north and west the Bedouin tribes and the more settled peoples of Syria were eager for any chance to strike at Assyria. Finally Shamashshumkin was won over, and in 652 a great coalition was formed against the hated rule of Ashurbanipal. Elam and the tribes along its border, Babylonia, the desert peoples of the west, Syria, Palestine and even Egypt, which had regained its independence a few years before, united under the Babylonian king's leadership and prepared for war. Shamashshumukin himself gave notice to his brother that he would no longer allow him to offer sacrifices in Babylonia and then turned on the Assyrian garrisons in the south. Soon he was joined by a marauding band of Elamites who captured Uruk and plundered the surrounding countryside. Then Ur, Eridu and all the Sealands joined in on Babylon's side, and for a time Shamashshumukin seemed to have the upper hand. But soon a Chaldaean called Belibni succeeded in winning back the

Sealands for Ashurbanipal, while in the north an Assyrian victory at Babsame somewhere east of the Tigris (650) opened the way to the heart of Babylonia. Soon Sippar, Kutha, Borsippa and Babylon were under siege, and the situation had turned entirely in favour of Assyria. Gradually the other cities were conquered, and by July 648 all hope for Babylon had gone. The streets were piled high with the bodies of those who had died of hunger or pestilence, and those who survived were forced to turn to human flesh for sustenance. An attempt by the desert Arabs to relieve the city was a complete failure. Finally, just before the city surrendered, Shamashshumukin set his palace on fire and threw himself into the flames.

Once Babylon was conquered, Ashurbanipal was surprisingly merciful. All those who were suspected of having been in any way concerned with the revolt were taken to Assur, where their blasphemous tongues were cut out before their execution. Then the conqueror turned to works of mercy. The streets of Babylon were cleared of corpses and ritually purified, prayers of placation were offered to the city gods, and the inhabitants who had escaped into the country were invited back and settled in their homes again. An otherwise unknown Babylonian, Kandalanu by name, was appointed governor of the city, and once more Babylon was firmly linked with the Assyrian empire. Most of the other members of the great coalition of 652 had faded quietly away, and only Elam and the desert Arabs continued to give trouble. In two campaigns Ashurbanipal defeated the Elamite army, captured and sacked Susa, and systematically ravaged the whole land. By 639 Elam had virtually ceased to exist, and it never again played an important part in Near Eastern history. About the same time a series of expeditions into the western desert resulted in the renewed subjection of the Arab tribes. Thus Babylonia was quiet and the lands on either side of it were reduced to impotence. Then suddenly the records of the period cease, and though it can be seen that local business carried on as usual, the silence is an ominous one. The end of Assyria was close at hand.

(5)
The Second Babylonian Supremacy

BY the second half of the seventh century B.C., the once mighty empire of the Assyrians was beginning to disintegrate. Their policy of continuous conquest and expansion was in itself the main cause of their decline, for their finest native warriors, the main strength of their army, had gradually been wiped out and replaced by subject peoples and mercenary troops, and soldiers drawn from these sources were naturally not so keen on wearing themselves out for the spread of Assyrian greatness. As well as this, geography was against them. Mesopotamia had no natural boundaries at which the Assyrians could halt and consolidate their power. They had continually to be expanding and subduing new peoples. What they did not realize was that these peoples—Elamites, Urartians, and others—were themselves of unique value to Assyria as buffer-states against the barbarous hordes who lay beyond them. It was these barbarians who were eventually to emerge as the rulers of the area and indeed of most of the known world.

Inside Mesopotamia, the Babylonians waited for another chance to gain their independence. Kandalanu, the governor appointed by Ashurbanipal after his capture of Babylon in 648, was at first an obedient servant of Assyria. His domain was much more restricted than that of his predecessor. It extended only to Sippar in the north and Uruk in the south, and in the middle was Nippur, which remained an Assyrian garrison-town and an effective deterrent to any subversive movement. As a further check, an "administrator of the Sealands" was appointed to look after Assyrian interests in the far south. Ashurbanipal's nominee for this post was his Chaldaean supporter Belibni, and he too proved to be a loyal servant. Thus it seemed that Babylonia was once again firmly in Assyrian hands.

After Ashurbanipal's death about 633, however, the situation

133

rapidly changed. A series of weaker kings followed on the Assyrian throne, and Kandalanu, after almost twenty years of loyal obedience, was inspired to seize the opportunity for independence. Sinsharishkun, the new Assyrian king, immediately took steps to meet the threat. The garrison at Nippur was alerted and a new administrator of the Sealands was appointed. Nothing is known of what happened to Belibni. It is possible that he had died naturally and that Nabopolassar, the new administrator, was his son. At any rate Nabopolassar was quick to move against the rebels, and conducted a successful raid on Uruk. The forces sent from Assyria had less success, and when Kandalanu died in 627, the Assyrians were unable to appoint a successor in Babylon. Assyria's weakness, in fact, was so obvious that Nabopolassar, elated by his success at Uruk, decided that it was better to work in his own interests than to try to prop up a falling empire, and instead of moving in on the rebels in Babylon, he turned towards Nippur and laid siege to the town. The inhabitants were so hard pressed that they were forced to sell their children to buy food, and eventually the Assyrian garrison was driven out.

By September 626, however, Sinsharishkun had reorganized his forces and advanced on Babylonia, capturing and burning the border-fortress of Shuznaku. He then divided his army, one body marching rapidly towards Nippur, while the other, larger and slower moving, headed for Babylon. Nabopolassar, who had now united with the Babylonian rebels, realized that he did not have the power to meet both Assyrian forces. As the smaller body neared Kish, which lay on the direct line of march to Nippur, he offered no resistance but removed the gods of the town to Babylon for protection, and as the Assyrians approached Nippur itself he prudently withdrew to Uruk, leaving the town undefended. After occupying Nippur and conscripting a detachment of its citizens, the Assyrians followed and attacked Nabopolassar's forces, but news from the north compelled them to make a hasty retreat. The main Assyrian army, which had been heading for Babylon, had been decisively defeated. The Assyrian supremacy in Babylon was at an end.

On November 23rd, 626, Nabopolassar was proclaimed king of Babylon. He had already been recognized in Sippar as king of Akkad, and with his accession, Babylon entered a period of renewed greatness. But first his main concern was with the consolidation of his position. He recognized far more than the Assyrians had done the value of buffer-states, and one of his first acts was to win the friendship of Elam by restoring to her the gods whom the Assyrians had removed. This secured his rear while he dealt with renewed Assyrian attempts to win back what they had lost. The following year Sinsharishkun's forces advanced again into Babylonia, causing the gods of Shapazzu, another border fortress, to be withdrawn to Babylon for protection, and then crossing the Tigris and moving towards Sippar. The gods of this city too were evacuated, and the neighbouring town of Sallat was taken and plundered. But although a Babylonian counter-attack was unsuccessful, the Assyrians were unable to follow up their advantage and withdrew to their own country. Further south the garrison at Nippur still held out, and the following summer an Assyrian campaign was undertaken to win some relief for it by gaining control of the Banitu canal which supplied the city with water. Apart from one unsuccessful attack on Nabopolassar's camp, however, there was little military action that year before the Assyrian withdrawal.

The following year (623) events moved nearer Nineveh when the city of Der in the border country between Elam and Babylonia proclaimed its independence from Assyrian rule. In the autumn, another attempt was made to relieve the garrison at Nippur, but by now Nabopolassar had the strength not only to defeat the Assyrians, but to follow up his victory by an advance northwards into enemy country. Soon after, the Nippur garrison broke out from the city in a last desperate attempt to assert Assyrian rule. For a time they were successful, and even managed to capture Uruk. But without help from the north they could not hope to hold out, and eventually they were overwhelmed by the rapidly increasing power of Babylon.

For the next few years Nabopolassar continued his policy of annual advances into Assyrian territory. Nothing is known of these campaigns until 616, when the Babylonian army, following the ancient trade route to Syria and the Mediterranean, advanced up the Euphrates almost as far as the Khabur River. Although local resistance was negligible, it was sufficient to encourage the Assyrian king to gather his army. A few months later he encamped at Qablinu, a short distance upstream from the Babylonian position. But when Nabopolassar closed in on the town Sinsharishkun lost his nerve and began a hasty retreat. Nabopolassar, however, quickly caught up with him and inflicted a heavy defeat. Qablinu fell and the Assyrians retired to Harran. Unable to attack this stronghold, Nabopolassar's forces plundered three towns south of it and retired with their booty to Babylon. For Assyria had found a new ally, and her army had been reinforced by a detachment of Egyptian troops. At first this seems a strange combination, for it was less than forty years since Egypt had freed herself from Assyrian domination. But pressure of events now drove them together. From the Egyptian point of view, Assyria was now a buffer against the barbarians from the north and east and, besides this, she served as a check on the rise of Babylonian power in Syria, which could only interfere with Egyptian influence there. Hence the presence of Egyptian troops in Syria, and Nabopolassar's hasty retreat. The Assyrian forces followed as far as Qablinu, but failed to overtake him and withdrew once more.

Despite his discomfiture in Syria, Nabopolassar did not hesitate to strike at other points where there was no likelihood of Egyptian intervention. An attack up the eastern bank of the Tigris ended in an Assyrian defeat south of the Diyala, followed by a pursuit as far as the Lower Zab. Early the next year this policy was continued by a more ambitious campaign up the Tigris into the heart of Assyria. Assur, the ancient capital of the country, was blockaded, but Nabopolassar had over-reached himself. An Assyrian counter-attack forced him to raise the siege and make off with all speed down the Tigris, hotly pursued by Sinsharishkun's forces. So hard pressed were the Babylonians that they were compelled to flee for refuge to Takrit, a natural fortress of immense strength well south of the Lower Zab. Here they were in their turn besieged for ten days until the Assyrians gave up the attempt and turned north again. A more dangerous enemy had entered the land. By November the country south of the Diyala, the very area where the Babylonian king had been operating the previous year, had been occupied by the Medes.

The Medes were only one of a number of Indo-European tribes which had been forcing their way on to the Iranian plateau since the beginning of the first millennium B.C. They are first mentioned in the Assyrian records in 834, in the region of Hamadan, but at this time they were a loose collection of related clans rather than a united nation. The union of the clans was achieved under Phraortes, who was killed in an attack on Nineveh in 653, but after this the Medes were subject for almost thirty years to the Scythians, a group of warlike nomads from the north who spread terror through Assyria, Asia Minor, Syria and Palestine. Eventually Cyaxares, the son and successor of Phraortes, succeeded in overthrowing the Scythians, and made good use of his knowledge of Scythian military tactics in reorganizing his army into a powerful war-machine. It was this army which now appeared on the borders of Assyria.

The following summer (614) Cyaxares marched directly towards Nineveh, and laid siege to it. But for some unknown reason he abandoned the siege and turned away to the north-west to attack the neighbouring city of Tarbisu. Perhaps he felt that he was not strong enough to take the capital by storm, or possibly Scythian intervention caused him to abandon his purpose. After the fall of Tarbisu, the Medes turned down the Tigris and launched an attack on Assur, which Nabopolassar had failed to capture the year before. The city did not escape a second time. It was totally destroyed and its inhabitants were taken prisoner or killed.

All this was too good a chance for Nabopolassar to miss, and he led his army north to give his help to the Medes. But so swift had the Median invasion been that the Babylonians did not reach the area until after Assur had fallen. Somewhere near the ruins of the city Nabopolassar and Cyaxares met and made a treaty of friendship which was perhaps sealed by a marriage between Nebuchadnezzar, Nabopolassar's son, and Amytis, the granddaughter of Cyaxares. Having agreed on their plans for the destruction of Nineveh, the two leaders retired to their homelands for the winter.

In 613 something went wrong with the master-plan. Instead of being penned in his capital, the Assyrian king was able to conduct a campaign in the central Euphrates valley in support of rebellious vassals of Babylon. The revolt brought Nabopolassar hurrying to the scene, and after capturing the island-town of Rahilu he moved on upstream against the fortress of Anatu, which was also built on an island. An elaborate causeway was built out from the bank of the river and siege-engines were moved against the walls. But in the midst of the attack the

Assyrian army appeared, and Nabopolassar hastily withdrew.

It seems obvious that in this year there was no siege of
Nineveh, and this was probably because there was no Median
invasion. No trace of a reason for this can be found in the
cuneiform sources, and it can only be assumed that the Medes
were occupied with domestic troubles and with persuading
the Scythians to side with them against Assyria. At any rate
in the next year Cyaxares appeared as leader of a combined
Median-Scythian confederacy which joined forces with the
Babylonians for a final assault on the Assyrian capital. Moving
up the Tigris the allies surrounded the city and began a siege.
Eventually in July or August, after almost three months of
fighting, an entry was forced where the walls had been
weakened by abnormally high floods. The city was taken,
looted and set on fire, and Sinsharishkun perished in his burning
capital. The Medes, loaded with spoil, retired once more to
their homeland, and Nabopolassar was left in control of the
countryside.

But although Nineveh had fallen, Assyria was not yet finally
destroyed. During the siege a number of Assyrians led by a
noble whose name was Ashuruballit, realizing that the city
was doomed, had contrived to break through the Babylonian
lines and escape to the west. Crossing the Khabur River, they
headed for Harran, the capital of the Assyrian province of which
Ashuruballit may well have been governor. Nabopolassar
pursued them as far as the Khabur, gathering still more booty
and causing the towns west of Nineveh to pay tribute to him,
but he was unable to cross and attack Harran. Heartened by
this, the Assyrians appointed Ashuruballit as their new king,
and settled down to await another attack.

In 611, nothing was heard of the Medes. The Babylonians
marched back up the Euphrates and spent the summer in
plundering and destroying the area round Harran. But despite
minor successes and the capture of at least one town Nabopolassar did not feel himself strong enough to attack the new
Assyrian capital single-handed, and retired once more to
Babylon. The next year the same procedure was followed with
an equal lack of success. By this time the Assyrians had been
joined in Harran by Egyptian reinforcements and the combination was much too formidable for the Babylonian king. In the

autumn however, perhaps in answer to an appeal from Nabopolassar, a Median army appeared to give him aid, and its
presence so frightened the Assyrians and Egyptians that they
abandoned Harran and fled across the Euphrates. The Medes
and Babylonians moved into the defenceless city and plundered
it, destroying the temple of the moon-god in the process, before
returning home for the winter. A Median garrison, aided by
a Babylonian contingent, was left to defend the town against
any Assyrian attack.

The following spring, Ashuruballit led a large force of Egyptians and Assyrians against Harran in the hope of recapturing
it before help could reach it from Babylonia. As soon as he
heard the news, Nabopolassar headed north, but before he
could reach Harran, the siege had been raised and his help was
no longer required. Again no reason has been discovered for
the Assyrian withdrawal. Perhaps the garrison which had been
left was itself sufficiently strong to break the siege, or possibly
the Medes had arrived before the Babylonians. Nabopolassar
promptly by-passed the city and moved into the mountains
to the north-east, burning villages and leaving garrisons to
watch over the unruly hill-men. It has also been suggested that
he was searching for Ashuruballit, of whom no further mention
has been found, or that he was helping the Medes in their
advance through Urartu towards Lydian territory in Asia
Minor. The campaign was continued in the autumn of 608 and
more hill towns were plundered and destroyed, although
details are rather obscure.

In the meantime, Egypt was on the move. Necho, the newly
appointed Pharaoh, was determined to sustain his interests
in Syria. The Egyptian troops already in the area had proved
inadequate for this, so he mustered his full army and set out
for Carchemish. To his surprise, when he reached the pass of
Megiddo, he found his way barred by the little army of Judah
under its king Josiah, a monarch who had some years before
won his country's independence from Assyria and now refused
to give help to his former masters' allies. The result was inevitable. Judah was heavily defeated, Josiah was killed, and the
Egyptian force moved on into Syria.

For two more years Nabopolassar contented himself with
comparatively minor operations in Syria. He had no intention
of allowing Egypt to fill the vacuum left by Assyria, but he

realized that for the moment he could not count on winning
a full-scale battle. Besides, he was growing old and his health
was beginning to fail. In 607 he was forced to return home after
less than a month in the field, and the crown prince Nebuchadnezzar was left in command. By the autumn Nabopolassar was
fit enough to lead his army once more and made a surprise
attack across the Euphrates which gained him the town of
Kimuhu, just south of Carchemish, and with it a bridgehead
on the Egyptian side of the river. Leaving a garrison to defend
the town, he returned to Babylon in 606.

Kimuhu was of vital importance to the Egyptians. Besides
commanding a river-crossing, it lay close to their supply lines
from the south. Their reaction was swift, and soon the town was
under siege. Again Nabopolassar called out his army and
marched up river, but again he was too late. After a four-month
siege Kimuhu fell. This habit of leaving garrisoned outposts
close to enemy territory but far from help in case of emergency
was a curious weakness in Nabopolassar's strategy. In this case
he attempted to retrieve the situation by crossing the river
further south at Quramati and seizing a few villages on the
Egyptian bank. But again he returned to Babylon, leaving his
garrisons in isolation, and when the Egyptian forces advanced
towards them, they were forced to retreat from their impossible
position.

In 605 the situation was completely reversed. Instead of
conducting another cautious and indecisive campaign, Nabopolassar was forced by age or ill-health to entrust his army once
again to Nebuchadnezzar. For some reason the Egyptians had
withdrawn from Kimuhu and Quramati, and Nebuchadnezzar
took them completely by surprise when in late May or early
June he crossed the river near Carchemish. The Babylonian
forces were inside the city before Egyptian resistance could
be organized, and bitter hand-to-hand fighting took place in the
streets as well as in the country round about. The city was set
on fire during the struggle and the Egyptian army was anni-
hilated. Isolated groups which had fled before the battle really
began were pursued to the south. Some were destroyed in the
area of Hamath on the Orontes while others managed to reach
the coast before being overtaken. Not a man escaped Nebuchadnezzar's fury. Jehoiakim, the new king of Judah, who had been
a humble vassal of Egypt, was quick to transfer his allegiance

to the Babylonian king and offer him hostages, one of whom may have been the prophet Daniel. By August Nebuchadnezzar had reached the borders of Egypt.

The comparative ease with which the Babylonian forces gained Syria and Palestine can only be explained by an almost complete lack of Egyptian arms in the area. Necho had failed to learn from Nabopolassar's mistakes in relying on isolated garrisons, and when Nebuchadnezzar caught the Carchemish garrison in equal isolation from Egypt, the loss of the whole province was bound to follow. Perhaps if in the previous year the Egyptians had followed up their successes by striking down the Euphrates the result would have been different. But their sphere of influence ended at the river and the conquest of Babylon did not interest them. So Nebuchadnezzar was allowed to strike back at Carchemish, and with his success the kingdoms of Syria and Palestine at once came to heel.

If Nebuchadnezzar had any plans for invading Egypt he was not allowed to put them into operation. On August 15th his father died. As soon as the news reached him Nebuchadnezzar took the quickest route across the desert and on September 6th, the very day on which he reached Babylon, he ascended the throne as Nabopolassar's successor. Later the same year he returned to Syria. No resistance was offered, and the campaign became a parade of military strength designed to impress local princes and remind them of the tribute they owed him. In the spring he returned once again to Babylon to take the hands of Marduk and celebrate the New Year Festival, and this was followed by another Syrian campaign to ensure submission to his rule. States such as Tyre, Sidon, and Damascus probably acknowledged him at this time, but Askelon, under its King Achon, preferred to appeal for Egyptian help. This did not arrive, and Askelon could not hold out alone. The city was destroyed, its king was deposed, and Aga', a Babylonian vassal, was appointed in his place. To ensure that he kept the peace, Nebuchadnezzar seized a number of hostages, including the king's two sons, before returning to Babylon.

Events in 603 and 602 followed the same pattern, and show that Nebuchadnezzar was undisputed master of his empire. Tribute flowed in from the Syrian dependencies, and the army, free from loss through war, grew steadily stronger. In 601, Nebuchadnezzar judged that he had the power for a direct

attack on Egypt. In this he was mistaken, for after an indecisive
battle somewhere near the Egyptian border he was forced to
retire to Babylon again. So heavy in fact were his losses that all
the next year had to be spent at home in manufacturing
chariots, training horses and re-equipping his men. Pharaoh
Necho must have been in similar difficulties, for he made no
attempt to advance into Asia but contented himself with
espionage in the Babylonian dependencies. In December 599
Nebuchadnezzar returned to Syria intent on retrieving his
losses. First he had to deal with the nomad Arab tribes of the
desert regions, who were friendly to Egypt and so would be
a threat in his rear. To ensure their submission he exacted
tribute and took their protective gods with him when he returned to Babylon in March 598.

In Palestine the news of the Babylonian losses against Egypt
had been sufficient for Jehoiakim, undeterred by the warnings
of the prophet Jeremiah, to stop his payment of tribute and
turn to Pharaoh once more. Reconstruction of what followed
is almost impossible without further evidence, but it appears
that by the autumn of 598 a Babylonian force had moved into
Jerusalem, removed Jehoiakim and appointed Jehoiachin in
his place. The death of Jehoiakim in early December may
or may not have been natural. About the same time the
main Babylonian army set out from home and headed for
Palestine.

Despite the change of king the allegiance of Judah was by no
means certain, and in January 597 Nebuchadnezzar began
a siege of the city. While it was going on, Lachish and other
towns in the area were captured and destroyed. Then on
March 15th, 597 Jerusalem fell, perhaps surrendered by
Jeroiachin to save it from destruction. At any rate, Nebuchadnezzar spared the city but demanded heavy tribute including
the treasures of the palace and Solomon's temple. A fortnight
after the capture of the city Jehoiachin with his mother, his
wives and the leading men of the land began the long journey
to exile in Babylonia. With them were a thousand skilled
craftsmen who might manufacture arms and up to seven
thousand soldiers capable of using them. Only the poorest and
least useful citizens were left, and Mattaniah, Jehoiachin's
uncle, was appointed to rule over them. As a final mark of
degradation and subservience he was forced to change his name

to Zedekiah. It seemed that Jerusalem's days of greatness were at an end.

Nebuchadnezzar's victory in Palestine was so convincing that later in the year he could afford to go tribute-gathering in Syria without even the protection of his army. The rest of the empire was probably quiet as well, and in Mesopotamia the Jewish exiles were settled in their new homes. Jehoiachin and his family were detained in the royal palace in Babylon, where tablets recording their allowances of food have been found. The common people were scattered, some at least, like the prophet Ezekiel, being given homes in the vicinity of Nippur.

In 596 there was trouble with an unnamed enemy on the eastern frontier, but on the approach of the Babylonian army the hostile forces retired. The general lack of activity on Nebuchadnezzar's eastern front over these years presumably shows that the alliance between Media and Babylonia was still active, thus leaving each free to pursue its own interests elsewhere. The year 595 was spent in Babylon and ended with the suppression of a palace revolt. Soon afterwards an official called Baba-ahuiddina was executed for treason and his property was confiscated, and it is probable that he was one of the leaders of the intrigue. So firmly did Nebuchadnezzar deal with his opponents that by the spring he was able to leave Babylon for his annual tribute-collection. The west was still quiet and again he could travel without his army. In the next few years however the situation began to change. Necho of Egypt died in 595, and his successors Psammetichus II (595–589) and Apries (589–569) were eager to extend their influence into Asia. In 590 Psammetichus led an expedition to Phoenicia to foment rebellion, and this policy was also followed by Apries, who occupied Tyre by sea and Sidon by land in an attempt to win a footing on the coast. As a result of this Zedekiah of Judah, trusting Egyptian promises and driven on by the anti-Babylonian ardour of his prophets, refused to pay his tribute to Nebuchadnezzar. Only Jeremiah had the foresight to see what would happen, but he could not change his king's mind. In January 587 the Babylonian king, stung by a petty vassal's insult to his majesty, appeared in Syria and established his headquarters at Riblah on the Orontes. There he could meet any Egyptian attack from the coast while a detachment of his troops moved south and surrounded Jerusalem. Hoping for Egyptian help, the city held out. Apries however realized that he could not by-pass Riblah to relieve Jerusalem, so he returned by sea to Egypt and entered Palestine from the south. His advance was dangerous enough to raise the siege for a short time, but when he saw the size of the Babylonian forces he retired discreetly from the fray. Nebuchadnezzar took the opportunity of re-covering Lachish and other towns in the area which had revolted, and then Jerusalem was surrounded again. In July 586, when famine was raging in the city and the walls had already been breached, Zedekiah found a way through the enemy lines and escaped towards the Jordan. He was captured near Jericho and brought to Nebuchadnezzar's headquarters at Riblah, where he was convicted of breaking his oath of subservience. His sons were killed before his eyes, and then he was blinded and sent in chains to Babylon. By this time Jerusa-lem had been occupied, and it was now systematically des-troyed. All removable valuables were taken away, the walls were pulled down, and the temple, palace and private houses were burned to the ground. Seventy of the most important citizens were taken to Riblah and executed, and most of the remainder were deported. Only the most useless of the inhabi-tants were left, and Gedaliah was appointed to govern them. A few months later he was murdered, and the few remaining Jews made their way to Egypt, where Apries welcomed them and gave them a home.

Having dealt with Judah, Nebuchadnezzar turned to the conquest of Phoenicia. This proved to be a difficult task, and although Sidon was quickly captured, the fortress of Tyre, unassisted by any Egyptian relieving force, held out until 573. About the same time as Nebuchadnezzar began this campaign, his Median allies were engaged in an indecisive battle with the kingdom of Lydia in western Asia Minor. The dispute was settled by arbitration in which the Medes were represented by Nabonidus, a high-ranking Babylonian official who at this time was probably engaged in the conquest of Cilicia. This again shows the good relations which were still maintained between the two great powers. But before the end of his reign, Nebuchad-nezzar must have begun to suspect Median intentions, for he built a great defensive wall north of Babylon from Sippar to Opis with a supporting network of canals to make attack from the north more difficult.

It is unfortunate that practically no historical records have so far been found for the final part of Nebuchadnezzar's reign. The only record of foreign expeditions from this time is a fragmentary text which tells of an encounter in 568 between Nebuchadnezzar and Pharaoh Amasis of Egypt. This can have been little more than a skirmish somewhere in the desert near the Egyptian border, and may indicate that the Babylonian king

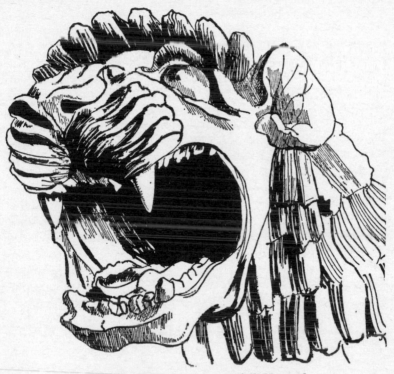

FIG. 8   Clay lion from Tell Harmal

was trying to gain control of trade routes in the Red Sea area. Apart from this there is a great gap in the history of the period which it is hoped will one day be filled by new discoveries. But the times must have been prosperous, if we can judge by Nebuchadnezzar's building activity all over his realms and especially in Babylon itself. The city revealed by Koldewey's excavations and described in another chapter is a monument to the prowess of its greatest builder.

Nebuchadnezzar died in 562 and was succeeded by his son Amelmarduk, concerning whom almost the only information preserved is that he ruled without law or restraint. The precise nature of his crimes is unknown. He showed mercy to the exiled Jehoiachin of Judah, who was brought out of prison and for the remainder of his life dined at the king's own table. Perhaps this indulgence towards foreigners was one of the reasons for his unpopularity in Babylon, and it is not clear whether he died naturally or was assassinated by a group of army officers eager to restore the military glory of Nebuchadnezzar's reign. Neriglissar, who came to the throne after Amelmarduk's death in 559, was an experienced general who had served in Syria and Palestine to such good effect that he had won the hand of Nebuchadnezzar's daughter. Until a few years ago it seemed that despite his military background Neriglissar paid more attention to building operations than to the extension of the empire. Temples in Babylon and Borsippa, a palace by the Euphrates and a network of canals—these seemed to be the sum of the general's activity once he became king, and his only known journey outside Babylon was to bring an exiled goddess back from Gutium. With the publication of new material in 1956 the picture abruptly changed, and Neriglissar could be seen to have lived up to the expectation of those who had supported him to the kingship. Details of only one campaign are given, but there is no reason to suppose that it was the only one of the reign. The operation began late in 557 when the fertile plain of Cilicia, which had been a Babylonian dependency for almost thirty years, was invaded by Appuashu, the king of the mountainous country to the west. On Neriglissar's approach Appuashu retired to the foothills and set his forces to guard the approaches, but the Babylonians smashed through his defences and followed him across the difficult mountain-country to his capital. After capturing and plundering the town they continued the pursuit for another forty miles before turning south to the coast where the island fortress of Pitusu, two miles offshore, was successfully assaulted. The country was ravaged as far as the Lydian border before the Babylonian forces returned home in February 556.

In April of the same year Neriglissar died. The circumstances of his death are obscure, but by the following year the Medes had gained possession of northern Syria, including Harran, and it is possible that he was killed in an attempt to defend the area. Alternatively the Medes may have taken advantage of the crisis that followed his death to seize the Babylonian province, for when Neriglissar's young son Labashimarduk was placed on the throne there was widespread discontent in Babylonia. Some cities refused to recognize him, perhaps because he was not the son of Nebuchadnezzar's daughter and so not of the royal blood, and within a few days a rival candidate had been widely accepted. Less than three months later Labashimarduk had been murdered and the rival was on the throne.

Nabonidus (556-539), the last king of the Neo-Babylonian Dynasty, was a man of middle age with a distinguished military and diplomatic career behind him, and his accession shows the power, not of the priesthood as was originally thought, but of the army which had been Nebuchadnezzar's chief support. Two of the great king's generals became king within a few years of his death, and another ex-general was to play a substantial part in the final overthrow of his empire.

Nabonidus was not a Babylonian by birth. His father Nabubalatsuiqbi was a Syrian of princely birth and political importance, and his mother was high priestess of the moon-god at Harran. So Nabonidus was brought up in the rarified atmosphere of a Syrian shrine until the arrival of Ashuruballit and his fugitives from the destruction of Nineveh. Two years later, when Harran was destroyed and its temples plundered, its citizens, including presumably the high-priestess and her son, were deported to Babylonia. After this a great deal must be left to conjecture, but by 597 a Nabonidus, the son of a prince, was a city-governor of some sort, and in 585, if Greek tradition is to be believed, Nabonidus was the Babylonian representative in the arbitration between Lydia and Media. This was remarkable promotion for the son of an exiled priestess, and there seems reason to accept the suggestion that when she reached Babylon, his mother had been placed in Nebuchadnezzar's harem, and there she had risen to be his favourite wife. Her son then must have been one of the most powerful men in the kingdom by 556, and there is little reason to doubt his own statement that he was the heir of Nebuchadnezzar and Neriglissar, elected by popular acclaim to the position which they had held.

Once he had secured his position, the king's first concern

was to win back the lost Syrian province. Since the Medes had sacked Harran in 610, the moon temple had lain in ruins, and Nabonidus had long cherished the ambition to restore it to its former glory. But first he had to get rid of the Medes, and he was doubtful of his ability to do this alone. Looking round for a possible ally he picked on the rebellious leader of the Median dependency of Anshan in southern Persia. Oracular advice was sought, and the desirability of the alliance was confirmed. Secret arrangements must have been made soon after by which Nabonidus was to attack Syria, and Cyrus, the vassal king of Anshan, was to take advantage of the destruction to strike at the Median empire from within.

In 555 Nabonidus kept his part of the bargain by a military levy throughout the empire, followed by a march on Harran. The campaign, which to Nabonidus was more like a crusade, ended in success, and while the foundations of the temple were laid lesser operations were conducted in Cilicia, the scene of Neriglissar's victories two years before. Meanwhile in Babylonia the effects of his Syrian upbringing were beginning to be felt. The priests especially found that although temples were restored and liberally endowed, the king's ideas on cult practices were scarcely their own. He regarded Marduk not as the national god, but merely as an intermediary for his own supreme deity, the Syrian moon-god Sin, whose statue was erected for worship in Babylon. At Sippar, Ur and other important shrines he insisted on changes in the cult, and although he tried to justify them by appealing to ancient records, his efforts were extemely unpopular. Other temples were insulted by the removal of their deities to a centralized cult in Babylon. In civil affairs, Nabonidus began to appoint foreigners to important administrative positions and thus alienated the ruling classes as well as the priests. As a final blow the New Year Festival on which the prosperity of the land depended was not held in 554, nor did it take place again until at least 545, and probably until the final year of his reign.

It may have been because of his waning popularity that Nabonidus planned the elaborate operations that were to follow. It was as a soldier that he had been placed on the throne, and he was perhaps determined to show that in the field he could rival the achievements of his great patron and predecessor. In 554 the building of the moon temple continued, and

Nabonidus spent the year in destroying pockets of resistance in Syria. The following spring he advanced into the Lebanon. There he had to stay for some time through illness, but by the end of the year he had recovered sufficiently to lead his army down the old caravan-route east of the Jordan as far as Adummu, the Biblical Edom, where the town of Shindini was besieged and captured. At this point his son Belshazzar was summoned from Babylon and the kingdom was entrusted to him before Nabonidus set out on his great military adventure.

The oasis of Tema lies in the north Arabian desert about a hundred miles east of the Gulf of Akaba, and is a natural centre of Arabian trade. It is the meeting-place of the caravan routes from Damascus to the north, Sheba to the south, the Persian Gulf to the east and Egypt to the west, and Babylonian control of it was becoming more and more essential. The constant silting of the Persian Gulf meant that ports under Babylonian control were becoming increasingly useless for overseas trade, and a new trading centre was urgently required to maintain the prosperity of the empire. The conquest of such a centre, perhaps planned by Nebuchadnezzar, would be an achievement worthy of the inheritor of his throne, and as he looked around his realms, Nabonidus cannot be blamed for thinking that he had found the ideal time for it. Egypt under the peaceful Amasis was unlikely to interfere, and to the north-east Cyrus of Anshan had played his part in the bargain made three years earlier and had rebelled from his Median overlord. Belshazzar had already proved himself a competent administrator in Babylon, and so Nabonidus felt himself entirely free to press on with his enterprise. After a march south from Edom, Tema was captured and its king was killed.

Although it is easy to give reasons for the Tema expedition it is more difficult to account for the fact that when Nabonidus had taken the town he stayed there at least until 545, and probably until 540. Many explanations are possible—voluntary retirement, forced abdication, desire to spread the worship of the moon-god, convalescence after his illness, and a host of others—but not one of them is really supported by the evidence. Had he been interested merely in securing the trade of the area, any competent general or member of his family—Belshazzar for instance—could have been appointed governor of the district. Certainly the continued presence of the king was not essential. If his withdrawal from Babylon was to decrease his personal unpopularity, then surely the omission of the New Year Festival and the king's other religious duties must have served the opposite purpose. If he was seeking an alliance with the king of Egypt he certainly would not secure it by interfering with Egyptian trade. It seems more likely that after his agreement with Cyrus Nabonidus decided that since expansion to the east and north was impossible, the future of his kingdom lay in the west. The Tema campaign was the beginning of this new expansion, and with it the centre of gravity in the empire moved. Nabonidus rebuilt Tema like a second Babylon because it was to be the new capital of his empire, and Belshazzar was left to govern Babylon because henceforth Babylon was to be a mere provincial town. This would account more than anything for the animosity of Babylonian opinion.

In planning this new conception of a western empire ruled from Tema under the supreme guidance of the moon-god Nabonidus made one fearful miscalculation. In 553 Cyrus of Anshan might have seemed a mere petty king, but by retiring to the Arabian desert Nabonidus failed to see the speed with which his power grew, and so he took no steps to counteract it until it was too late. The king of Anshan belonged to an Indo-European people who had entered the area at the same time as the Medes. They are first found in Assyrian records about the middle of the ninth century, when they were living west and south-west of Lake Urmia, but in the next hundred and fifty years they moved gradually south into Elamite territory, finally settling in the area known as Parsumash, east of modern Shustar in south Persia. At first they were vassals of the Elamites, but the decline of Elam allowed them a period of quiet expansion into the surrounding districts of Anshan, north-west of Parsumash, and Parsa, the modern Fars, from which they gained their name of Persians. The increasing power of Media after the fall of Nineveh led to another period of vassaldom, during which Cambyses, a prince of the junior Persian line, married the daughter of Astyages, king of the Medes. The son of this marriage was Cyrus, who became king of Anshan in 559 and immediately began to look for aid in securing his country's freedom. His agreement with Nabonidus in 556 was followed by revolt from his overlord in 553, just when Nabonidus was leaving for his Arabian campaign, and after a three-year struggle he succeeded in overthrowing his grandfather and seizing the Median throne. The next two years were spent in winning over other parts of the empire. About this time too Gobyras, a former general in the army of Nebuchadnezzar and now governor of the Babylonian province of Gutium, offered his services to the Persian king. In 547 Cyrus was ready for expansion. Crossing the Tigris near Arbela, he led his army westwards across the Khabur, through north Syria, and on into Asia Minor.

By the autumn he had reached the Halys, where a battle was fought with Croesus of Lydia. When neither side gained a decisive advantage, Croesus retired to his capital at Sardis and sent out an appeal for help. Among those to whom it was addressed was Nabonidus. Babylon had presumably allied itself with Lydia, perhaps towards the end of Nebuchadnezzar's reign, in an attempt to curb the power of the Medes, but now Nabonidus found himself in the uncomfortable position of being asked to supply troops to fight against his own allies the Persians. Fortunately Cyrus did not leave him time to make a decision on this awkward question. Following Croesus rapidly to his capital he caught him completely unprepared. Sardis fell, and Croesus was executed.

Thus within a few years the balance of power in western Asia was entirely altered. Babylon was no longer secure to north and east; instead she was faced by a single power, young, vigorous and rapidly expanding, backed by all the resources of Asia Minor and Iran. It must have been obvious that the Babylonian empire would be the next objective, but for some unfathomable reason Nabonidus in his desert capital failed to see this. The only event in Babylonia which was thought worthy of mention at the time was the death of the king's mother, which took place in 547 at Durkarashu, near Sippar. Belshazzar and the army in Babylonia held a three-day period of mourning, and word was sent to Nabonidus at Tema. Two months later instructions for a more elaborate mourning were brought back from Arabia, but there is no indication that Nabonidus himself returned to Babylon.

After his defeat of Croesus, Cyrus was able to expand into Syria without much trouble. Even if Nabonidus was engaged in Arabia, it is surprising that Belshazzar apparently made no effort to hold the northern area for his father, and he must take a large share of the blame for allowing Cyrus to succeed in a blatant propaganda campaign, winning over local priests and princes by lavish bribery and by persuading them that he was freeing them from Babylonian tyranny rather than indulging in colonialism on his own account. In this way Syria and Palestine were whittled away from the Babylonian empire with scarcely any fighting, and by 540 Cyrus had won over the Bedouin sheikhs of the desert areas towards Tema. When this happened the position of Nabonidus became completely untenable. His lines of communication with Babylonia could be cut at any moment, and his new capital was in imminent danger. There was nothing he could do except abandon it and head with all speed for Babylon. Thus the new western empire on which he had set such high hopes collapsed without a struggle.

On his return to Babylon, Nabonidus found little to comfort him. There was famine in the land, the sea-peoples along the Persian Gulf were already in revolt, and the armies of Cyrus were massed on the Diyala, ready for the final assault. Babylon's only hope lay in Nebuchadnezzar's Median fortification wall from Sippar to Opis, and there Nabonidus awaited the Persian attack. In March 539 the New Year Festival was held for the first time in many years, but already Cyrus was assaulting the Median wall. Hastily the deities of the surrounding towns were called to Babylon for protection, but Cyrus's propagandists had been at work in several cities, and they refused to send their gods. As the assault continued, desperation grew, and when Opis was about to fall, an abortive rebellion broke out in Babylonia. This was rapidly crushed by Nabonidus, but the effort was too much for him. Opis was captured and the Persian troops moved across the Median wall. Nothing was ready for a final stand—the tradition of Belshazzar's feast is supported by Greek testimony which tells of feasting and revelry as the city was about to fall—and the invading forces met practically no resistance in a two-pronged thrust which took Cyrus to Sippar, and Gobyras, the Babylonian governor of Gutium who had deserted to Persia some ten years earlier, straight to the capital. Sippar fell on October 11th, and two days later Gobyras and his Gutians entered Babylon. Thus the empire which Nebuchadnezzar had created was finally destroyed by one of his own officers.

Nabonidus was not in his capital when it fell. When he heard that Sippar had been captured, he made a last desperate attempt to flee to the south-west, towards the desert region where he had tried to found his new capital. But soon he was cut off by the Bedouin tribes who were Cyrus's allies and forced back towards Babylon, where he was captured and probably executed by the victorious Gutians. Apart from this, Gobyras was careful to take no punitive measures. His soldiers made sure that there was no interruption to the temple ceremonies, and the people were carefully prepared for the arrival of their new master. When on October 29th, 539 Cyrus entered Babylon, his route was lined by cheering crowds waving palm-branches, and he was hailed as the saviour and liberator of the country.

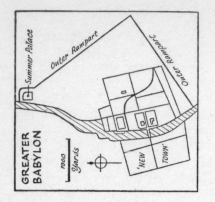

(6)
The City of Babylon

THE surrender of Babylon to Cyrus marks the end of the city's greatness. From 539 B.C. onwards, there was a steady decline to final desolation. But before describing this decline we must consider the appearance of Babylon in the days of its power. Fortunately ancient description and modern archaeology have combined to give us a fairly accurate picture of the city as it was reconstructed by the Neo-Babylonian kings.

The most important, as well as the earliest, of the descriptions given by classical authors is that of the Greek traveller and historian Herodotus, who visited Babylon about the middle of the fifth century B.C., when the city was still largely as it had been before the Persian conquest. Despite his uncritical acceptance of measurements given by his Babylonian guides, Herodotus gives a surprisingly accurate account. He says:

The city of Babylon is situated on a large plain. It is square in shape, and each side is fourteen miles long, so that the complete circuit is fifty-six miles. It is built like no other city known to the Greeks. A wide deep moat full of water runs round it, and inside the moat is a wall 330 feet high and 86 feet thick. I must tell you where the earth was used when it was taken from the moat, and how the wall was built. As they were digging the moat they formed the mud which was brought out of the excavations into bricks, and when they had moulded a sufficient number of bricks, they baked them in kilns. With these bricks they built the banks of the moat, and after that the wall itself, using hot bitumen for mortar and inserting reed-mats every thirty rows to strengthen it. Along the edges on top of the wall they put one-roomed buildings facing each other, with sufficient space between them for a four-horse chariot to turn round. There are a hundred gates in the wall, all made of bronze with posts and lintels of the same material. The Euphrates, a wide, swift and deep river which rises in Armenia and flows into the Persian Gulf, runs through the city, dividing it into two parts. The wall runs down to the river on either side, and the ends are joined by fortifications of baked bricks along each bank of the river. The city itself contains many houses three or four storeys high, and all the streets are straight, some running parallel to the river and some at right angles to it. At the end of each street which runs down to the river there is a gate made of bronze in the wall to give access to the river.

These walls form the city's outer defence. Inside them there is another wall, narrower than the first but almost as strong. In each half of the city there is a fortified building; on one side of the river there is the royal palace with its great defensive wall, and on the other is the temple of Bel, the Babylonian Zeus. This is an enclosure a quarter of a mile square, with bronze gates, and was still in existence when I visited Babylon. In the middle of the enclosure is a solid square tower with its sides more than two hundred yards long. On top of it there is another tower, and another on top of that, and so on up to eight stages. The staircase to the upper storeys runs spirally round the outside, and about halfway up there is a platform with seats where people going up can rest. On the top storey there is a large temple in which there is a great couch covered with fine draperies, with a table made of gold alongside it.

There is another temple in the sacred enclosure at Babylon. It is at ground level, and contains a large seated figure of Bel, made of gold. The base of the statue, the throne on which it sits, and the great table alongside are also golden. The Babylonians told me it took more than eighteen tons of gold to make them.

As the river divides the city in two, anyone who wanted to cross from one part to the other had at first to go by boat, and this must have caused a good deal of inconvenience. Queen Nitocris however found an answer to this. When she was altering the course of the Euphrates upstream from Babylon so as to improve the defences of the city, she made use of these operations to bridge the river and add to her own fame. She had long blocks of stone cut, and when they were ready and the basin for the river had been dug, she diverted its waters into the basin. While this was filling, the old river bed became dry, and Nitocris used bricks baked in the same way as had been done for the walls to build embankments on either side of the river where it ran through the city, and ramps leading to them from the gates that opened on to the river. At the same time she used the stone blocks which had been prepared to build piers for a bridge at the city centre, binding the stones together with iron and lead. On these piers she laid squared timbers over which the inhabitants were allowed to cross during the day. At night however the timbers were removed to stop people crossing in the dark and committing burglaries.

Further information is given by Ctesias, a Greek who was court physician to the Persian king Artaxerxes II. The royal palace, he says, was built by the legendary queen Semiramis.

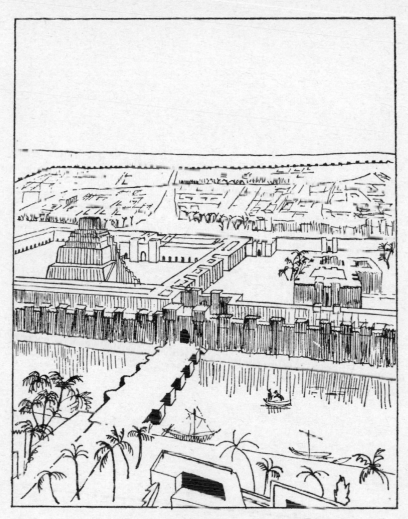

FIG. 9   View of Babylon from the New Town
(after Unger)

She made its outer circuit-wall over seven miles long, and the high wall was built from baked bricks with no sparing of expense. Inside this she built a second circuit-wall. Before the bricks for it were baked, all sorts of wild animals were engraved on them, and these were so ingeniously coloured that they seemed almost real. This wall was almost five miles long, 300 bricks wide and 300 feet high, and it had towers which were 420 feet high. Inside there was a third wall which enclosed a citadel with a circumference of two and a half miles. The height and width of this wall were even greater than those of the middle wall. On it, and on its towers, there were again wild beasts of every kind, cleverly drawn and realistically coloured to represent a complete big-game hunt. These animals were more than 6 feet long, and Semiramis was portrayed among them, mounted and hurling a javelin at a leopard. By her side was her husband Ninus, dispatching a lion at close quarters with his spear.

Beside the citadel was the building known as the Hanging Garden. This wooded enclosure was square in shape with sides four hundred feet long, and sloped like a hillside with terrace built on terrace as they are in a theatre. During the building of the terraces galleries were built underneath them which carried the entire weight of the gardens, each rising a little above the one before it on the ascent. The uppermost gallery, which was 75 feet high, supported the highest level of the garden, and this was the same height as the battlements of the city-wall. The walls of this structure, which cost a fortune to build, were 22 feet thick, and were separated by passages 10 feet wide. The galleries were roofed with stone beams 16 feet long and 4 feet wide. Above these beams there was first a layer of reeds set in great quantities of bitumen, then two courses of baked brick bounded with cement, and then a covering of lead so that moisture from the soil would not be able to sink through. On this was piled earth, deep enough to contain the roots of the largest trees, and when it was levelled over, the garden was planted with all sorts of trees which would appeal to those who saw them either by their great size or by the beauty of their appearance. Because of their arrangement the galleries were all open to the light, and contained royal apartments of all kinds. One gallery had shafts leading from the highest level and machinery for raising water in great quantities from the river and supplying it to the gardens. This machinery was entirely enclosed, and so could not be seen from the outside.

These descriptions convey well enough the impression made by Babylon on Greeks who worked and travelled in the orient. It was one of vast size, enormous wealth and magnificent buildings. Post-classical visitors found only a desolate wilderness, but despite this the site of the city was not forgotten, and from time to time western travellers brought back information about the place, most of it picturesque rather than accurate. In the early nineteenth century interest in the antiquities of the Middle East took a more scientific turn, and small excavations at Babylon were undertaken by C. J. Rich, (1811), Layard (1850), Oppert (1852–1854) and Rassam (1878–1889). These yielded tablets and other objects, and various plans of the city were made, but almost all our detailed information on the site is due to the excavations conducted from 1899 to 1917 by the Deutsche Orient Gesellschaft, directed by Robert Koldewey, an architect who perfected a technique of field excavation which has been the basis of all later investigation in the area. It was one of the main aims of the German expedition to reveal the *buildings* of the city, and not simply to search for texts and museum objects. This involved tracing the remains of mud-brick walls which were practically indistinguishable from the soil surrounding them. The success of Koldewey's workmen at this difficult task can be judged from the plans of the areas they laid bare: the Babylon excavations were the beginning of modern scientific archaeology in the Middle East.

The site itself lies on the broad plain of the Euphrates some fifty miles south of Baghdad, and is today nothing more than a desolate series of mounds with a few scattered villages surrounded by their little patches of cultivated land. But in its heyday Babylon had an abundant supply of water and lay in the centre of a magnificent "green-belt" of palm-trees and cultivation. Surrounded by its mighty wall, with the ziggurat towering above, it must have been an impressive sight to the approaching traveller.

The outer rampart of the city was a complex construction. It consisted of an inner wall of unbaked brick 23 feet 4 inches thick, and an outer wall of baked brick 25 feet 7 inches thick. The space between these two walls, almost 40 feet wide, was filled with rubble; and immediately in front, and fitted to the outer wall beneath ground level, was another wall, 10 feet 10 inches thick and also of baked brick. This was to protect the main rampart from damage by the waters of the moat which circled the town as an additional defence. The width of this moat is uncertain, but it may well have been over 300 feet. On top of the inner wall there were towers about 27 feet wide at intervals of approximately 130 feet. These projected beyond the wall on either side. The outer wall also probably had towers, but all trace of these has now vanished. Between the two sets of towers a roadway about 37 feet wide was constructed on top of the rubble filling so that troops defending the city could be moved at speed to any part where danger threatened. The exact length of the outer rampart is not known. The north-east side is almost three miles long, and on the south-east it stretched for just under two miles, of which about a mile and a quarter has been traced. These two sides with the Euphrates enclose all the ruins of Babylon which we know at present. Despite the authority of Herodotus, it seems unlikely that the outer rampart extended to the western bank of the river, and that the city was in the form of a quadrangle with the river flowing diagonally through it. No traces of these western ramparts have been found, whereas there are signs that after the Persian conquest, but before Herodotus visited the city, the river changed its course and cut off part of the old town, including the royal palace, from the rest, where lay the sanctuary of "Bel, the Babylonian Zeus". The idea that the outer rampart formed a square was probably based on a rather confused recollection of the approximately quadrangular shape of the inner city which was projected, falsely, onto the outer wall as well.

The idea of building this outer bastion was formed by Nabopolassar, and work was begun on digging the moat, for this provided clay for bricks and foundations. The rampart was however completed in the early years of Nebuchadnezzar's reign, and with the river provided a complete defensive ring. But the river itself was still regarded as the weakest section, and the ends of the greatest rampart were joined along the eastern bank of the river by a single fortification constructed by Nabonidus. This wall was about 28 feet wide and also had towers as well as a quay-wall 11 feet 6 inches wide along the river. There were portals and passage ways in the wall with steps down to landing-platforms, and other openings to allow water to flow into the city. These passages were protected by screens of limestone to prevent any enemy from entering the city through them.

The total length of Babylon's outer defensive ring is thus seven and a half to eight miles, a completely different figure from that of Herodotus who, as has been seen above, gives a figure of fifty-six miles. If this figure is to be accepted, then the neighbouring cities of Borsippa and Kish have to be included

FIG. 10 The Ishtar Gate (after Unger)

within one enormous wall for which there is no archaeological evidence. Besides, contemporary inscriptions show that the outer rampart of the Herodotean description must be the one which has been revealed by excavation. Koldewey, who accepted Herodotus's statement that the city was square and bisected by the river, calculated that if the existing rampart had been continued to form a square with the river running

11

diagonally across it, the length of this hypothetical outer rampart would have been about eleven and a quarter miles. He
also uses a smaller unit in calculating the length of the rampart in the Greek description, and arrives at a length of about
fifty-four miles for Herodotus, and just over forty miles for
another estimate by Ctesias. These figures, he claims, are so
close to four times the correct figure that foreigners must mis-
takenly have taken the figure they were given for the total
length of the rampart as being the length of one of the sides,
and simply multiplied by four. That different foreigners should
do this independently is unlikely, and in any case there was
no rampart west of the Euphrates, so it has been suggested that
the figures refer not to the length of the outer rampart, but to
a supposed "sub-satrapy" or administrative district of which
Babylon was the centre. This "greater Babylon" may have been
approximately square and have included neighbouring towns
like Borsippa and Kish. However, in the absence of any evidence
for its existence, it is perhaps better to assume that Greek
travellers accepted uncritically the figures which local guides
gave them. This is certainly true of Herodotus's information
on the height of the rampart—approximately 330 feet. From
our knowledge of other walls, and from Assyrian pictures of
Babylonian walls, it can be calculated that the height of such
defensive walls was at most three times their thickness, and that
therefore the two walls forming the outer bastion cannot have
been more than about 65 feet high. Not even Herodotus could
have been credulous enough to accept a five-fold exaggeration
of what was before his eyes; but it is likely that the walls
were in a semi-ruinous state by the time he visited the city,
and he had no way of checking on their original height. He
could himself check the thickness of the rampart from the
remains which he saw, and his figure of 86 feet is surprisingly
accurate.

It must be understood that this outer rampart did not enclose
an entirely built-up area. Some houses had been built beyond
the old inner wall, and Nebuchadnezzar had extended his
palace beyond it as well, but the main purpose of the outer
rampart was to provide protection for people from the surrounding countryside in times of war. Also inside it, at its northern-
most corner, Nebuchadnezzar built another palace for summer
use (Map II). As far as can be seen, it consisted of a series of court-

yards with rooms opening off them, on a raised terrace about 60 feet high. The floor was of sandstone, each paving-stone inscribed with the king's name on its edge. Unfortunately not much more could be discovered about this building because most of it had been destroyed by systematic quarrying for bricks. Ancient Babylonian bricks have in fact proved admirable for building modern houses and even dams. The mound that is left is about 72 feet high, and its summit forms a rough square with sides about 270 yards long. It is known locally as Babil and thus preserves unchanged the ancient name of the city.

The old city itself is more than a mile south of the summer palace, and lay along both banks of the river, which flowed slightly to the east of its present course. It was surrounded by a second defensive rampart (Map II), again a double structure, and by a moat. The original city-walls, built by Sumuabum and other kings of the first dynasty, were not found, and all the remains date from the Neo-Babylonian period. The inner and probably higher wall of this rampart was known as Imgur-Enlil, and was 21 feet 3 inches thick, and 23 feet 7 inches in front of it was another wall called Nemetti-Enlil 12 feet 2 inches thick. Both were built of unbaked bricks, and both had reinforcing towers at intervals of 65 feet or less. In this case the space between the walls was unfilled, and was presumably used as a military road. Sixty-five feet in front of the outer of these walls was a moat-wall of burnt bricks bordering a moat more than 250 feet wide in places which was connected with the river at either end. Along the river itself were bulwarks to strengthen the banks and steps leading down to landing-platforms. These bulwarks were later replaced by defensive walls. West of the river was the "new town", which was contained within the inner rampart and remains unexcavated. The total length of this inner rampart was about five and a quarter miles, of which about two and a quarter miles were on the western side of the river. Access to the city was by eight gates, each approached by a dam over the moat, and each bearing the name either of a god who had a temple nearby or of the town towards which the gate faced. Four of these gates have been excavated—the Marduk and Zababa gates on the east, the Urash gate on the south, and the Ishtar gate to the north. The other four were the Sin gate on the north, the Enlil gate on the south, and the Shamsh and Adad gates on the western bank of the river.

Besides these, there were smaller gates such as Lugalgirra, Kellek and Bel whose sites have not been identified.

The most elaborate of the gates is that of Ishtar (Map II). A traveller approaching this gate from the summer palace would first have reached a broad road between high brick walls. This processional way leading up to the gate itself was paved in the centre with limestone slabs 3 feet 5 inches square, and on either side with blocks of red and white marble 2 feet 2 inches square. The roadway sloped upwards towards the gate, and on the walls on either side were figures of lions in enamelled brick advancing to meet the incoming traveller. These lions, some white with yellow manes and some yellow with red manes, were on a light or dark blue background and were about 6 feet 6 inches long. The road led between the friezes for some 200 yards and there were sixty lions on either side, the figures of which are so alike that they must have been cast in a mould.

At the top of the slope was the gateway itself (Fig. 10). Its original appearance must be largely conjectural, as practically nothing above the level of the roadway has been preserved. But from the broken remains and from pictures of similar gateways we can gain some idea of its appearance. It consisted in fact of two gateways, one in each of the two walls of the inner defences. Behind the outer façade lay a room across the space between the walls, and behind the second gateway, inside the inner wall, was a long chamber running back into the town. The outer gateway was flanked by twin towers with battlements, and the inner gateway was probably similar but taller. All this was fairly typical; what made the gate unusual was its decoration. On the sides of the outer gateway, on the faces of the two outer towers, all along the inner faces of the gatehouses and the façade on the city side were rows of alternate bulls and dragons in enamelled brick (Fig. 11). The animals were arranged in such a way that they appeared to be advancing towards the incoming traveller, for on walls running north and south they faced the entrance, while on walls at right angles to the road they faced inwards. As the gate was about 40 feet high, and each animal was 3 feet 6 inches tall, there were probably seven rows visible on the decorated walls. The animals were in yellow and white on a blue background, while at the pavement level was a band of rosettes with yellow centres.

Fig. 11*a*   Bull from the Ishtar Gate (after Koldewey)

Fig. 11*b*   Dragon from the Ishtar Gate (after Koldewey)

In all probability each row contained fifty-one animals, so that in the finished gateway as many as 357 animals may have been visible. Our knowledge of this decoration is due almost entirely to the fact that the level of the roadway was raised several times during Nebuchadnezzar's reign. The result is that there are no fewer than ten rows of animals beneath the stone road surface, and there are signs of older pavements between the sixth and seventh, and between the eighth and ninth rows. The six lowest rows of animals were probably never meant to be visible, for the bricks are irregularly laid and asphalt from the joints protrudes and has run over the faces of the bricks. The next three rows were carefully finished, and coated with mud or plaster before the roadway was filled in. It is from these animals, and from the mass of fragmentary enamelled brick, that the decoration of the upper part has been reconstructed.

Passing through the Ishtar Gate, the Processional Way (Map II) crossed a high open space, still artificially raised, between the temple of Ninmah, the Great Mother, on the left, and the Royal Palace, or Southern Citadel, on the right. It then crossed a canal and descending gradually to ground level passed the temple of Ishtar of Akkad on the left before reaching the residential quarter, again on the left but set back so as not to mix secular with sacred. On the right was the great precinct-wall of Etemenanki, "the house of the foundation-stone of heaven and earth", the Tower of Babel itself. As far as the gate of the precinct the road was paved entirely with marble, the blocks of which carry Nebuchadnezzar's inscription. Some of them also have an inscription of Sennacherib, and were presumably used by him during building-operations undertaken by him before his destruction of the city and then re-used at a later date by Nebuchadnezzar. At the south-eastern corner of the precinct, almost a thousand yards south of the Ishtar Gate, the processional way turned right to run between the tower of Babel and Esagila, "the house that lifts up its head", the lower temple of Marduk, and so onwards until it passed through a gate in the river-wall, across the Euphrates on a bridge over 400 feet long, and into the "new town", which has not been excavated. Thus in its course it passed most of the important buildings of Babylon. These will now be described in greater detail.

The Royal Palace or Southern Citadel (Fig. 12) lay just

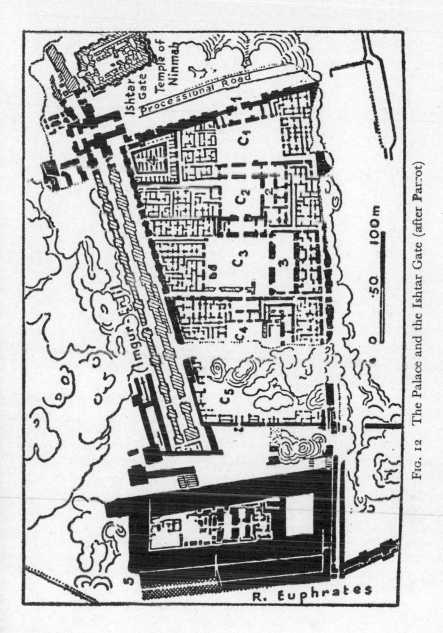

Ishtar Gate

Temple of Ninmah

Processional Road

(Imgur-Enlil)

C1

C2

1

2

C3

bb

3

C4

C5

G

S

S

R. Euphrates

0   ·50   100 m

Fig. 12   The Palace and the Ishtar Gate (after Parrot)

inside the Ishtar gate. It stretched from the Processional Way to the river, just inside the inner walls, and was roughly 350 yards long by 200 yards wide. It was surrounded by a fortification wall of burnt brick and was almost entirely the work of Nebuchadnezzar, who enlarged and almost completely eclipsed the former palace on the site built by his father Nabonidus. The older palace had lain at the western end of the enclosure, and in front of it, towards the Processional Way, there had been a large open courtyard. It was in this courtyard that Nebuchadnezzar began to build while he lived in the older palace to the west. When the new building was finished he moved into it, demolished the old one, and re-built it on the old foundations. The complete structure consisted of five parallel courtyards, each with buildings to north and south. The main entrance was from the Processional Way, where there also survives a section of older wall with a doorway which may belong to the older fortification of Nabonidus. Inside the main gateway was a small court with two rooms opening from it which may have been for the use of the palace guard. Then came the first courtyard with offices and houses on the north and south sides. As in the other courts, the larger and more important apartments were on the south, where they would be in shade throughout the day. The courtyard was paved first with brick and then with tiles set in asphalt.

The next courtyard was entered by a double gateway with side-chambers which could also be entered from the adjoining houses. Koldewey suggests that these gateway chambers were used as courts of justice which the judges entered from the houses, and he may well be right. The buildings on either side of this court may have been used by high court officials. There is a large reception room on the south side of the court, and passages lead to the private offices of the king on the south side of the third court. The main entrance to this court was by a larger and more imposing gateway with a staircase in one side-room which led to an upper storey or to the roof. The gateway was decorated, like the others, with lions in enamelled brick, and the courtyard was larger than the others, being 197 feet long and 180 feet wide. To the north were houses and offices, and to the south was the largest and most magnificent room in the palace, Nebuchadnezzar's throne-room, 170 feet long and 56 feet wide. On its outside wall facing the court it

FIG. 13 Detail of the wall of the throne-room at Babylon (after Koldewey and Wetzel)

was richly ornamented in enamelled brick (Fig. 13). On a dark blue background there were yellow columns about a yard apart, with light blue capitals, each consisting of three sets of double volutes. Above the uppermost of these volutes part of a daisy-like flower with white petals and a yellow centre could be seen, and between each set of volutes there was a bud in a sheath, forming a trefoil pattern in light blue, yellow and white. These buds were joined to the volutes by light blue curved bands which serve to link the whole composition. Higher up the wall, between formal borders of yellow, black and white bricks, was a frieze formed of linked curved lines with daisies appearing above and below. Groups of four columns were surrounded by an elaborate border again composed of curved lines and daisies, while underneath the whole composition was a row of striding lions similar to those outside the Ishtar Gate. The entire effect must have been quite unusual in a land of mud-brick architecture.

The interior of the throne-room, like all Babylonian rooms, was very dim indeed, for there is no evidence that windows were used. It was decorated only with a wash of white gypsum. The long walls of the room are so much thicker than the others that it is probable that they supported a barrel-vault. In the rear wall, opposite the centre of the three doorways which gave access from the court, was a doubly recessed alcove which must have contained the royal throne. Thus the king could be seen not only by those inside the room, but also by those in the central part of the Great Court. It is pleasing to imagine with Koldewey that this was the very room in which Belshazzar's famous feast took place.

The rooms behind the throne-room were obviously intended for the king's service. They opened off three small open court-yards, and in the south-west corners of the two rooms immediately behind the throne-room were circular wells. The walls of these rooms were carried down through the foundations to water-level, and the space between walls and wells was firmly packed with mud, asphalt and broken brick to ensure that the king's water-supply was absolutely pure.

West of the Great Court, and quite distinct from it, was the domestic part of the palace. This was re-built by Nebuchadnezzar on the foundations of his father's home, and consisted of two more courtyards with buildings to north and south. The

king's own residence was on the south side of the fourth court,
and round the fifth and innermost court were buildings which
may have been the women's quarters. Beyond this again, on
the river-bank, was a huge fortification begun by Nebuchadnezzar and completed by Neriglissar. Although Nebuchadnezzar claims that it was to protect Babylon from flooding, it
seems likely that it was intended also as a final stronghold in
the event of attack.

There was one important building inside the palace which
has so far not been mentioned. This was in the north-east
corner of the citadel, and was entered by a wide passage from
the second court. The central core of the building was a strong
wall forming an irregular rectangle roughly 140 feet by 100
feet, with fourteen cells inside, seven opening on either side of
a central passage. A narrow corridor ran round this central
building, flanked to the north and east by the outer wall of
the palace, and on the south and west by further small rooms.
These outer rooms were on the same level as the rest of the
palace, but the central building was beneath ground level
and was reached by a brick stairway in one of the rooms on the
southern side. Semicircular arches show that each chamber
was roofed with a barrel-vault, and the whole structure was
capable of supporting an enormous weight. This building is
unique in the ruins, and it seems likely that it is in fact the
foundation of the famous Hanging Gardens of Babylon.

There are several reasons for this identification. Firstly,
the late Babylonian historian Berossus places the Hanging
Gardens among the buildings by which Nebuchadnezzar enlarged his father's palace, which means that they must have
been either here or in the later Central Citadel just to the north.
Secondly, the many fragments of hewn stone found in the
vaulted building show that stone was used somewhere in its
construction, and in all the literature on Babylon, including
the cuneiform inscriptions, there is mention of stone used for
buildings in only two places—the north wall of the citadel and
the Hanging Gardens. Thirdly, there is the existence in one of
the little rooms near the south-west corner of the building of
a remarkable well, quite different from any other well which
was excavated. It consists of three shafts close to each other, the
one in the centre being square and the others oblong. The most
natural explanation is that above the well stood a wheel,

and an endless chain with buckets attached passed over it, up one oblong shaft and down the other. The centre shaft was used as an inspection-pit into which a man could descend to clean out the well or repair the machinery. This type of well is still used in the area, and is usually propelled by animals. Owing to the lack of room, slaves probably supplied the power in the Hanging Gardens.

There are two possible reconstructions of the upper part of the building. Perhaps the central core, designed as it was to support an enormous weight, was the base of a series of terraces from which the gardens hung, as it were, above the surrounding chambers and the palace wall. Or perhaps the vaulted roof of the subterranean chambers was covered with a thick layer of earth, and formed a garden court at ground-level, surrounded perhaps by a pillared colonnade with rooms opening on to it on the south and west. In either case the vaults would have been used as store-rooms or granaries, probably the latter, as tablets found in the staircase room deal with matters relating to grain.

Such, then, is in all probability the site of what was one of the seven wonders of the ancient world. Tradition has it that the Hanging Gardens were the work of Semiramis, but Berossus more accurately refers them to Nebuchadnezzar, who, we are told, built them to remind his Median queen of the mountains and trees of her homeland. If the identification of the site is correct, then the Hanging Gardens cannot have been as impressive as we might have expected from the classical descriptions. The measurements in particular seem much smaller than those given by authors like Strabo and Diodorus, who describe the central core as being almost 400 feet square. But as we have seen in the case of the outer walls, the measurements of classical authors are not altogether trustworthy.

Despite the size of his royal palace Nebuchadnezzar felt that it was too cramped for a monarch of his dignity. He had no desire to move away from Babylon, and expansion to the east was impossible because piety forbade the alteration of Marduk's sacred street. So he turned to the north, to the area beyond the city-wall. A grandiose first scheme was abandoned soon after the foundations of a mighty defensive wall, 56 feet thick, had been laid. An even more elaborate plan was then prepared, and an enormous terrace of rubble, 26 feet thick, was laid down outside the city-wall. On this terrace the foundation walls of a new palace were built, and the spaces between them were again filled with rubble laid down with great care and regularity to prevent damage by water. Frequent changes of plan were made during the operation and this makes it highly unlikely that Nebuchadnezzar completed the work in fifteen days, as he claimed. The Principal Citadel, as it has been called, again consists of buildings grouped round courtyards which were paved in white and mottled sandstone, limestone, and black basalt. Large basalt lions, like those in Assyrian palaces, stood at the entrances, and the rooms had ceilings made from cedar, cypress and other wood. The decoration must have been even more splendid than that of the southern palace.

One of the most surprising features of the excavation here was the number of foreign objects found. These included statues of Puzurishtar, governor of Mari about 2200 B.C., a relief of Shamashreshusur, Assyrian governor of Mari about 900 B.C., steles and inscriptions of Assyrian monarchs, a seventh-century stele of the god Teshub with a "Hieroglyphic Hittite" inscription, various building-cylinders, and a basalt statue of a lion trampling on a man, the origin and date of which are uncertain. In fact the palace must have been used as a museum to house the collection of antiquities made by Nebuchadnezzar and his successors.

Immediately to the north of the principal citadel was another defensive structure, the Northern Citadel, the outer bastion of which was stengthened by a fortress-wall of large limestone blocks, in front of which ran a moat. The wall to the east of these two citadels, 825 feet long, formed one side of the Processional Way where it led up to the Ishtar Gate. On the other side of the street was another wall, part of a defensive structure which lay to the east, but which has been largely destroyed by a later change in the course of the Euphrates.

Just inside the Ishtar Gate, to the left of the roadway, lay the temple of Ninmah, goddess of the underworld (Fig. 15a). This was an approximately rectangular building, 175 feet long and 116 feet wide, built of unbaked brick coated with white plaster. The line of the walls was broken by slightly projecting towers at regular intervals giving the building the appearance of a fortress rather than a religious structure, an impression which was heightened by the fact that there was only one entrance, flanked by rectangular towers and fitted with double

doors. Besides the usual bolts a wooden beam was provided
which could be propped against the door to make it even
stronger. The door itself was on the northern side of the temple,
facing the city-wall, and a short connecting-wall with a doorway cut off the sacred precinct from the view of casual passers-
by. Immediately in front of the entrance was a small altar on
a pavement of baked brick, and just inside was an entrance
chamber which led to an open courtyard. Doors on either side
of this led to priests' rooms, store-rooms and other apartments,
while on the south side, opposite the main entrance, was a doorway, again flanked by rectangular towers, which led through
an ante-room into the shrine itself. On a low platform opposite
the doorway stood the cult-statue where it could be seen from
the open court. Long narrow chambers on the east and south
sides of the building may have contained staircases or ramps
leading to the roof. An interesting feature, characteristic of
religious buildings but never found on secular structures, is the
use of vertical grooves to decorate the towers of the main
entrance and the doorway leading from the court to the shrine.

South of the Royal Palace, to the right of the Processional
Way, was the wall which surrounded the temple of Marduk,
the principal shrine of Babylon (Fig. 14). The sacred precinct
was almost square, and the length of each side was about a
quarter of a mile. There were twelve gates, the principal one
of which was near the centre of the eastern wall. Here the line
of the wall was broken by an open paved area about 260 feet
long and 80 feet broad, the inner end of which was probably
closed by a large ornamental gateway, perhaps the very "Gate
of God" from which Babylon took its name. Other gates were
recessed in a similar way but on a smaller scale. Inside the courtyard on the south side were the houses of the priesthood, while
on either side of the main gateway were large store-buildings,
each consisting of narrow rooms opening off a central court.
Small rooms in the thickness of the wall on the north and west
may well have served as lodgings for the many pilgrims who no
doubt flocked to the shrine.

In an isolated position immediately opposite the main gate,
but towards the west of the courtyard, stood the ziggurat or
temple tower of Babylon. This mighty building (Fig. 14),
rising to a height of almost 300 feet, must have been a dominant
feature of the Babylonian landscape, and certainly accounts

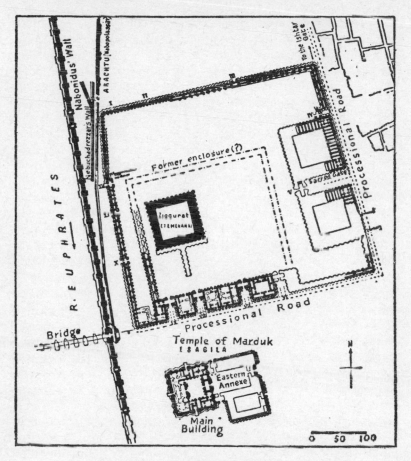

FIG. 14 Esagila and Etemenanki (after Parrot)

for the Biblical narrative of the Tower of Babel. Only the ground plan was recovered by excavation, and there has been a great deal of scholarly argument on the details of the upper portion, but thanks to descriptions given by Herodotus and in contemporary inscriptions, the general shape of the building is clear. The tower was square in plan, and rose, probably in eight stages, to a temple at the summit. The lowest stage was 300 feet square and about 108 feet high, the second 256 feet square and 60 feet high. The third, fourth and fifth storeys were each about 20 feet high, with sides of 197 feet, 167 feet and 138 feet. The size and shape of the sixth, seventh and eighth storeys are disputed, but it seems most probable that the sixth was 108 feet square and 20 feet high, while the seventh stage, 50 feet high, was no longer square but rectangular, measuring probably 79 feet by 69 feet. On top of this may have been a small "ward-room", the dimensions of which are not known, forming an eighth storey.

An alternative theory, based on a different interpretation of the Babylonian text which gives the measurements of Etemenanki, would omit the sixth stage as described above. By this theory the sixth stage was 79 feet by 69 feet, and 50 feet high, while the seventh and final stage, containing the "ward-room", was 20 feet high, and covered the same area as the sixth. In fact from a distance it would have been indistinguishable as a separate storey. This, together with the fact that Herodotus mentions eight rather than seven storeys, makes this interpretation rather less likely.

The whole of this structure was apparently faced with baked bricks over a core of unbaked bricks. The core of the first stage was 200 feet square, while the facing on all sides was 50 feet thick, and finished with the usual recesses between flat "towers". The upper storeys may also have been finished in this way, but this is not certain.

Another problem is that of the stairways which led to the temple at the top of the tower. According to Herodotus there was a stairway which encircled the towers, with a resting-place halfway up. Excavation revealed two stairways running along the south face from the south-east and south-west corners, and if these were carried on upwards on the other sides of the upper stages they would correspond roughly to the description of the Greek historian. But the main stairway, not mentioned by

Herodotus, was at right angles to the southern face of the building. It was 30 feet wide and its lowest step was 168 feet from the base of the tower. According to the general rule in this area a stairway is approximately as high as its length along the ground, so Koldewey reckoned that it was also 168 feet high. This would make it reach to the top of the second stage. Other reconstructions suggest that it led only to the first stage or even to the entrance to the temple at the top. But the exact correspondence between the horizontal measurement of the stairway and the height of the first two storeys of the tower seems to favour the first interpretation.

Details of the temple itself are uncertain. It was probably decorated with blue enamelled bricks, and contained in one room a large couch which was used during the ceremonies of the New Year Festival in re-enacting the marriage of Marduk and his consort Zarpanit.

South of Etemenanki and separated from it by the Processional Way was the other part of the sacred precinct of Marduk. This contained his principal temple Esagila, "the house that lifts up its head" (Fig. 14). Unfortunately the remains of this lay some 70 feet beneath ground level, and Koldewey was able to excavate only part of the building and trace the outer lines of the remainder by tunnelling galleries. The plan thus revealed is of a rectangular building, 281 feet 6 inches by 262 feet, joined on its eastern side to a larger group of buildings, 380 feet by 293 feet, of which only the outlines are known. This eastern annexe projected to the south beyond the line of the principal building, and the main entrance was towards the north of the eastern wall, where a recessed gateway with a towered façade and the vertical grooves which are characteristic of religious structures led across a courtyard to the entrance of the main temple. The most striking feature of the plan of this building is its regularity. Exactly in the middle of each side was a gateway with flanking towers, and there were two stepped towers between each gateway and each corner. The gateways were flanked by bronze dragons placed there by Neriglissar. Although the gates were similar in size, the eastern one, access to which was gained through the eastern annexe, was certainly the principal one, for while the other three led to small entrance-halls and side-passages, the eastern gateway had a passage through a large vestibule to the temple-court itself. Here

12

again towers and doorways were arranged symmetrically. Immediately opposite the main entrance, marked as usual by a towered façade, was the shrine of Marduk. This room, roughly 130 feet long by 66 feet wide, was famed for the richness of its decoration. Nebuchadnezzar especially boasts of the magnificent way in which he adorned it, plating the gypsum walls and cedar roof-beams with gold, and embellishing it with alabaster, lapis lazuli and precious stones. Herodotus too speaks of the gold altar, throne, footstool and statues of the god, a total weight, he was told, of about eighteen and a half tons of gold. All this gold had of course disappeared long before Kolde-wey's workmen opened up the site, but the size of the building in comparison to other Babylonian temples still gives some idea of its former magnificence. Besides the shrine of Marduk him-self, there were chapels devoted to Nahu, Adad and other deities, of which less is known. One of these chapels, which lay to the north of the temple court, is of particular interest. In it Koldewey found the remains of a carved wooden throne, on which could still be distinguished goddesses holding flowing water-vases, a fish, and the head of a dragon. All these are attributes of Ea, god of the primeval waters, and the shrine was presumably dedicated to him. If so, it was here that the generals of Alexander the Great came to ask the god (whom they identi-fied with Serapis) if the dying king should be brought to the temple to be cured.

Esagila was entered from a side-street leading south from the main Processional Way, which passed between Marduk's two temples towards the Euphrates. At this stage the surface was of tiles laid over a foundation of brick set in asphalt. Just before reaching the river the road passed through a towered gateway in the river-wall, and then over a bridge into the new town. This bridge (Figs. 9, 14) was over 400 feet long, and the piers were made of baked brick strengthened with wooden beams and asphalt. There is evidence that stone too was used in its construction, probably as a roofing for the brick piers. It is thus, as Koldewey notes, the oldest stone-built bridge of which we have any record. The piers, 69 feet long, 30 feet wide and 30 feet apart, were shaped like boats with their prows pointing upstream, and were obviously modelled on an earlier bridge of boats. The roadway, probably 16–20 feet wide, was laid over these piers, and the remark of Herodotus that the wooden

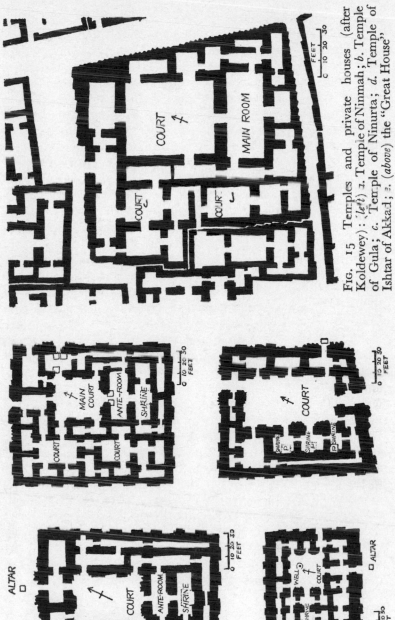

Fig. 15 Temples and private houses (after Koldewey): *(left)* a. Temple of Ninmah; b. Temple of Gula; c. Temple of Ninurta; d. Temple of Ishtar of Akkad; a. *(above)* the "Great House"

ALTAR

COURT

ANTE-ROOM

SHRINE

0 10 20 30 FEET

COURT

MAIN COURT

ANTE-ROOM

SHRINE

COURT

0 10 20 30 FEET

WELL

SHRINE

COURT

0 10 20 30 FEET

ALTAR

SHRINE

SHRINE

SHRINE

COURT

0 10 20 30 FEET

COURT

COURT

COURT

MAIN ROOM

FEET
0 10 20 30

beams could be taken up at night to prevent thefts across the river probably means that part of the roadway could be removed to allow the passage of river traffic. The bridge is the work of either Nebuchadnezzar or Nabopolassar.

Besides the temples already mentioned, several others were discovered by Koldewey in the course of his excavations. The essential plan, consisting of buildings surrounding a courtyard from which the cult-statue on its dais inside the shrine could be seen, was always the same. In every case there were gateways flanked by grooved towers leading through vestibules to the courtyard and the shrine. But there are differences of detail in each temple. For instance in a temple south of Esagila, dedicated perhaps to Gula, goddess of health (Fig. 15b), a west wing was added containing rooms round two additional courtyards, and as well as the main entrance to the north of the main courtyard, opposite the shrine, there were two other doorways on the eastern side, one leading through a vestibule into the principal courtyard, and the other into a smaller room in the north-west corner where presumably the public could transact temple business without entering the shrine proper. Another temple, slightly to the east of the temple of Gula and dedicated to Ninurta, god of war (Fig. 15c), had also three entrances. In this case the principal gateway was in the eastern wall, while the other two may have been used by processions passing through the shrine from south to north. Opposite the eastern gateway the main shrine was flanked by two others, each with its own entrance from the courtyard and dais for a cult-statue. These subsidiary shrines may have been dedicated to the god's wife Gula and son Nusku. Finally a temple lying among private houses to the east of the Processional Way and dedicated to Ishtar of Akkad (Fig. 15d) had two entrances, the principal one being to the south, and a shrine area to the west consisting of six inter-communicating rooms accessible only from the courtyard. As usual, there was an altar in the roadway facing the main entrance.

As well as the public buildings already mentioned, Koldewey found considerable traces of private houses in Babylon. These appeared in the excavations in three areas, between the Royal Palace and the ziggurat, in the southern part of the city around the temples of Ninurta and Gula, and to the east of the Processional Way opposite the main gate of Etemenanki. In the first two areas only exploratory trenches were cut, but in the third houses were cleared over a considerable area, thus revealing the street-plan as well as details of the buildings. It could be seen that the direction of the streets was determined largely by the course of the river, for most ran either parallel or at right angles to it. Apart from the Processional Way most streets were fairly narrow, varying in width from 4 feet 6 inches to 20 feet, and unpaved. As well as giving access to the houses they served as rubbish dumps for the householders, and thus the surface was continually raised until steps were necessary to go down into the houses or until the houses were rebuilt at the new level.

The houses themselves were of unbaked brick and, like the temples, consisted of rooms grouped round one or more court-yards. Each house had only one entrance, and there were no windows at all in the outer walls. Light and air entered the rooms only from the courtyard, either through the door or through ventilation-channels high up in the walls. As the principal consideration was to avoid the heat, the main sitting-room was normally on the south side of the court. Rooms were usually rectangular, and if the plan of the house was irregular, the outer face of the walls were often stepped to allow rooms to have the correct shape, thus giving a "saw-toothed" appearance to the building. The houses were whitewashed inside and outside, and there were brick pavements in the courtyards. Bathrooms, toilets and kitchens can often be identified, but the uses of other rooms can only be guessed at. Houses varied greatly in size. A small house for instance measured about 42 feet by 59 feet, and consisted of a living-room about 30 feet by 10 feet and a courtyard about 20 feet square with eight smaller rooms opening off it. On the other hand a large house (Fig. 15e), owned presumably by a prosperous merchant or tradesman, measured about 130 feet each way. It had three courtyards and twenty-six rooms, the largest of which was 52 feet long and 23 feet wide.

Although Babylon was the centre of an enormous trading area no trace of any group of buildings that could constitute a market was found. Presumably buying and selling was done in an area as yet unexcavated. But from the areas revealed by Koldewey it can be clearly seen what a prosperous city Babylon was, well fitted to be the capital of a powerful empire.

Beneath the residential quarter of the Neo-Babylonian city the excavators found traces of older buildings dating from the First Dynasty. At this time the street-plan had been roughly the same as it was in the Neo-Babylonian period. Houses were built of mud-brick on a foundation of baked brick, and were roofed with palm-trunks covered with clay and rush-matting. These houses were built at the top of a slight hill, and so remain above the modern water-level, which is considerably higher than it was in the time of Hammurabi. The remainder of First Dynasty Babylon lay beyond Koldewey's reach beneath the water which seeped through into his trenches from the nearby Euphrates.

(7)
The Babylonian Civilization

THE life led by the people of Babylon has to a certain extent been dealt with in an earlier chapter. It is time now to deal with other aspects of the civilization which is known as "Babylonian". But to interpret that civilization fully it is necessary to look first at the language and script of the Babylonian documents and to consider how it developed and how it was deciphered.

The language of Babylon belongs to the great group known to us as Semitic, a name adopted by eighteenth-century scholars to describe the language spoken by the "sons of Shem" who are listed in the tenth chapter of Genesis. These sons include Aram, Ashur and Eber, that is, the Aramaeans, the Assyrians and the Hebrews, and since the eighteenth century the family has been extended to include many other languages which share the common features of these three. The most notable characteristic of the Semitic languages is that they are based on a system of "roots" consisting in the main of three consonants. These roots express a basic meaning without any grammatical connection, and words are formed by the addition of vowels and consonantal prefixes, suffixes and infixes. Thus in Babylonian, the consonants P R S form a root which gives the general meaning of "cutting". The root itself does not exist as a word, but words are formed from it by the addition of vowels, prefixes and so on. So *parāsu* means "to cut", *iprus* "he cut", *iparas* "he is cutting", *aparas* "I am cutting", *purus* "cut", *iprusu* "they cut", *parsu* "cut off, inaccessible", *pirištu* "something cut off, a secret", and so on through a whole range of meanings connected with "cutting".

Closer examination of the Semitic languages shows that they can be divided into various groups which have closer relationships among themselves. The main dividing-line is between West and East Semitic, and West Semitic itself is divided into several smaller groups. First there is a northern branch consisting of the Canaanite languages—Phoenician, Carthaginian, Ugaritic, Moabite and Hebrew among them—on the one hand, and the "Aramaic" languages—including Syriac, Samaritan and Nabatean—on the other. The southern group of West Semitic languages includes Arabic, Ethiopic and the ancient languages of southern Arabia. East Semitic is represented only by the ancient languages of Mesopotamia—Assyrian and Babylonian. These are practically identical in matters of grammar and vocabulary, and the main difference was probably one of pronunciation. The general name for the two languages is Akkadian, a name derived from the old Sargonic kingdom of Akkad.

It is out of fashion today to seek a "cradle" or "original homeland" for a group of languages. Such a search carries us so far into the realms of supposition and hypothesis that it is of very little value. What can be seen from the historical evidence is that in general Semitic migrations have come from the area of the Arabian desert, and it may be supposed that the first Semitic immigrants to the Mesopotamian region came from the same direction. Whether the "Semitic" language first evolved in Arabia or was brought there by immigration at a still earlier period is a question that will probably never be answered.

Although the official language of the rulers of Babylon was Semitic, the script in which it was written had a very different origin. Long before it began to be used for writing Akkadian it had been developed by the Sumerians both in Mesopotamia and in the area (wherever that may be) from which they originally came. In origin it was pictographic, that is, pictures were used to represent the word for the object in the picture. Thus * would represent the word for "a star", ∬ the word for "a man", and so on. A natural extension of this was that the sign should denote not the object itself, but something associated with it. So *, as well as denoting "a star", began to be the sign for "heaven", "the sky", and then by a further extension it came to be used to represent "god".

But despite its extended use this type of script is of little value for anything beyond the simplest ideas. While it is easy to depict objects it is much more difficult to picture the relations between them, and abstractions are well-nigh impossible. A similar problem is to be seen in modern strip-cartoons, where it is unusual to be able to tell a story or make a point simply by means of illustrations. As a general rule, sub-titles or "balloons" of conversation are required as well. The Sumerian answer to this problem was to let a picture represent, not the object depicted, but the *sound* of that object's name. To use a modern example, if a scribe wanted to write the word "carpentry", the old method would have been to draw a picture of a man cutting up wood, which might have meant "carpentry" or "he is sawing" or "firewood" or a dozen other things. Using the new method, the scribe would represent "carpentry" as something like ⟨⎯⟩ ／ 𑀈 . This was all the easier in Sumerian, because words were largely monosyllabic, so that most pictures came to represent a *syllable*. When the script was taken over by the Babylonians for their own polysyllabic Semitic language, the Sumerian syllables were easily used in writing down Semitic sounds. But at the same time relics of the old system lingered on, and a sign like the old Sumerian star, now formalized into ⊏╪, not only represented the syllable "an" (the Sumerian for "heaven"), but could also be used by itself as a sign for the Akkadian word *šamû* "heaven" as well as for Akkadian *ilu* "god". This use of the same sign as both a syllable and an ideogram continued until the very end. Other complications were caused by the fact that one sign could have several syllabic values, due to the fact that each sign had originally represented several Sumerian or Semitic words, and that several signs representing originally words of approximately similar sounds came in the end to be used indifferently for the same syllable. The script was thus very complicated and cumbersome, and efforts were made to make it clearer by the use of "determinatives". These were signs which were placed before words to show the class of word into which they fell.

Thus all gods' names were preceded by the star-sign ⊣╪ to show that a god's name was in fact meant, all towns were preceded by ⊏⊒‖ *alu*, "town", and so on. To clarify the reading of ideograms, they were often followed by a sign representing the final syllable of the word which was intended. So the star-ideogram ⊏╪ would be followed by ⎗⊒‖, "lu"

to show that it represented *ilu*, "god" and not (say) *šamû*
"heaven". But these aids to reading are often no great help.
The Akkadian script remained a clumsy method of writing,
and reading must often have been difficult even for professional
scribes.

The fact that so many Babylonian records of all kinds have
been preserved is due to the fortunate chance that the most
easily accessible writing-material was clay. This was formed
into small tablets, usually cushion-shaped, and writing was
incised with a stylus, normally a shaped piece of reed. The
stylus was held at an angle, and the end was pushed down into
the clay, forming a hole which was deeper and wider at one
end, wedge-shaped, in fact, or "cuneiform". When the scribe
finished writing the tablet was left to dry in the sun or baked in
an oven for greater permanence. Texts could also be put into
clay envelopes which were baked with the tablets, thus ensuring
that the contents could not be tampered with or altered in any
way.

The story of the decipherment of the cuneiform script is one
which has often—perhaps too often—been told. Here a short
summary must suffice. The story begins in the early days of
the seventeenth century when reports and specimens of "wedge-
shaped" writing began to attract the attention of European
travellers in the Middle East. During the eighteenth century
such reports, especially from Persia, increased in number, and
the first important step towards their decipherment was made
by a Dane called Karsten Niebuhr, who not only brought back
accurate copies of inscriptions from Persepolis but pointed out
the fact that they were in three different scripts, all of them
cuneiform. Of these scripts, one used a great number of different characters, a second was much less complicated, and the
third, with (according to Niebuhr's calculations) only forty-two
characters, seemed comparatively simple and possibly alphabe-
tic. Soon it was recognized that in the simplest script words were
separated by a diagonal wedge, and that the inscriptions were
probably the work of the great Persian kings of the Achaemenid
dynasty, Darius, Xerxes and the other monarchs so well known
from Classical sources. If this were so, then the language in
which they were written must be close to that of the Avesta,
the ancient scripture of the Persians, and this was already
known. Despite this, the problem of beginning the decipherment

remained, for without some clue to the information contained in the inscriptions it seemed impossible to decide on the value of any character. The problem was largely solved by a twenty-seven-year-old German schoolmaster called Grotefend, who worked on the theory that the inscriptions began with the name, titles and ancestry of the various kings who had commissioned them. This theory was supported by the form of other such ancient inscriptions, and by the fact that where he suspected "son of So-and-so" in one inscription, So-and-so's name was represented by a group of characters which reappeared at the beginning of another inscription, except for the final character. This Grotefend decided must be a genitive ending. All that remained now was to find in Herodotus the names of Persian kings which fitted the characters of his inscriptions, and in fact only Darius and his son Xerxes seemed possible. By substituting what he thought were the Persian forms of these names, Grotefend succeeded in establishing the values of fifteen Old Persian characters, eleven of which later proved to be correct.

The decipherment thus begun by Grotefend was carried on during the first half of the nineteenth century by scholars like Rask and Lassen. At the same time Henry Rawlinson, a British officer in the service of the Persian government, was working independently towards the same end. His discovery of a lengthy inscription of Darius on a rock-face at Bisutun (more widely, if less correctly, known as Behistun) enabled him to recognize such great similarities between the language of the Persian inscriptions and that of the Avesta, as well as Sanskrit, that a close relationship could no longer be denied. After this, further work on Old Persian was on matters of detail only. The decipherment had been accomplished.

This cleared the way for the other two scripts of the Persian inscriptions. Of the syllabic Neo-Elamite script nothing need be said here as it contributed little to the progress of the decipherment, and many problems remain to be solved. The third and most complicated script proved more rewarding, for it was known to be used on a constantly increasing mass of documents which turned up at various points in the Middle East. It was in fact the Akkadian script of the Babylonians and Assyrians. Once more the first step was the identification of proper names. At first the difficulties of the Akkadian script, some of which have been mentioned above, were too great for would-be decipherers. The conclusions of Löwenstern (1845) that the language of the inscriptions was Semitic, and of Hincks (1850) that the different signs represented syllables, were of fundamental importance. Gradually, as texts were compared, instances were discovered where ideograms were spelt out in full, and so the phonetic values of the ideograms could be determined. Finally the discovery of ancient Babylonian vocabularies giving translations or equivalents of ideograms and Sumerian words helped towards a definitive solution. From this point the process of decipherment was rapid, and when in 1857 the Royal Asiatic Society gave copies of a newly discovered text to four scholars, Rawlinson, Hincks, Fox Talbot and Oppert, with a request to produce independent translations, the similarity of their results gave conclusive proof that the problem had been solved. From then on research in Akkadian, like that in Old Persian, was concerned much more with details of interpretation and philology.

Documents written in Akkadian are of many kinds and varied value. Some—details of rituals, for instance, or economic documents from different periods—are of interest mainly to specialists, but besides these there is a considerable body of Babylonian literature which demands attention in its own right. This literature, like so much else in Babylonian civilization, is in origin not Semitic but Sumerian. Recent research on Sumerian documents has shown the existence of an extensive literature, much of which was translated or adapted to suit Semitic tastes and needs. The story of Gilgamesh, the hero of Babylonia's finest epic poem, for instance, can be shown to have its origins in a number of separate Sumerian legends concerned with the early kings of Uruk, and may reach back to a Sumerian "heroic age" like that which historians have postulated in the development of the Greek and Germanic epics. However this may be—and at present it is incapable of proof—it seems certain that the transformation of these Sumerian stories into the epic *as we know it* was the work of the Semites.

The epic is the story of a king, semi-divine but in character essentially human, and of his unavailing struggle to combat the one thing which could prevent him enjoying complete mastery of himself and of the world—the fact that he is mortal. Death, in fact, is the subject of the poem. It opens with the mighty Gilgamesh showing such disregard for the feelings of his people that they appeal in desperation to the gods. In answer to their prayer an opponent is created for Gilgamesh, Enkidu, an unspoiled hero of the wilderness, who lives with wild beasts. But Enkidu is seduced from this life by the attractions of civilization, and is defeated by Gilgamesh when they wrestle in Uruk. The friendship that springs up between them is reinforced by their adventure together in defeating the demon-guardian of a distant forest, an adventure which gives Gilgamesh such a high opinion of himself that he scorns the love of the goddess Ishtar. She in anger sends down the "bull of heaven", a monster which is also killed by the heroes. But retribution must come, and although Gilgamesh is saved for the moment by the intervention of his protector Shamash, Enkidu is condemned to death. When he dies, Gilgamesh is brought face to face with his fundamental enemy. Death is not something abstract, something in the remote future, a mere risk that adds spice to a life of adventure; it is immediate, final and outside human control. The death of Enkidu convinces him of the frailty of his merely human strength. Life, which had been so vital and joyous before, now becomes a constant search for a means of avoiding death. The search takes Gilgamesh beyond the ends of the world to the garden of the gods on the shores of the waters of death. On an island in this lake lives Utnapishtim, the Babylonian Noah, the only mortal to have gained eternal life. But Utnapishtim can offer him no comfort. He can only retell the story of the flood, of his building of a boat and escape from the waters, and of Enlil's grant of eternal life. These were special circumstances which can never recur, and he can offer no solution for Gilgamesh's problem. One thing only can he suggest, a plant which grows on the sea-bed and can be eaten to renew a man's youth. This plant is brought to the surface by Gilgamesh and the journey home begins. But while he is bathing in a pool by the wayside, a snake eats the plant. Gilgamesh's last hope is lost. He returns to his city, the mighty walls that he has built, the walls that despite all his efforts will long outlast their builder.

This surely is the end of the epic. The Sumerian "Death of Gilgamesh" has no place in it, nor has "Gilgamesh, Enkidu and the Nether World", another Sumerian poem which was translated almost word for word into Akkadian and added to the Assyrian version of the epic. It ends, as the *Iliad* and the *Aeneid*

end, when the author has made his point and there is no more
to say, no need to round it off with a death which is known to
be inevitable anyway. It is the inevitability, not the death
itself, which is the point of the poem. Its cumulative effect
is remarkably like that of the Orpheus myth. Here too is the
hero almost triumphant over death, but at the last moment
frustrated by his own humanity. The Greek myth ends as
Eurydice slips back to the world of the dead ; with the loss of the
plant of renewal of youth, the Babylonian epic reaches its
natural and magnificent conclusion.

The other great epic of Babylonian literature is entirely
different in content. It deals, not with humanity and human
problems, but with the origins of the universe and the establishment of world order. Again its roots are deep in the Sumerian
period, and again it has been re-shaped by the later Semites. Its
hero was almost certainly originally Enlil, the Sumerian god of
Nippur, but when the myth was translated and adapted at the
time of the Babylonian first dynasty the opportunity was taken
to substitute the Babylonian Marduk for Enlil, and the epic,
incorporated in the Babylonian New Year Festival, became the
main justification for the supremacy of Babylon. A similar
process took place a thousand years later when Assyria became
the supreme power of the area, and Assur was substituted for
Marduk in the official dogma.

The epic begins with primaeval chaos, an undefined mixture
of Apsu, fresh water, and Tiamat, salt water. Gradually gods
are produced from this chaos, Lahmu and Lahamu, then
Anshar and Kishar. Eventually Anu, god of the sky, is born,
and then Enki, god of the earth. These younger gods have a
restless energy and a longing for order which soon rouses the
wrath of their progenitors, and Apsu and Tiamat resolve to
destroy them. However, they are defeated by the magic of
Enki, who kills Apsu and establishes his house on top of him.
In this house a son is born, Enlil, or in the later version Marduk,
and when Tiamat has reorganized her forces it is Marduk who
saves the situation. For when the older gods, Anshar, Enki and
Anu, prove powerless against her, Marduk agrees to face her—
on his own terms. He is to have full authority over the gods and
the power of fixing destinies. Possessed of this authority, he
sets out against Tiamat, succeeds in catching her in his net, and
kills her. He then cuts her body in two and uses half of it to

form the sky, where he founds a house for himself. Stars are arranged in constellations, and the sun and moon are organized for their regular duties. The gods are divided into two communities, one for the sky and one for the underworld, and to relieve them of any need for work man is created to serve them and look after their needs. To show their gratitude the gods build Marduk a mighty temple and his position as king is fully confirmed.

Myths of the "aetiological" type, dealing with the origins of particular objects, arrangements and so on, are fairly common in Mesopotamian literature. The Creation Epic is the longest and finest example, but other myths deal with arrangements in the regions below the earth, and show again the characteristic Babylonian preoccupation with death. One such story tells how Ishtar, the goddess of fertility, goes down to the underworld to visit its queen, her sister Ereshkigal. On her arrival, Ereshkigal looses sixty diseases on her and prevents her from returning. Meanwhile in the world above, fertility has ceased with the departure of the goddess. Crops and vegetation wither, and beasts and humans are sterile. This worries the gods to such an extent that they send orders to the queen of the underworld, and Ereshkigal is compelled to sprinkle Ishtar with the water of life and allow her to ascend to earth again. With her return growth and fertility on earth are renewed. Parallels in other mythological accounts of the year-cycle are many and obvious. Another underworld myth is that which accounts for the fact that Nergal, originally a sun-god, became the king of the nether regions. When Ereshkigal was unable to come to a feast of the gods, she sent her representative Nantar to take her place. All the gods acknowledged him except Nergal, and Ereshkigal was so angry at this insult that Nergal was summoned to her presence. On his arrival, he attacked Ereshkigal and, dragging her from her throne, threatened to kill her. Ereshkigal begged for mercy and offered her hand and her throne to her conqueror. So Nergal won the underworld kingdom for himself.

The transience of human life, so well brought out in the Gilgamesh epic, can be seen in myths like that of the childless King Etana who tried to reach heaven on an eagle's back to win the talisman of childbirth for his wife. His attempt was of course a failure, and he fell back to earth again, for men cannot exercise any control over life. Another hero who fails to gain eternal life is Adapa, son of Ea, a fisherman who broke the wings of the South Wind after it had overturned his boat. Summoned before Anu to answer for his crime, Adapa followed his father's advice and because he suspected he would be poisoned refused to eat or drink anything which Anu offered him. Unfortunately, Anu was so impressed by Adapa that he offered him the food and water of life. Again the impassable barrier between mortality and immortality is emphasized.

Another type of poetry which was common in the Mesopotamian world was lyric. This was concerned entirely with matters of religion, and there are examples of prayers, hymns of praise and psalms of penitence. Though cast for the most part in formal moulds, many lyrics show remarkable vigour and vivid imagery reminiscent of passages in the Old Testament. The resemblance is heightened by the use of balance and parallelism of phrase and by the powerful sense of personal aspiration which characterizes some of the poems.

The essential pessimism of the Mesopotamian attitude to life has already been seen, and it emerges even more clearly in compositions which deal with moral and ethical values. The most famous of these treats of a problem which has puzzled religious thinkers of many ages, that of the righteous sufferer. How is it that a man may fulfil his duties to the gods in every way, and yet still suffer all the evils that should be reserved for the wicked? The hero of the poem has throughout his life been careful to show the gods every respect, but now he has fallen sick. Prayer and exorcism do nothing to allay his sufferings; the gods have abandoned him. The problem is a very real one, and the Mesopotamian moralist finds only a pessimistic answer. Man cannot hope to understand the ways or the standards of the gods. Man is the creature of a moment, and cannot hope to judge true good and true evil. "The thoughts of a god are like deep waters", and man must continue to suffer, and to pray.

A conclusion of this sort, though often confirmed by the evidence of life, is not one which men will easily accept, and in the heyday of the first dynasty of Babylon, when Marduk was established as the supreme god of all mankind, a postscript was added giving a happy ending to the story. When the righteous sufferer had given up hope Marduk restored him to health and happiness. But this "wish-fulfilment" type of ending is scarcely typical of the Mesopotamian attitude to the problems of life. Much more characteristic is a composition cast in the form of a dialogue between a master and his slave. The basic idea of the dialogue is very simple; the master tells the slave that he intends to do some particular thing, go to the palace, have dinner, find himself a woman, and so on, and on each occasion the slave enumerates good reasons for doing so. When he has done this, the master changes his mind, and on each occasion the slave finds equally good reasons for not carrying out the plan. In this way the author emphasizes the lack of true values in life. Nothing is really good or bad. Life is vain and values non-existent. The only answer is death.

Although they form only a small proportion of the documents we possess, the works which have been mentioned comprise practically all that can be described as "literature" in the modern sense. On their merits as literature it is not easy to form a balanced judgement. Style in documents such as these is difficult to assess, but in content there is no doubt that some are of considerable value. The Gilgamesh Epic especially shows an awareness of fundamental human problems and a sure handling of epic material which make it rank with the Homeric epics. Other poems, such as the master-slave dialogue, betray a crudeness of form which lessens their literary value, but it is still possible to see that their authors made a fairly accurate assessment of the problems of their time. Although their answers were negative, it is difficult in the light of twentieth-century events to see that better answers have since been provided.

An approximation to a Mesopotamian prose literature was provided by the annals compiled by kings, in which the chief events of their reigns were described. While Assyrian kings provided details of their military campaigns, the kings of Babylon were more interested in matters of religious importance, and their records are of little use in reconstructing their reigns. Other historical information is provided by inscriptions in the foundations of buildings, by lists of years named after important events in them, and by documents like the "Babylonian Chronicle", which did make some attempt at combining the history of Babylonia and Assyria.

More historical information can be found in the voluminous correspondence, both royal and private, which has survived. Much of what we know of Hammurabi's empire, for instance,

13

is gained from his letters to his provincial governors, and the same is true of many other Mesopotamian monarchs. Private letters too can tell us a good deal of the problems of finance, trade and so on which faced ordinary Mesopotamian citizens, although their brevity and abrupt transitions from subject to subject often make them difficult to interpret. Similarly contracts, accounts and other business documents are of enormous value in re-creating the economic life of the time.

Two other types of document must also be mentioned. Those dealing with religious ritual and magic practices are of enormous value to historians of cult and religion but of little interest to the general reader, while documents dealing with the law, notably the Hammurabi code, have been dealt with in another chapter.

The art of Babylonia, like its literature, had its origin in the Sumerian period, and really began with the foundation of the first cities towards the mouths of the twin rivers. Further north, where settlement had been much earlier, independent traditions had arisen which were gradually ousted by the spread of the southern culture. From the beginning features can be observed which were to remain typical of Mesopotamian art throughout its long life. An alabaster vase (Fig. 2) found at Uruk, for instance, depicts in relief a religious ceremony with processions of animals and bearers of offerings, and one of the strongest characteristics of Sumerian art is its connection with ritual and religion. The darker side of religion, also a typical theme in later periods, can be seen in a limestone monster with a human body and the head of a lioness (Fig. 4a). Again, a granite stele from Uruk (Fig. 4c) shows men killing lions, and is the ancestor both of later commemorative reliefs and of the hunting scenes so vividly portrayed in Assyrian art. Although they stand at the beginning of Sumerian tradition, these works betray no lack of confidence in design or execution. They show a remarkable adaptability in their approach to relief work or work in the round, and make excellent use of their materials. The vigorous naturalism of the hunters and the offering-bearers, and the latent monolithic power of the monster, are characteristics which are typical of much Sumerian art. A contrast is to be found in the head of a woman, also found at Uruk (Fig 6a), for as well as its naturalistic qualities it shows, particularly in the lips, the cheeks, and the areas round the eyes, a delicacy and sensitivity in modelling which seems strangely un-Sumerian.

The period of the early Sumerian dynasties was a flourishing one for art. Religion still provided the main motive for sculpture, which was used for cult-statues, temple-furniture and for numerous representations of worshippers which were intended to stand constantly in the god's presence and intercede for their donors. In the Diyala region an evolution from a concentrated abstract style to one of greater realism can be traced, but over the rest of the area the naturalistic style prevailed. It can be best seen in the well-known metal sculpture found by Sir Leonard Woolley at Ur, or in the bearded bull's head now in the City Art Museum of St. Louis (Fig. 5). Relief sculpture in this period developed an efficient narrative technique which proved ideal for commemorative accounts of royal campaigns, and this technique was also used in other mediums, such as shell-mosaic set in bitumen. The "standard" from Ur, for instance, shows on one side the various stages of a campaign, and on the other the feast which followed the victory, and has been described as the world's first animated newsreel.

The emergence to power of the Semitic element of the population under Sargon of Akkad and his successors was marked by no real break in artistic traditions. But there is in works of this period a sense of character and personality which can only be due to Semitic influence. Loyalty to tribe and tribal chief tended to replace the old Sumerian loyalty to city and city-god, and this resulted in a secularizing and personalizing of art which can best be seen in a bronze head which may represent Sargon himself (Fig. 1). At any rate it is clearly a portrait. The formal elaboration of the hair and beard is offset by a face of striking sensitivity in the modelling of eyes, lips, cheeks and nostrils. A commemorative stele set up by Naramsin, Sargon's grandson (Fig. 7), also shows the change of attitude. The king strides high above his advancing troops, dwarfing them and the enemy he tramples underfoot. The gods are present, but only in the form of their emblems in the sky— the king is the all-important figure. No attempt is made to follow the Sumerian serialization of incidents. The sculptor has represented the advance, the victory, the rout and the divine backing in a single unified composition.

The overthrow of the Akkadian empire by the barbarous

Gutians led to a Sumerian revival in the south, artistic as well
as political. Gudea, ruler of Lagash about this time, has left
a series of statues of himself (e.g. Fig. 6b) which show both the
religious fervour of the Sumerians and the mastery of modelling
technique inherited from the Akkadians. But the arrival of the
Amorites finally ended the Sumerian ascendency and
established the Semites as masters of the area. Artistically,
however, works of the Isin-Larsa period which followed are
closely connected with the Neo-Sumerian period, although the
best work which has survived, coming as it does from sites like
Mari and Eshnunna, shows an interest in personality and personal adornment which emphasizes the northerly position of
these cities. By the time of Hammurabi the qualities which we
have taken as Semitic had returned to full prominence. The
head of a monarch, possibly Hammurabi himself (Fig. 3),
shows, like the Sargon portrait, a formal framework to a face
of great character and individuality. The sculptor has caught
exactly the careworn features and innate power of the great
monarch in his old age. Once again the modelling around the
mouth and eyes is of the highest order. It is interesting to see
the same technique—realism framed by formalism—in animal
sculptures such as the roaring lion in clay from Tell Harmal
near Baghdad (Fig. 8).

A complete contrast in subject is provided by a number of
clay reliefs showing domestic subjects—a man riding an ox
(Fig. 18a), a carpenter at work (Fig. 18d), a musician (Fig.
18b–c), a showman with his monkeys. While the artistic
standard of these works is not very high, they provide a lively
glimpse of the everyday life of the period.

A branch of art of which very little has survived is painting.
By a lucky chance, some wall-paintings from Mari have been
preserved, although there is no reason to suppose that the
technique was limited to that city. As well as geometric
patterns, human figures appear in scenes of religion, war and
daily life. Individually the figures are of no great merit, but
the total decorative effect is enhanced by organized composition
and pleasing use of colour.

The Kassite conquest of Babylonia did not lead to any violent
reaction against old artistic styles. On the contrary the Kassite
monarchs were deeply interested in the repair and restoration
of ancient cities and temples. But on the whole their artistic

ambitions exceeded their technical skill. Remains of wall-paintings found in the palace at Dur Kurigalzu are of poor quality, and a similar clumsiness and lack of style can be seen in the wall decoration of a Kassite temple at Uruk where figures of deities holding vases of water (a typical Mesopotamian motif) stand in niches linked by wavy lines simulating running water. What is important about these figures, however, is that they show a completely new technique in being made from moulded brick, a technique which was to reappear to good effect in the Neo-Babylonian period.

The objects most typical of the Kassite period are sculptured boundary-stones, which occur in great numbers. These normally bear relief sculptures of the king of the time or emblems of the gods, and are on the whole more interesting to students of religion than to students of art. But in one respect at least the Kassites achieved complete mastery of an earlier technique —that of naturalistic animal sculpture. The head of a lioness from Dur Kurigalzu (Fig. 4b) is a fine example of this.

With the Kassites artistic inspiration in southern Babylonia came temporarily to an end. But while there was stagnation in the south, a vigorous new civilization was developing further north which, although at first culturally dependent on Babylonia, soon achieved both political and artistic independence. The history of the period of Assyrian domination, however, has no place in this volume. With the fall of Nineveh the south came into its own once more, and for a time Babylon was the artistic capital of the world. Unfortunately the works which have survived from this period are so few that no real appraisal of their value can be made. In fact the period has to be judged almost entirely by what can be reconstructed from the remains of Nebuchadnezzar's Babylon. Of these remains, the most striking are those of the Ishtar Gate (Fig. 11), with its decoration of bulls and dragons in moulded brick enamelled in yellow and white on a blue background. The bulls, despite their rather contrived attitude and the decorative formalism of their manes and body-hair, have an appearance of liveliness and restless energy, while the smooth relentless stride of the dragons is emphasized by their balanced composition and the regular treatment of their scales. The repetition of these beasts in brilliant colour all over the massive gateway must have made it a work of impressive power and grandeur.

Mention of the great Ishtar Gate leads naturally to the subject of architecture in Mesopotamia, for both in size and in decoration it shows a triumphant answer to the eternal problems of the area—lack of most building materials and the natural dullness of what was available. In the alluvial plain there was no stone and practically no timber. But other materials, less promising architecturally but nevertheless useful, were there in abundance. Reeds grew in the marshes, and mud was everywhere. So it was from mud that the earliest farmhouse settlements at Hassuna were built. In the south reed huts must have been very common, but as well as this the early settlers brought the technique of brick moulding down with them from the Iranian highlands, and throughout the area mud remained the principal building material.

The development of sacred architecture can be seen almost from the start in southern Mesopotamia. Excavations have revealed shrines which reach back to the earliest days of human settlement. The earliest shrine at Eridu, for instance, dating from the fifth millennium, is a simple rectangle 12 feet long and 15 feet wide, but it has two features which remain constant in later periods, an alcove in one wall with a pedestal for the image of the god, and an altar or offering table in front of it. When the shrine was rebuilt on a larger scale the builders were faced with the practical problem of supporting the roof, and their answer to this was to strengthen the walls with buttresses where roof-beams rested on them. In doing so they also found a solution to one of the fundamental problems mentioned above, for buttresses provided a means of breaking the monotony of mud-brick walls. At first shrines were the only buildings large enough to need external buttressing, and when they became purely ornamental their use was still confined to religious buildings. In fact buttressing served to distinguish sacred from secular architecture until the conquest of the area by Alexander the Great.

As the importance of the temples grew, so their size continued to increase. The central shrine was surrounded by subsidiary rooms and the number of doors was increased to allow for freer movement of worshippers. Another basic feature of Mesopotamian temples also appeared, for by the beginning of the protoliterate period some had already been built on a raised platform of mud brick. This was the ancestor of the ziggurat or temple tower, and was an effort, not to raise man nearer god, but to raise god's shrine towards him so that he could more easily descend to man. With the increased prosperity of the cities, man-power and resources became available to raise temple-towers to ever-increasing heights. In Uruk, for instance, the so-called White Temple in the second half of the fourth millennium was built on an artificial hill some 40 feet high, a height which would be very impressive in the utter flatness of the plain. The temple itself, being intended for the god rather than his worshippers, was small in comparison with temples at ground level, but otherwise it followed the same pattern with its platform and offering table. Decoration was by buttresses and whitewash frequently renewed to preserve its colour. Another type of decoration found at Uruk was the use of coloured clay cones, each about 4 inches long, which were inserted point first into a thick coating of mud on walls and pillars to form mosaics in black, red and brown. Patterns which have survived intact are purely geometric, but friezes of animals may have formed part of the original designs.

As the cities increased in size and complexity a new problem arose. Older temples had been open on all sides, and at the top of an artificial hill this was still possible; but in a confined space among other buildings it often proved impracticable. At Khafaje for instance only one entrance was possible, and cult activities which had earlier taken place on the open ground round the temple were now confined to the irregular space that happened to be available in front of the door. This space was walled in to preserve it from profane eyes, and, at least at Khafaje, was later extended to a series of three courtyards opening from each other, with the result that the shrine was no longer a central hall, but an innermost holy-of-holies. By the Early Dynastic period courtyards had been given tower-flanked entrances from the street, and had become an integral part of the temples. This is true even of temples in open spaces. These were built to a rectangular plan, or sometimes in an oval form which is characteristic only of this period and passed out of use before the Sumerian revival under the Third Dynasty of Ur. Ziggurats or temple-platforms remained the rule, and foundations of untrimmed stone have been found at Mari and Al 'Ubaid. Also at Mari temple courtyards have been found decorated with columns or pilasters to give a cloister-effect.

Another development which gradually became the rule in the south was the division of the shrine-room into two by pillars or cross-walls so that the statue of the deity was cut off still more from ordinary mortals. The altar was then relegated to the outer part of the shrine-room or, in some cases, to the open court which was substituted for it. During the Kassite period religious architecture remained highly conservative, as can be seen from the ziggurat at Dur Kurigalzu, which was in all respects like earlier Mesopotamian temple-towers. However, some elements such as corner-buttresses can be best explained as showing the retention of traditional northern styles, perhaps an inheritance from the Kassite homeland. The development of Assyrian architecture cannot be traced in this book, but with the Neo-Babylonian revival it can be seen that the old traditions were still preserved. A fuller description of the temples of Babylon can be found in the chapter dealing with Koldewey's excavations.

The development of domestic architecture is more easily traced. The adobe farmhouses at Hassuna dating from the early part of the fifth millennium have already been mentioned. With their pitched roofs and farm-buildings grouped around them, they probably looked little different from farm-cottages of many more modern periods. Later flat roofs became the rule and houses were built, first round a central main room, and then round an open courtyard. Sometimes the courtyard was roofed in and provided with clerestory lighting, and by the Neo-Sumerian period some houses had an upper storey with rooms opening from a balcony round the courtyard. The principal room was normally on the shady side of the court for the greater comfort of the inhabitants, and usually there were no windows as these would have added to the heat of the interior. Palace architecture was simply domestic architecture on a larger scale with facilities and amenities which would be beyond the reach of private citizens. The early dynastic palace at Kish shows in one section at least a series of rooms opening off a courtyard, and at Eridu, too, public buildings were arranged round interior courts. Later palaces were arranged with their throne-rooms opening directly from the main court, and as rulers grew in importance their palaces were often enlarged to include further offices and more grandiose apartments. The palace of Zimrilim at Mari, for instance, extended over

FIG. 16 Cylinder seals
a. and *b*. Protoliterate

c. and *d*.
Early Dynastic

e. Akkadian

more than eight and a half acres and in its time was considered
one of the wonders of the world. Surrounded as it was by a
strong defensive wall it was a fortress as well as a residence.
Even this vast complex was eclipsed in size by Nebuchadnezzar's residence in Babylon, which was more than twelve acres
in extent, but the principle of rooms around courtyards was
still preserved. Once again the remarkable continuity of architecture in the area can be seen.

One aspect of Mesopotamian art which cannot be omitted
here is the practice of seal-engraving. The predominant type
of seal was cylindrical, so that as it was rolled across a surface of
soft clay, its design was indefinitely reproduced. The demand
for seals was a constant challenge to Mesopotamian engravers,
especially as the themes employed were curiously limited, but
it was a challenge which on the whole they triumphantly met.
At first scenes were found which had a "narrative" interest
(Fig. 16a), but on the whole this was found to be unsatisfactory.
An impression on a small surface gave only part of the narrative,
while on a wider surface the first part had often to be repeated,
and so narrative continuity was destroyed. The result was that
closely connected groups were designed which could effectively
bear repetition. Most of these designs were religious in content—
offerings to deities, acts of supplication and herds of sacred
animals, as well as mysterious beasts like serpent-headed lions
(Fig. 16b) and lion-headed eagles. At the beginning of the
Early Dynastic period a simplification of design took place by
which motifs—limited as a rule to running animals—were
reduced to repetitive patterns whose effect was purely decorative (Fig. 16c). Later in the period the range of subjects was
increased, but the interest in continuous design was retained.
Favourite subjects were taken from the rich Sumerian mythology. Struggling men, animals and monsters half human and
half beast were linked in close-knit patterns of deadly conflict
often suggesting incidents in the adventures of Gilgamesh
and Enkidu (Fig. 16d). Towards the end of the Early Dynastic
period a new interest in the plastic modelling of figures appeared, and inscriptions were used first to fill in odd spaces and
preserve the continuous nature of the design but later to give
variation and even become the central feature. The beginning
of the Akkadian period was marked by a greater interest in
physical reality, but the realism is one of treatment rather than

a. Akkadian

b. Third Dynasty of Ur

c. First Dynasty of Babylon   *d.* Neo-Babylonian

FIG. 17   Cylinder seals

of content, for the mythical struggles of beasts and beast-men continue to be important themes. But while earlier artists had concentrated on the decorative possibilities of such conflicts, Akkadian seal-engravers gave them a swashbuckling vigour unequalled in previous periods (Fig. 16b). The feeling for life and personality, noted also in Akkadian sculpture, is very obvious, and presumably represents Semitic influence. At the same time there is a return to the "narrative" technique which had earlier been rejected. The scenes normally chosen were from the world of the gods, who were shown performing the many activities, beneficent and malevolent, which Akkadian religious thinking ascribed to them (Fig. 17a). In all these scenes there is a precision and clarity of craftsmanship which distinguishes them from earlier work.

With the revival of Sumerian fortunes under the Third Dynasty of Ur, the richness and variety of glyptic design was reduced to the monotonous repetition of a single theme in which a human figure is introduced to the presence of a deity (Fig. 17b). As designs became standardized, seals depended more and more on their inscriptions to distinguish their owners' property, but there was a temporary revival of glyptic art under the first Babylonian dynasty, when variation of design was attempted by the introduction of "secondary motifs", such as animals in various positions, into the gaps in the presentation scenes (Fig. 17c). The results, however, could never be unified compositions, and towards the close of the dynasty the habit dropped out of use. Kassite seals merely continued the old style of presentation scene plus inscription, but new vitality was introduced in the north when Assyria appeared as an independent power and her seal-cutters combined their natural vigour with the best traditions of previous periods. Too few seals are known from the Neo-Babylonian period to form a true judgement of their merit; what is immediately obvious is a loss of Assyrian liveliness without any striking innovations in design. The usual motif is a worshipper before the symbols of the gods (Fig. 17d). By this time Aramaic was becoming the principal language of the area, and as writing in cuneiform gradually disappeared, the cylinder seal dropped largely out of use.

In the sphere of religion the separation of Semitic from Sumerian is again a virtually impossible task. It is clear that when the Semites came into contact with the older civilization, they adopted the Sumerian religious system almost in its entirety, and although Semitic aspects of certain deities may be established, the system as a whole remained unchanged. But before any description of the Babylonian pantheon is given, an attempt must be made to adjust our mental sights in order to understand an attitude to religion and to the world which is fundamentally different from our own. It seems inevitable that when men are faced with a world that is strange and beyond their control, they should react to it by providing explanations for its strangeness and for the powers that transcend their own. In earlier periods they could not stand apart from the world and examine it impersonally, as modern "scientific" observers can. They were only too conscious of the fact that they were part of the universe about them, and that the universe stood in an immediate relationship to them. So the universe was personalized in terms of human experience, and human experience found its explanation in cosmic events. This attitude of mind—mythological rather than scientific— is prevalent in much ancient religion. "Something is as it is because so-and-so happened"; "man cannot do such-and-such because someone else tried and failed". Such stories are certainly useless as scientific explanations of phenomena, but within the mental framework of their creation they are completely and satisfyingly true.

So in any myth-making community a body of myth is created and a cosmic order established. Any such order must of necessity be based on the only order which is known to its creators— the order of the community in which they live. Thus the government of the gods is a projection to the divine place of the government among men, and the gods themselves behave as humans do. Admittedly they live for ever and have superhuman powers, but they have the passions and emotions which are those of mankind. Surprise is sometimes expressed because ancient peoples felt nothing odd in the fact that their gods were surly, selfish and often cowardly. How could men possibly worship such gods? The answer to this question lies in another fundamental distinction which must be made. The explanations offered by the myth-maker were of facts in the world about him, and emotions like cowardice and anger were as much part of that world as emotions like mercy and love. His explanations, in fact, dealt with the world as he knew it, not with the world

as he would have liked it to be. Why should the gods be
paragons of moral virtue when the world was not at all like
that? The gods to a Babylonian were not examples of how he
ought to live; they were personification of the vital forces of the
universe. Man was in their power, and his duty lay in service
and obedience to them even when he could not understand
their motives. He made no attempt to console himself with
rewards in a life after death, for again the idea that because
there is no justice in life there must be justice hereafter was
a form of wish-fulfilment quite alien to his mode of thought.

Mesopotamian religion can now be approached with a
clearer mind. The world in the formative period of civilization
in the river-valleys was not an easy place to live in. Man was in
constant danger from the violence of flood and storm. Neither
his crop nor his life was assured, and this lack of certainty is
reflected in his religion. In his eyes the greatest powers of the
universe were the sky, the air and the earth, and these powers
became the greatest deities of his pantheon. Anu, the god of
the sky, was originally the principal god, but like the sky itself
he was always rather remote, and before the Akkadian period
he had lost his pre-eminence to Enlil, god of the air. Enlil
represented all that was powerful in the space between earth
and heaven, and the might of the storm was his manifestation.
As the god who wielded power, he performed an executive
function in the assembly of the gods, and it was by him that
their orders were carried into effect. So he was responsible not
only for the organization of prosperity on earth, but for any
destruction that was deemed necessary—the Flood, the sack
of a city and so on.

The other great power of the universe was the earth. Con-
ceived in mythology as the wife of heaven and the mother of all
the gods, she was regarded as the source of all life and fertility.
She was known as Ninmah, Ninhursag, and by various other
titles. But the earth also contains another power, the creative
power which causes the great mother to conceive, the water
which fertilizes the earth and makes it productive. This power,
known as Enki, later as Ea, was the third great god of the pantheon. Wells are deep and streams are devious, and it has been
suggested that it was these aspects which gave Enki his position
as god of wisdom, and so, as minister of Anu and Enlil, as
creator and organizer of all that is good in the world.

Beneath these great deities was the rest of the hierarchy of the gods, organized like a human state, each diety with his or her functions, so that every aspect of life was included. No distinction was ever made between sacred and secular : in fact to a Mesopotamian the word secular would have had little meaning, for religion embraced all life, and life itself *was* religion. Building, wood-carving, even playing a musical instrument, were subject to divine ordinance and supervision in exactly the same way as kingship, law and justice. The "explanations" provided by mythology covered everything.

Religions, it has already been said, reflect the world as it exists for those who create them, and as the world changes, so religions must reflect those changes. The Mesopotamian world was one of city-states, each the property of a god, and as the political fortunes of a state waxed and waned the city-god's importance in the divine assembly grew or shrank with them. Thus the kingship of the gods changed from time to time and deities of various cities assumed power for as long as their cities held the leadership among men. One god, however, seems to have been above this. In the Sumerian period Enlil retained his executive functions at all times, and his city, Nippur, was always the principal holy city of the area, although there is no trace of any period of political supremacy to establish this. Enlil, in fact, was a national rather than a local god, and it was largely through him that the Sumerians, politically divided as they were, retained a sense of kinship and nationality. One of the greatest achievements of the first dynasty of Babylon was to win for Marduk a position much like that which had earlier been allotted to Enlil.

Other deities of the Mesopotamian system do seem to show signs of Semitic influence. Sin, the god of the moon, has a Semitic name, and is thought to be of nomadic origin. If so, he was equated with a Sumerian moon-god called Nanna. His special concern was with the regulation of the calendar. His son Shamash, the sun-god, if one can judge by his name, was also introduced by the Semites, and he too was equated with a Sumerian deity, Utu or Babbar. As the god who surveys and sheds light on all mankind he was the god of truth and justice. Finally mention must be made of Ishtar, another goddess of fertility who eclipsed all the others in the area. While Ninhursag continued to be a universal mother-figure, Ishtar

represented the more immediate aspects of love, reproduction
and fertility. Her cult, as might be expected, was widespread
and popular, and features of it such as the employment of
temple prostitutes have been roundly condemned by moralists
of later ages whose life was perhaps not as close to the earth as
that of the average citizen of Babylonia.

The Mesopotamian world, as has been said before, was a
difficult place in which to live, and it is easy to see why the
Babylonians believed that man had been created for one
purpose only—to serve the gods and save them the trouble of
working for themselves. A monarch might be inspired to the
service of compiling a law-code which would make the divine
justice shine out over all his peoples, but for the most part man
was simply a slave who must make sure that his masters lacked
for nothing. In return his masters gave him—or at least ought
to give him—a life of ease and prosperity. The trouble was that
life was seldom so simple and straightforward, and, as has already been seen, this could lead to an attitude either of complete
cynicism or of complete resignation. But for most people any
misfortune meant simply that they had failed in some duty to
the gods. Serious failure meant personal intervention by the
greater gods; neglect in smaller matters meant only that the
gods turned away for a time, and allowed the sinner to be
attacked by the numerous demons who were waiting for such
opportunities. Ill-health, bad harvests and similar misfortunes
were caused by the demons, and only by performing the neglected duties could a man regain the favour of the gods. Death
was the ultimate punishment. Only a bird-like shadow lived
on in the gloomy halls of the underworld. The idea of reward
after death was unknown.

The architectural development of the Mesopotamian temple
has already been traced. It was regarded as the home of the
god when he descended to earth, and it was man's duty to look
after that home and the estates belonging to it. This involved
a good deal of manual labour performed by a retinue of temple
servants of all kinds—shepherds, brewers, cooks, musicians,
and many more. As well as this, all members of the community
had at first to take their turn in the cultivation of the temple
lands and the clearing of the temple-canals. All this work was
supervised and co-ordinated by the god's *ensi* or chief steward
upon earth, an official charged with the maintenance and pre-

servation of the estate under the direction of his divine master. This gave the *ensi* a position of great power in the community. In fact in many cases he was sole and absolute ruler of the city-state, and later, as his dominions were extended, he sometimes took on the title of king. But it must be emphasized that throughout Mesopotamian history the king remained a servant of his god. Only in a very few cases did kings make a claim to personal divinity, and it has been reasonably suggested that this happened only when a monarch was regarded as the personal genius of the community, commanded by the mother-goddess to share her couch in a ceremony to ensure the continued fertility of the land. By this personal contact, however it may be presumed to have taken place, a few selected humans gained a measure of divinity, but on the whole kings remained to the end as human as their subjects.

It has been pointed out in an earlier chapter that the *ensi* was not the only person who could aspire to permanent kingship. In some cities elected war-leaders or internal administrators were also able to perpetuate their rule. In many states there must have been a considerable struggle before the question of kingship was settled, but the eventual winner always took over the functions of the loser and by the historical period no distinction was made. The king, whatever his origin, was administrator and leader in war, but primarily he was god's chief priest and steward. Under him were large numbers of lesser priests, divided into classes according to their functions. A large and important class was concerned with the propitiation of the gods and the warding off of evil spirits. This entailed knowledge of a vast collection of spells and incantations for almost any circumstance, and it is easy to understand how the priestly duties of Babylonia soon became the property of a few families who closely guarded the secrets of their trade. The same is true of the other classes such as the musicians whose performances were designed to gladden the hearts of the gods, and the soothsayers who observed omens and interpreted dreams. The theory behind their function was that the gods gave signs of man's destiny in material objects, and that any object could yield up its meaning to a correctly trained priest. Some objects, however, proved much more useful than others. The livers of sheep and goats were considered especially potent, for the liver was thought of as the seat of life and clearly

14

reflected the intentions of the god to whom a victim was sacrificed. Letting drops of oil fall into a jar of water was also regarded as a useful method, and any out-of-the-ordinary happening was laden with hidden meaning. Not only men were involved in the work of the priesthood, for women too could perform most of the priestly functions. Princesses of the royal blood were often content to spend their lives in the employment of a temple.

The central feature of the Babylonian religious calendar was the day on which spring began. This was celebrated by a twelve-day festival of particular magnificence when the gods of neighbouring towns were gathered into Marduk's shrine. The chief features of the festival were the procession along the Sacred Way to the procession-house outside the city (it was here that the king "took the hands" of the god to lead him from his temple), the re-enaction of the creation myth, the stripping and reinstatement of the king, the sacred marriage of the god and goddess (probably represented by the king and high-priestess), and the fixing of destinies for the coming year. This elaborate festival ensured the renewal of the earth's life-cycle and the continued prosperity of the state.

Medicine and astronomy would nowadays scarcely be considered matters of religion, but to the Babylonians they were ancillary to what were regarded as the more important processes of exorcism and astrology. Illness was essentially a matter of possession by demons, and, as has been said, a large class of priests was concerned with driving out these demons by spells and incantations. Often enough a doctor's task seems to have been merely to administer medicines so unpleasant that it would be uncomfortable for the demons to remain any longer in the patient's body. But as early as the third millennium a body of more reasonable medical knowledge had grown up, based presumably on folk-medicine and practical experience. Drugs were extracted from local plants and minerals and mixed in beer to give them a pleasant flavour. Surgeons performed operations at least as early as the time of Hammurabi, and by the Neo-Babylonian period physicians had formed themselves into a professional body and had developed a technique of prognosis and treatment which, though crude, was at least more likely to produce cures than were priestly incantations.

The study of the heavens was always of great importance in Babylonia, for it was one of the principal methods of discovering the will of the gods. The sun, moon and five planets then known were associated with the principal divinities, and a system of interpreting their motions was evolved which was later extended to include the main fixed stars. Temple towers were ideal observatories from which the courses of the stars could be plotted and the cycles of the planets studied. Moreover the continuity of Babylonian civilization meant that records were preserved over a sufficiently long period for the recognition (at least at the end of that period) of features such as the precession of the equinoxes and the regularity of eclipses. From an early date the sky was divided into zones, the most important being that which lay along the celestial equator. This was in its turn divided into twelve sections, each named after the principal constellation in it, and these constellations, through which the sun, moon and planets appear to pass in their yearly journeys, have largely come down to us as our Signs of the Zodiac. The Bull, the Twins, the Crab, the Lion, the Scales, the Scorpion, the Archer, the Water-carrier and the Fish were all named by the Babylonians. The Goat was known as the Goat-fish, the Ram as the Day-labourer, and the Virgin (for obvious reasons) as the Great Mother. Many other constellations—the Raven, for instance, and the Eagle—also received their names from the astronomers of ancient Mesopotamia.

Another interesting survival which owes much to ancient Babylonia is the seven-day week. Every hour of every day was thought to be dominated by one of the seven planetary gods (in modern terms the sun, the moon, Mercury, Venus, Mars, Jupiter and Saturn), and each day was called after the deity who dominated its first hour. Thus there were the days of Shamash, Sin, Nergal, Nabu, Marduk, Ishtar and Ninib. Greek contact with late Babylonian astronomy brought this idea of time-reckoning to the western world, but the divine names were naturally replaced by those of Greek deities. By a similar process Roman gods replaced the Greek ones on the transfer of the system to Rome, and these names can still be seen in several modern European languages. In English the process of change has gone one stage further, and Norse deities have given their names to several of the days; but the system remains in essence Babylonian.

Mesopotamian calculations concerned with the stars, as well as those dealing with everyday problems, show a considerable knowledge of mathematics, based on a system partly decimal and partly sexagesimal. The main units were ten, six times ten, ten times six times ten, and so on, but by far the most important was sixty. On this basis systems of weights, measurements and time-divisions were evolved, and complicated problems could be solved by extracting roots, raising to powers, and solving complex equations, as well as by the use of ordinary addition, subtraction, multiplication and division. Perhaps the most important achievement of the Mesopotamian mathematicians was their discovery of the "position-concept" in numeration. This involves the use of a very limited number of numerical symbols, the magnitudes of which are determined by their positions within a compound figure. It is in fact the system in use today. For example, 21 does not mean $2+1$ (as it would in Roman number, for instance), but $2 \times 10+1$, and 221 means $2 \times 100+2 \times 10+1$. That is, moving a figure one place to the left multiplies it by ten, and similarly moving it one place to the right divides it by ten. The Babylonian base was sixty, so moving a figure one place to the left multiplied it by sixty. Thus a figure which may be represented 2,1 would mean $2 \times 60+1$, that is 121. For a system like this to be workable it is important to have a symbol for zero to indicate an empty place between two other figures, and this too is to be found at least in later Babylonian texts. Another important feature of the system was its extension to sub-multiples of the unit as well as multiples, in other words the invention of a system of sexagesimal fractions comparable to our decimal fractions. It can be seen that the Babylonian system was essentially "modern" in its methods, and far superior to any other in the ancient world. Unfortunately its merits were not appreciated by posterity. The "position-concept" was lost until its revival in connection with Arabic numbers, and the idea of sub-multiples disappeared until its revival in the late sixteenth century in connection with decimal numbers. Only elements of the sexagesimal system have survived without interruption to the present day, but although efforts are now being made to replace what remains of it by a purely decimal system, its long survival is a tribute to the mathematicians of ancient Babylonia.

(8)
The Decline of Babylon

AFTER his arrival in Babylon on October 29th, 539
Cyrus was careful to maintain the good impression
that he had created. He offered his friendship to all
Babylonians and immediately began to compensate them for
the injuries which they had suffered at the hands of Nabonidus.
Buildings destroyed by him were restored, the forced labour
which he had imposed was abolished, and priests and citizens
were allowed to return to the worship of the days before his
rule. At the same time a systematic campaign was begun, the
sole object of which was to blacken the memory of the former
king. A long proclamation was issued which told in detail of
his evil actions and his insults to the gods, and how Marduk in
desperation had turned to the righteous Cyrus to save his land
from disaster. Another account, written in verse to make it
easier to remember, was obviously aimed at those who had not
the education to read the royal pronouncement. Throughout
the empire the story was spread that Cyrus was the liberator
sent by the gods, and everywhere details were arranged to give
local authenticity. To the Babylonians Cyrus proclaimed that
it was Marduk who had given him victory; to the citizens of
Ur it was their own god Sin who had guided him, while the
Jews considered that he had been led by Jahweh himself.
Every trace of Nabonidus was removed from the temples and
cities. Inscriptions were destroyed, statues were burned, and
nothing was left which might remind the Babylonians of their
former king.

The policy which Cyrus adopted towards his new subjects
certainly had the results he wished. While he was in Babylon
all the kings from the Persian Gulf to the Mediterranean
brought their tribute and kissed his feet. Throughout the land
there was rejoicing that an oppressor had been overthrown, and
if any remnants of support for Nabonidus remained they were

CAUCASUS Mts

ARMENIA

ARTU

Lake Van

Lake Urmia

Upper Zab

Lower Zab

R. Tigris

R. Diyala

ZAGROS Mts

MEDIA

CASPIAN SEA

Area covered by MAP 1

Bisutun.

PARSUMASH

ari

R. Euphrates

nana

BABYLON

Susa.

ANSHAN

Pasargadae

Persepolis.

FARS

CHALDÆA

Basra

DESERT

THE MIDDLE EAST

Showing ancient sites
Modern names in *italics*

PERSIAN GULF

Tilmun

0   100   200   300   400

Miles

MAP III

so thoroughly destroyed by Cyrus that no memory of them remained. In the outlying provinces temples were rebuilt and their gods restored to them. In Babylon itself the administration was entrusted to Gobyras, but this was probably not the governor of Gutium, who died a few days after Cyrus entered the city. Babylonian officials were for the most part retained in their offices and as far as possible nothing was changed which was not directly connected with the evil government of Nabonidus. Even when the former king's wife died in November 539 a four-month period of official mourning was decreed and strictly observed.

The private life of the citizens of Babylonia remained unaltered by the change of dynasty. Only a few days after the fall of Nabonidus documents were being dated by the accession-year of Cyrus, and they show clearly that there was no interruption of the city's commercial prosperity. The great merchant-families and banking-houses continued to flourish and Babylon's markets were as busy as ever before. Only in the highest administrative offices were changes made. Cyrus himself remained in the city during the winter of 539–538 to supervise his new province, and when he returned to Ecbatana in the early spring he left his son Cambyses as his representative in Babylonia. In March 538 Cambyses took the hands of Marduk at the New Year Festival and thus received the god's approval for his father's assumption of the title "King of Babylon". For the next eight years he lived in Sippar, concentrating on routine administration and on the performance of religious duties. In Babylon Gobyras continued in his office as satrap or governor of the province of "Babylon and the land across the river", a territory which included Syria, Phoenicia and Palestine. This meant that he was virtually king of an enormous area, but it was a kingship so limited as to be almost powerless. Although he was in complete charge of the civil and legal administration of his province and could organize levies of troops within it, a satrap was kept from plotting complete independence by the fact that his secretary, his treasurer and the commander of the garrison in his capital city were directly responsible to the Great King. As well as this, there was the annual visit of the notorious "King's Eye", a royal inspector who made a thorough enquiry into the state of each province.

During the reign of Cyrus Babylon was quiet and presumably contented. Early in 530 the Great King decided on an expedition against the Massagetae on his far north-eastern frontier. According to the Persian custom he had to appoint a successor before leaving the country, and Cambyses was recognized as King of Babylon and regent of the empire. When in the summer of 530 Cyrus was killed in action Cambyses succeeded him as ruler of all the Persian dominions. This caused little change in Babylonia, where the new king had been in residence since 538, and Gobyras continued to hold office as satrap. But during the king's absence on an expedition which ended in the Persian conquest of Egypt, there seems to have been a good deal of disturbance in the area. In March 522 Bardiya, a brother of Cambyses who had been left in charge of Media, Armenia and Cadusia, proclaimed himself king. By the middle of April he had been accepted in Babylonia, and by July he was recognized all over the empire. Cambyses, who was on his way back from Egypt, was so startled by the news that he took his own life—or so at least we are told by Darius, the royal spear-bearer, who took it upon himself to revenge his master's death. The whole of the history of this period is in fact coloured and complicated by the fact that our primary source of information is Darius, and he, like Cyrus, was much more interested in spreading propaganda on his own behalf than in giving a truthful account of his accession and achievements.

The story, as given by Darius, is as follows. Soon after his accession Cambyses had suspected the loyalty of his brother Bardiya, and had seen to it that he was quietly murdered, although nobody knew or suspected this. Afterwards a man called Gaumata pretended to be Bardiya, and had himself proclaimed king. All the people went over to him, and so Cambyses committed suicide. But Darius, a member of another branch of the royal family who was serving with Cambyses in Egypt, hurried back, and with the aid of six conspirators killed Gaumata and took the throne for himself. Now it seems unlikely that the murder of a powerful prince would be completely suppressed for several years, and Darius's accounts of his campaigns are full of details of usurpers pretending to be someone else. In all probability this was only his way of concealing the fact that he had destroyed a legitimate ruler with a greater claim to the throne than he had himself. The suicide of Cambyses is also highly suspicious, and suspicion is heightened by the tradition, carefully prepared for later generations and possibly quite unfounded, that Cambyses went mad while in Egypt and committed various acts of impiety. On the whole it seems at least possible that the Bardiya who rebelled from Cambyses was the real Bardiya and not an imposter, and that the death of Cambyses, so unexpected and so convenient for Darius, was in fact murder rather than suicide. The year of hard fighting which followed the death of Bardiya scarcely suggests that the provinces were willing to accept Darius as the legitimate successor to the Persian throne. Certainly Babylon refused to do so. As soon as news of Bardiya's assassination reached the city, it rose in rebellion (October 3rd, 522) under Nebuchadnezzar III, son of Nabonidus—or rather, if we believe Darius, under Nidintu-Bel son of Ainaira pretending to be Nebuchadnezzar son of Nabonidus. The Babylonians stationed their army along the Tigris, which they considered could not be forded, but Darius floated his army across on inflated skins and defeated them in open battle. The Persians marched on towards Babylon, and were met by Nebuchadnezzar with the remainder of his army at a town called Zazana on the banks of the Euphrates. The Babylonian forces were driven into the water, and their king fled to his capital, where Darius caught and killed him. By the end of December 522 Babylon's short-lived independence was at an end.

The months that followed were busy ones for Darius. Rebellion had broken out all over his empire, and there is little doubt that if the rebels had worked together they could easily have dealt with the scanty forces which he had at his command. But no unified action was attempted, and Darius was able to deal with each rebel separately. By September 521 most of the eastern provinces were in his hands, but just when final victory seemed to be in sight news reached him of another revolt in Babylonia. Its leader again claimed to be Nebuchadnezzar son of Nabonidus, and though his real identity is unknown, he may have been, as Darius claimed, an Armenian called Arkha son of Haldita. The rebellion began in the obscure village of Dubala, somewhere in southern Babylonia, and quickly spread to the cities of the area. By the end of September 521 Babylon had been occupied and the rebel proclaimed himself king. Darius cannot have considered the situation critical, for instead of intervening in person he dispatched an army under his general Intaphernes and this force quickly suppressed the revolt. Before the end of November Nebuchadnezzar IV and his principal followers were impaled, the royal tombs of the city were plundered and its defensive walls were at least partially destroyed. Nothing more is heard of the satrap Gobyras. Presumably he had been killed in the revolt, and Hystanes was appointed governor in his place.

Darius's primary aim once he had achieved peace throughout his dominions was to make sure that such unrest could never happen again. The system of satrapies was extended, and though national feelings were largely respected a much closer watch was kept on the provinces than in the reigns of Cyrus and Cambyses. At the same time a uniform system of law was imposed on the entire empire, and gradually the number of Persians in legal and administrative posts increased. A carefully maintained road system was created joining the principal cities, and though this was intended primarily for the use of the king's servants it served also to facilitate trade and the rapid movement of armed forces. Of the campaigns of Darius, which included expeditions to Egypt, India and Scythia and culminated in the great invasion of Greece and the Battle of Marathon, there is no space to speak here. In Babylon, trade and commerce continued unimpaired by the recent disturbances. However, rapidly rising prices and increased government interference show that without strong anti-inflationary measures the economy was liable to collapse at any minute. Doubtless the satrap Hystanes levied and led his satrapal contingents to the Great King's wars, and during the winter Darius probably spent some of his time in the northern extension of Nebuchadnezzar's palace. During his absence on campaigns he had by Persian law to appoint a successor. At first his eldest son Artobazanes held this office, but later he was supplanted by a younger son Xerxes, and Darius followed the example of Cyrus by making his son his personal representative in Babylonia. Between 498 and 496 a new palace was built to the west of Nebuchadnezzar's southern citadel and Xerxes was installed in it. The principal feature was an *appa danna* or hall of pillars with porticoes in front and on either side flanked by square towers. The pavements of the palace were coloured in red and the column-bases were of black limestone, while decoration was by means of brilliantly coloured glazed bricks like those which Nebuchadnezzar had used. Many of the figures were those of animals, but the face of a woman in white enamel was discovered, and it is easy to see that this is the palace described by Ctesias as the work of Semiramis. In it Xerxes conducted the routine business of Babylonia, and from it in 486 B.C. he issued a decree that fresh taxes were to be levied to pay for a second expedition against the Greeks. Soon after, in November 486, Darius died, and Babylonia loyally accepted as king the prince who had lived among them for a dozen years. Soon after his accession Xerxes paid a visit to Babylon, and what he found there must have aroused his suspicions, for on his return to his capital a series of repressive measures was directed against the city, and a change was ordered in the Great King's titulary. Since the conquest by Cyrus Persian kings had been known as "King of Babylon", but now a new title "King of Persia and Media" was prefixed to it to emphasize the city's subordinate position. There were already rebellious elements in Babylon and these measures served only to inflame them. The city rose in revolt and its satrap Zopyrus was killed. First Belshimmani proclaimed himself king of Babylon (August 482), and he was followed in September by Shamasheriba. Soon after, the Persian army arrived under the command of Megabyzus and the Babylonian revolt was quickly crushed. The walls of the city were demolished, its temples, including the great sanctuary of Marduk, were destroyed, and the gold statue of Marduk himself was melted down. In this way Xerxes hoped to make it certain that no future rebel could take the hands of Marduk and thus legitimize his rule. The satrapy of Babylonia was abolished and incorporated with Assyria, while the lands across the river were formed into a separate and independent satrapy. Babylon was heavily taxed and the great estates of the rich merchants were taken from their owners and given to Persians. Xerxes himself no longer used the title "King of Babylon", and the use of the name "Babylonian" was officially forbidden. As far as the Great King was concerned Babylon had ceased to exist.

The story of Xerxes' campaign against the Greeks and of the battles of Thermopylae, Salamis, Plataea and Mycale again has no place in this narrative. Embittered by his defeat, Xerxes retired to his capital cities and for the remainder of his life

a. Man riding ox   b. Musician (Chicago)

FIG. 18   Clay reliefs

c. Musician   d. Carpenter at work (Louvre)

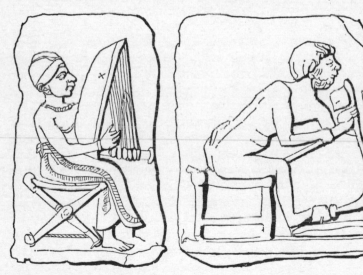

concentrated on building and matters of religion. After his assassination in 465 B.C. he was succeeded by his younger son Artaxerxes, who seems to have been more lenient towards Babylon. By 462 the priests of Marduk had had their lands restored and were re-installed in the remains of their temple, and about the same time a stele was dedicated to Ishtar of Babylon. But the effects of the punishment inflicted by Xerxes were still being felt, and information collected by Herodotus when he visited Mesopotamia about 450 shows how great a burden the city had to support. An annual contribution of about thirty tons of silver was exacted, by far the highest of any province in the empire, and besides this the country had to provide supplies for the Persian army and court for four months out of every year. Even the upkeep of the satrapal court was a considerable burden, for Tritantaechmes, the satrap at the time, made a daily collection to cover his expenses, and this was sufficient to fill a thirteen-gallon jar with silver. He also expected free fodder for his war-horses, his eight hundred stallions and his sixteen thousand mares, and he owned so many dogs that four large villages were exempted from taxation on condition that they fed and looked after them. The result of all this was a constant draining of Babylonian resources with very little return. So much silver was required by the Persians that there was a scarcity of coined money and business had increasingly to be conducted on credit. Prices, already high, began to soar in a quickening spiral of inflation, and many families found that the only method of survival was to sell their daughters into prostitution. To add to their misery, every year the Great King required five hundred Babylonian boys to be made eunuchs. In a situation like this, made more intolerable by the rapid increase in the number of Persians in legal and administrative positions, the province must have been ready for rebellion at any minute, but throughout his long reign Artaxerxes was strong enough to ensure that no revolt took place. After his death in 424 a period of assassination and palace intrigue was ended in 423 when Ochus, the son of Artaxerxes and a Babylonian concubine, was recognized in Babylonia as Darius II. After a tumultuous reception in Babylon, Darius moved on to Susa and the kingship, but soon the city had another royal governor to maintain, for Darius followed the custom of his ancestors in appointing his eldest son Arsaces as

official successor with his residence in Babylonia. Under his
watchful eye the province remained quiet until in 404 Darius
became ill and retired to his mother's house in Babylon, where
he died.

Arsaces, who succeeded as Artaxerxes II, soon had to deal
with trouble from his discontented younger brother Cyrus, the
satrap of Asia Minor. Backed by a force of thirteen thousand
Greek mercenaries, Cyrus in 401 set off down the Euphrates
to contest the throne. There was little opposition until they
reached the village of Cunaxa, only sixty miles from Babylon.
There a battle took place which Cyrus might well have won
had he not rashly exposed himself and been killed. The news
of the defeat brought Parysatis, the mother of both Artaxerxes
and Cyrus, hurrying to Babylon. A native Babylonian herself,
she had always supported her younger son, and now she was
quick to torture and kill those who had struck him down. The
man who at Artaxerxes' order had cut his head off was flayed
alive and crucified. At the same time the generals of the Greek
mercenaries who had supported Cyrus were treacherously
captured by Artaxerxes' followers and sent to Babylon for
punishment. Despite the efforts of Parysatis to save the supporters of her favourite son they were executed and buried in
the city. The story of the march by which Xenophon and the
ten thousand remaining Greek mercenaries eventually reached
the Black Sea belongs to the history of Greece rather than that
of Babylonia.

The evil work of Parysatis was by no means finished. The
following year she poisoned Artaxerxes' wife in Susa, and as
a result was banished for a time to Babylon. But apart from this
the city played little part in the politics of the time. The Persian
king still used it as a winter residence, for he was staying there
in 395 when he was visited by the Athenian admiral Conon who
was seeking the help of Persian gold for his struggle against
Sparta. This struggle eventually ended with both sides ex-
hausted and a peace imposed by the Persian king, but at the
moment when Artaxerxes seemed to have gained by gold what
his predecessors could not achieve by force his empire was
shattered by a rebellion of all the lands west of the Euphrates.
By a series of accidents the revolt was crushed, and when
Artaxerxes was killed in 358 and succeeded by his son Artaxerxes III the throne came into the hands of a bloodthirsty but

capable man who might well have renewed the glories of
Persia. The rebellious satraps were firmly dealt with and the
empire was completely restored, but in November 338 the king
was poisoned and replaced by his son Arses, a man quite incapable of dealing with the emergency which quickly arose. Just
before this, Athens and the new power of Macedonia had been
vying for Persian support, but in the same year as Artaxerxes
was assassinated Philip of Macedonia had succeeded in crushing
all Greek resistance to his power. Seeing his opportunity
in the Great King's death, Philip prepared to lead a crusade
against the Persian Empire.

In June 336 Arses, too, was poisoned, and succeeded by
Darius III. Then in July of the same year, and possibly with
Persian prompting, Philip was stabbed to death. He was succeeded by his son Alexander, a young man who was destined
to end the Persian Empire and change the course of world
history. Details of Alexander's campaigns can be found in many
text-books and do not concern the historian of Babylon until
after the conquest of western Asia and Egypt, when in the summer of 331 he advanced with seven thousand cavalry and thirty
thousand infantry to the Euphrates at Thapsacus and prepared
to cross into Mesopotamia. Two pontoon bridges had been prepared for him, although their construction had been hindered by
the cavalry of Mazaeus, satrap of Babylonia, and when Mazaeus
retired Alexander's forces crossed without opposition. Their
obvious course would have been to follow the river down to
Babylon, and Darius in expectation of this had stationed his
army beyond the upper Tigris, from where he could easily
move in and cut Alexander's supply-lines. But the Greek king,
anticipating this move, struck straight across towards the Tigris
through country where food and water were more easily
obtainable than in the burning plains of the south, and crossed
the river above Nineveh without any sign of Persian interference. Darius, confident in his strength, held back to await
a decisive battle, but when it came the result was not at all
what he expected. The ground he had chosen for the battle was
on the carefully levelled plain of Gaugamela, some sixty miles
from his base at Arbela. Here he hoped that his chariots would
be able to deal with the Macedonian phalanx, but when the
armies met on October 1st, 331, his plan proved a complete
failure. Despite gallant work by Mazaeus on the Persian right

Darius was put to flight, the battle was lost and the Persian
Empire was at an end.

From Gaugamela Alexander's route led rapidly southward
to Arbela, and then on across the Lower Zab and the Diyala
towards Babylon. As he approached the city, he was met by
a great crowd of its citizens bringing gifts and promising their
allegiance. The satrap Mazaeus, who considered that by his
desertion at Gaugamela Darius had forfeited all claim to the
loyalty of his servants, surrendered the city and the province,
and was rewarded by the renewal of his governorship. Bago-
phanes, who commanded the Persian garrison in the city,
handed over the treasures which he had been left to guard.
Amid great rejoicing Alexander ordered the restoration of the
temples destroyed by Xerxes, especially the great shrine of
Marduk, and himself took the hands of Marduk as king of
Babylon. The city's great days seemed to have returned, although the real power—control of the army and of finance—
was in the hands of Macedonians.

Alexander lingered for a month in Babylon before beginning
his march to Susa and the east. Babylonia did not see him again
until 324, by which time his conquests had been extended to
Bactria and India and had been halted only by the refusal
of his soldiers to go further. In the spring of that year he came
down to Opis to supervise the demobilization of Macedonian
veterans and found that he had to deal with the beginnings of
a mutiny. When he had succeeded in pacifying his troops he
returned to Ecbatana, where his greatest friend Hephaestion
died. Among the honours paid to him was that of a funeral
pyre in Babylon, and this was prepared at a cost of ten thousand
talents. To form a platform for this great construction part of
the city-wall was demolished and the rubble was piled up and
levelled in a prominent position east of the royal palace. There
Koldewey found it, its upper surface scorched and reddened by
the heat of the fire.

In the spring of 323, Alexander returned to Babylon. As he
approached the city he was met by a group of anxious priests
maintaining that the omens were against his entry. In reality
they hoped to conceal the fact that they had not obeyed his
orders to rebuild the temple of Marduk, but Alexander was not
deceived. Despite their protestations he entered the city and
soon work on the temple was begun in earnest. By this time the

15

tower of Etemenanki had completely collapsed, and the first
task was the removal of a vast amount of rubble. It was
estimated that it would take ten thousand workmen two months
to do this, and when work began the debris was deposited not
far from the site of Hephaestion's pyre, where again it was discovered by Koldewey. At the same time Alexander was planning even greater military exploits. His first interest was in the
circumnavigation of Arabia, which would open up the sea
routes to Egypt and India. For this purpose ships had been
built in Phoenicia and moved overland in sections to the
Euphrates, where they were fitted together and sailed down
river to Babylon. Plans were drawn up for an enormous
harbour and dockyards in the city, and there is no doubt that
if Alexander had lived Babylon would once more have become
one of the great cities of the world. But it was not to be. On
June 2nd, a few days before the Arabian expedition was due
to leave, Alexander began to feel feverish and had his quarters
transferred from the palace to a garden-house across the river
where the air was cooler. He had increasing difficulty in carrying out his official duties, but insisted that the expedition should
go on. By June 10th his condition was critical and he was
moved back to the palace. When his generals came to his bed-
side he knew them, but could not speak. For two days he lay
in a high fever, but on the 12th, when his soldiers burst in sus-
pecting that he was already dead, he was able to move his head
and hand a little to show that he knew them. That night some
of his generals went to the shrine of the healing god Ea in
Esagila to ask if Alexander should be brought there to be cured,
but were told that it was better to leave him in the palace.
On June 13th, 323, in the heat of a Babylonian evening,
Alexander died at the age of thirty-two.

The death of the great king caused consternation throughout
the empire. Immediately the question of a successor arose.
Alexander had no children, but his wife Roxane was pregnant,
and the Macedonian nobles who were with Alexander when he
died would have been content to wait for the birth of this child.
But the common soldiers of Alexander's army were unwilling
to face the prospect of a long regency and proposed Alexander's
half-brother, a youth of weak mind whose name was Arrhi-
daeus. Eventually a compromise was reached by which the two
were to rule jointly, and the Macedonians settled down to

working out the disposal of the empire. From the beginning Perdiccas took a leading part, and it was soon clear that he intended to retain effective control in Babylon. As commander-in-chief of the armed forces in Asia, he was in an excellent position to do this, and when satrapies were allocated to Alexander's commanders he made sure that Babylon was given to Archon of Pella, a man of no particular ability. Elsewhere in the empire there were many who were prepared to dispute Perdiccas' claim to absolute authority, and for many years there was almost continuous fighting before any sort of settlement was reached. The signal for this fighting to begin was a dispute over the funeral of Alexander, for instead of being taken to Macedonia his body was removed to Egypt by Ptolemy, the far-sighted general who had been given command of that province. This was too much for Perdiccas, and he made preparations for war. Early in 321 Archon, the satrap of Babylon, went over to the opposition, and Perdiccas, who was in Cilicia at the time, sent an officer called Docimus to replace him. Archon tried to retain his hold on the province by force, but Docimus had the support of the local population and Archon was defeated and killed. Soon after, Perdiccas led his army into Egypt against Ptolemy, but after failing to cross the Nile he was murdered by his mutinous army. Prominent among the mutineers was an officer called Seleucus who had served with Alexander since he first crossed into Asia and had reached a high position on Alexander's staff during his campaigns in India. Transferred to Perdiccas' service in the settlement of 323, he now received his reward for the murder of his leader, for in the arrangements which followed the conclusion of a truce he was appointed satrap of Babylon. Docimus was driven out and Seleucus took up residence in his capital.

This settlement could only be temporary. A new struggle for power was beginning among Alexander's generals, and Seleucus was determined that, precarious as his position might be, he was going to retain his hold on it. Little is known of his administration of his province, but it is clear that his object was to win the goodwill of his people so that he could be certain of their support in time of danger. The settlement of 321 had left Antigonus and Antipater as the two strongest men in the empire, and the death of Antipater in 319 led to a new crisis. Antipater had appointed Polyperchon as his successor, but this

was opposed by Antigonus. Naturally Eumenes, a former
lieutenant of Perdiccas and an inveterate enemy of Antigonus,
gave his support to Polyperchon and attempted to win Asia
for him. In 318 he invaded Babylonia and summoned Seleucus
to the aid of the legal authority. This placed the Babylonian
satrap in an awkward position, for although he protested his
loyalty, Eumenes had been declared an outlaw after the death
of Perdiccas, and Antigonus was commander-in-chief in Asia.
Finally Seleucus refused to treat with a rebel, and Eumenes
took Babylon by force (October 318). A counter-attack by
Seleucus was driven off, and Eumenes set out for further conquests in Media.

Early in 317 Antigonus arrived in northern Babylonia and
summoned Seleucus to his presence. Unwilling to leave the
garrison of Eumenes in his rear, Seleucus tried a direct assault on
the Babylonian citadel, but failed to capture it. A second attack,
which involved the alteration of the course of the Euphrates, was
successful and Seleucus then joined Antigonus in a campaign
against Susa. There Eumenes was captured and executed.

The success of Seleucus gave Babylon a short period of peace,
and work was started once more on Alexander's grandiose
scheme for the clearing and rebuilding of Esagila. But this did
not last long. Antigonus was determined to leave no prospective
opposition in the east, and in 316 he turned to Babylon. A
visit to the city must have roused his suspicions, for he demanded that Seleucus should render an account of his administration. The governor answered that he was accountable to
no one for a satrapy awarded to him by the Macedonians
for his services in the army of Alexander. The reply of Antigonus
was to blockade Seleucus in his palace, but when the building
was carried by assault the satrap had slipped out and headed
with all speed for refuge in Egypt. In his anger Antigonus
pillaged the country, set fire to the town and made Peithon son
of Agenor governor of Babylonia. A policy of continuous
plundering was followed by Peithon's troops. The fighting in
Babylon had made many of its houses uninhabitable and the
people were forced to move out into the open fields, where they
suffered great distress. The price of corn was high, and there is
no doubt that the support which Seleucus had won by his good
administration was vastly increased by the violent behaviour
of Antigonus's troops.

In Egypt, Seleucus was quick to persuade the other Macedonian leaders of their danger. Early in 315 an ultimatum was delivered to Antigonus, and among its demands was one that Seleucus be restored to Babylon. When the ultimatum was scornfully rejected preparations were made for war. At first fortune seemed to be against Ptolemy and his supporter Seleucus. The Egyptians were driven from Syria and Antigonus left a garrison there under his son Demetrius. Elsewhere Antigonus was not so successful, and in 312 Ptolemy entered Syria again and recaptured Gaza. Although he held it only for a short time, his victory was decisive enough to give Seleucus the chance he was waiting for, and with eight hundred infantry and two hundred cavalry he set out to regain Babylon. His personal popularity now began to show results, for reinforcements came over to him as he marched, and his former subjects flocked to greet him. Peithon, Antigonus's satrap, had been killed at Gaza, but his garrison commander Diphilus retired to the citadel and prepared to defend himself. With no great difficulty the stronghold was stormed and Seleucus installed himself in Babylon once more. Soon he was strong enough to ambush a force sent by Nicanor, the satrap of Media and a supporter of Antigonus, and to move on against Media and Susiana. A new Babylonian conquest of the east had begun.

But in the absence of Seleucus there was to be no peace for Babylon. While he was away, Antigonus sent his son Demetrius to attack the city, and once again it was captured and pillaged. Demetrius then withdrew, possibly seeing that a long campaign rather than a raid would be necessary to subdue the country, and Babylon came into the hands of Seleucus once more. Perhaps it was on his son's advice that Antigonus in 311 came to terms with his adversaries. At any rate it is notable that Seleucus was excluded from the truce, and that Antigonus retained his claim to Babylon. Shortly after it was made he descended on the province. Babylon was ravaged in 310 and again in 309, but despite everything Seleucus was unconquered. Finally in 307 Antigonus was forced by events in the west to come to terms.

Now at last Seleucus had a period of peace in which to consolidate his rule. At some time between 307 and 305 he assumed the title of king. One of his most immediate problems was the rehousing of the people of Babylon, and in doing so he made a

decision which proved fateful for the city. In its long history
it had survived many destructions and risen again to a position
of eminence and affluence, but its powers of recovery lay in its
general situation as a centre of trade routes rather than in any
paticular virtue of the site itself. Any town in the area was bound
to be prosperous. When Seleucus looked round for a site on
which to rebuild Babylon, several factors influenced his decision.
First, he knew from experience how expensive in money and
labour the removal of vast piles of rubble could be. Second, and
more important, he intended to revive Alexander's schemes for
sea-trade with India, and for this purpose the Tigris was much
more suitable than the sluggish Euphrates. So he chose for
his site a position on the Tigris some forty miles north of Babylon and began to build there a city which he named Seleuceia
after himself. The birth of Seleuceia meant the final elimination
of Babylon. Seleucus by an act of kindness achieved what many
conquerers had failed to do.

From 308 onwards Seleucus was also engaged in campaigns
in the eastern satrapies, and gradually he built up an empire
which reached as far as India. In the west, the struggle for
Alexander's dominion continued, and eventually in 303 the
opponents of Antigonus, led by Cassander and Lysimachus,
persuaded Ptolemy and Seleucus to join them. In 302 Seleucus
moved towards Asia Minor for a final battle while Lysinachus
crossed from Europe with the same purpose. Antigonus in a
last attempt to keep the two armies apart sent a small force to
occupy Babylon behind Seleucus' back and succeeded in holding the city during the winter of 302–301. But Seleucus was
not to be diverted. In the spring of 301 he joined forces with
Lysimachus, and at Ipsus in Phrygia the decisive battle was
fought. Antigonus was defeated and killed.

After the battle Lysimachus and Seleucus divided the empire.
The eastern half was awarded to Seleucus, and the history of
Babylonia thereafter was the history of the Seleucid Empire.
Of the city of Babylon, which has been our primary concern
throughout this narrative, there is little more to say. The
foundation of Seleuceia had left it little more than a depopu-
lated ruin, and many buildings in the new city were built from
the rubble of the old. In 275 Antiochus I, the son and successor
of Seleucus, gave orders for the remaining civil population
of Babylon to be removed to Seleuceia and commandeered land

and cattle which had been distributed to the people five years earlier. At the same time however he continued the building of Marduk's temple Esagila, perhaps because Alexander had encouraged the idea of honouring the gods of all nations, perhaps because he was interested in the revival of Babylonian history and literature. Certainly Berossus, a priest of Marduk, dedicated to him a work written in Greek on Babylonian history which was written during his reign. Another suggestion is that Antiochus favoured Babylonian religion as a bulwark against Zoroastrianism, the creed of Persian nationalism. At any rate Antiochus was proud of his work in Babylon, for among his titles he used "King of Babylon" and "Restorer of Esagila".

Seleucid policy in Babylon seems to have veered from time to time. The land which had in 275 been removed from the citizens of Babylon was handed back again in the reign of Antiochus II (261–247) and finally in 237 B.C. it was given as an eternal holding to the Babylonian temple. Here, in the midst of desolation, the priests of Marduk were presumably carrying out their sacred duties and pursuing their studies in their ancestral ways. The same was true in other temples throughout the land, and the revival of cuneiform literature is a feature of the period. Older documents were frequently copied and studied, and there was a special interest in astronomy. By the second century Babylonian astronomers were translating their native material into Greek, and western astronomy and astrology owe much to Babylonian scholars of this period.

With the accession of Antiochus IV (175–163) a new period of Babylonian prosperity began. Antiochus, like his predecessors, based his policy on the Hellenizing of Asia, and one of his Greek colonies was placed in Babylon. A local inscription hails him as founder of the city and saviour of Asia. The new city flourished for a time and documents have been discovered dealing with trade, taxes and royal regulations. The imported Greek population was provided with its festivals and amusements, and a theatre and gymnasium of sun-dried brick and rubble was constructed to house them, but despite these efforts Antiochus failed to make any great changes in the inhabitants' way of life. Babylonian language and writing survived, and business was still conducted as it had been before. The temple continued to play a leading part in the life of the city, and could not be superseded by the pleasures of the gymnasium or the theatre.

With the death of Antiochus IV in Persia in 164 Babylon entered another period of warfare. Timarchus of Miletus, who had been left in charge of the eastern provinces, took advantage of the confusion to set himself up as king of Babylon, but in 160 he was defeated and killed by Demetrius I (162–150). It was during his reign and that of his successors Alexander (150–145) and Demetrius II (145–139) that the real menace appeared. A hundred years before, the Parthians, a semi-nomadic tribe of Indo-European origin, had settled in northern Persia and begun a period of steady expansion at the expense of the Seleucid Empire. Between 153· and 140 their king Mithridates I forcibly annexed many of the eastern provinces, including Babylon in July 141. Early the following year the city was recovered by Demetrius II, but a year later it was captured once more by the Parthians. In 136 Mithridates died and the Seleucid king Antiochus VII began a partial recovery of the lost provinces. He was ruler of Babylon in 130, but in 129 he was routed and killed by Phraates II of Parthia. On his death Hyspaorsines, the governor of the province of Characene along the Persian Gulf, broke away, and by 127 he was calling himself King of Babylon and minting his own coins. During his reign the religious functions of Esagila were still maintained. But soon the Parthians returned and destroyed Babylon yet again. The market-place and some of the temples were set on fire, the few remaining parts of the defences were pulled down, and many of the inhabitants were deported to Media as slaves. Himerus, the Parthian in charge of operations, even seems to have set himself up as king of Babylon for a time, but in 122 he was defeated by Mithridates II of Parthia and Babylon was recovered.

By this time not much was left of it. The priests continued their duties in the ruins of Esagila, and just south of the temple traces of Parthian buildings have been discovered which show that some sort of civic life still existed. In fact the city seems still to have been important enough to have its own city-governor subordinate to the governor of the province. Shortly after the beginning of the Christian era Babylon saw a final short period of prosperity with the foundation (about A.D. 24) of a colony there by merchants from the great Syrian caravan city of Palmyra. Half a century later, however, the main Palmyrene colony was moved to the new Parthian town of Vologesia, across the Tigris from Seleuceia. With the departure of the merchants, Babylon was left to its fate. Shortly afterwards the Latin author Pliny stated that the temple of Marduk was still standing, but that in every other respect the place had become a desert. In A.D. 116 the Roman emperor Trajan wintered in the city during his campaign against the Parthians. Attracted to it by its widespread fame, he found nothing but mounds and stones and ruins. All he could do was to offer a sacrifice in the remains of the room where Alexander had died. Perhaps the final word on Babylon was written by the Greek satirist Lucian in the second half of the second century A.D., in a dialogue on the vanity of human hopes and endeavours. "Nineveh," he wrote, "has already perished, and not a trace of it now remains. As for Babylon, the city of the magnificent towers and the great circuit-wall, soon it too will be like Nineveh, and men will look for it in vain." His words were not quite true. Something of Babylon remained alive in the minds of men, although it is only today that its history has been rediscovered.

APPENDICES

A NOTE ON CHRONOLOGY

One of the greatest difficulties in compiling the history of a remote period is the establishment of a system of chronology. Often it is easy enough to find out the order in which events took place; what is much more difficult is to pin the period down, as it were, by relating it accurately to the rest of world history. To do this an absolute chronological system, based on some fixed point in time, is the prime necessity. For modern history a fixed point is supplied by the birth of Christ, and events are accurately arranged by the number of years before or after this took place. The fact that Christ was not in reality born in the year conventionally assigned to his birth makes no difference at all to its usefulness as a chronological landmark. It is the existence of a fixed point rather than its accuracy that is important.

Conventional fixed points are by no means lacking in ancient history. The foundation of Rome provided one for the Romans, and the holding of the first Olympic Games was similarly used by the Greeks. Often it requires only simple arithmetic to transfer dates based on these systems to their appropriate places in our own chronological framework. But in the ancient Near East no such fixed point was used. This does not mean that the Assyrians and Babylonians were unaware of the importance of accurate chronology. Lists of rulers and the years of their reigns were carefully compiled and preserved, and sometimes chronicles were composed which showed synchronisms between rulers of different states. The difficulty is to transfer these records to our own system, and this entails the discovery of an event which can be fixed in terms of modern chronology. Fortunately this is a relatively easy matter, at least for the latter part of Assyrian history. From the earliest period the Assyrians named their years after an annually appointed official called a *limmu*, and accurate lists of these officials were compiled, often including the chief event of each year as well as the *limmu's* name. One of these entries records that in the year named after Pursagale, governor of Gozana, there was an eclipse of the sun, and this has been astronomically fixed as having taken place on June 15th, 763 B.C. From this point the *limmu*-lists take us back to the eleventh century B.C. Among those who served as *limmu* were the kings of Assyria, and as they normally held office in the first or second year of their reigns it is a relatively simple matter, subject to no great

margin of error, to transform the *limmu*-lists into lists of kings and
their reigns. For the period before the eleventh century no *limmu*-
lists have been preserved, but there are lists of kings which are
demonstrably based on earlier *limmu*-lists. These king-lists carry the
record back to about 1700 B.C. before damage and deficiencies make
them unreliable.

For the chronology of Babylon no astronomically fixed point has
been discovered, but there are king-lists which cover the entire
period from the First Dynasty to the death of Kandalanu in 626.
As well as these there are the chronicles, mentioned above, which
relate the reigns of Babylonian kings to those of contemporary
Assyrian monarchs. As a result of these synchronisms it is possible
to establish the reigns of Babylonian kings as far back as about 1350
with a fair degree of accuracy, the maximum margin of error being
about fifty years either way. Before 1350 figures for reigns are lacking
until the end of the First Dynasty, but for this and several earlier
dynasties dating material is more abundant. This is due to the unique
method of dating used in the earlier period in southern Mesopotamia.

From the beginning of the Kassite period the Babylonians dated
by regnal years. That is, events were recorded as having taken
place in the *x*th year of king So-and-so. When a king died the remainder of the year in which he died was known as "the accession-
year" of his successor, and the following year became his successor's
"first year". Before the Kassite period all years had names. At first
they were named after the most prominent event of the year—"the
year in which the king conquered Ur", or something of that sort.
This system had very severe drawbacks. Sometimes the only important event was a defeat or some other happening which the state
had no desire to commemorate. In this case the year could be named
after some comparatively unimportant occasion such as the dedication of a statue to a god, or it could simply be called "the year
following the year in which the king conquered Ur", or whatever
the last important event had been. Even greater difficulty was
caused by the fact that until an important event took place the year
would have no name at all. Soon this was overcome by naming each
year at its beginning by the most important event of the *previous*
year. Thus if a king conquered Ur in his eighth year his ninth would
officially be "the year in which the king conquered Ur". This was
palpably untrue but provided a reasonable basis for chronology as
well as giving a great deal of information to later historians. Lists
of these "date-formulae" were compiled and these, together with
the king lists, mean that the sequence of events from the rise of the
Third Dynasty of Ur to the fall of the First Dynasty of Babylon is
fairly well established. But from this point until the resumption of
figures for reigns about 1350 B.C. there is a gap, and it is the length
of this gap which provides the main difficulty in Babylonian
chronology.

Various methods of bridging the gap have been attempted. One
of the most important has been the search for an astronomically

fixed point by the use of records of the movements of the planet Venus during the reign of the Babylonian king Ammizaduga. Unfortunately the evidence yields several possible dates for the end of the Babylonian First Dynasty. Of these the most probable are 1651, 1595, 1587 and 1531. Other evidence must therefore be sought in an attempt to confirm one of these dates. The Assyrian king-list, as has been mentioned above, gives fairly reliable dates as far back as about 1700 B.C., and this list tends to support 1531 as the date for the end of the Babylonian Dynasty. On the other hand the Babylonian lists lend support to the theory that it ended in 1595 (or 1587—for practical purposes it is impossible to distinguish between these two dates; it is usual to take 1595 as the end of the dynasty, but arguments for it could equally well be applied to 1587), and it can also be maintained that the Assyrian list supports this date. Archaeological evidence from Mesopotamia and the surrounding areas has been used to support all three dates as well as several others which ignore the Venus-tablets. All that can be said is that at present the "medium" chronology, with the First Dynasty ending in 1595, is the most probable on the evidence available. All dates which are based on this evidence must however be regarded as approximations.

The period earlier than the Third Dynasty of Ur is for dating purposes much more poorly documented. The primary evidence is the Sumerian king-list, of which something has already been said in Chapter 1. Archaeological evidence to supplement the king-list is fragmentary, and this is reflected in the fragmentary nature of the narrative in this book. But it is reasonably certain that the beginning of writing in Mesopotamia took place about 3500 B.C. and that the earliest kings mentioned in inscriptions ruled about 2700 B.C. From then until the Third Dynasty of Ur a combination of figures from the king-list and other documentary evidence, generation-counting and the study of the development of writing yields a chronology which seems approximately correct.

For the earliest periods of Mesopotamian history the most important method of dating is by radio-carbon testing. This is based on the fact that when organisms die their radio-activity runs down at a known rate, so that if specimens of organic matter are found in the course of an excavation it is possible by accurate measurement of the remaining radio-active carbon to estimate the length of time since death. There are still many limitations to this method, the chief ones being the possibility of contamination by contact with other materials either in the ground or while the specimen is being collected, and an inherent element of uncertainty, due to the random disintegration of atoms, which means that only a proportion of results can yield an approximately correct answer. Yet despite these drawbacks the agreement of several tests from the same site can go a long way towards yielding an absolute date for that site, and it is hoped that with further research the method may become still more accurate.

CHRONOLOGICAL TABLES

(a) Early sites and cultures of Mesopotamia

N. MESOPOTAMIA		S. MESOPOTAMIA
c. 10,000	Zarzi, Palegawra	
9000	Karim Shahir	
7000	Jarmo	
5000	Hassuna	
4750	Samarra	
4500	Tell Halaf	
4200		Eridu
4000		Hajji Muhammad
3900		Al 'Ubaid
3600		Uruk
3400		Protoliterate { Later Uruk
3300		Jemdet Nasr
3000		Early Dynastic I
2800		Early Dynastic II
2600		Early Dynastic III
2340		Dynasty of Akkad

N.B. There is a good deal of dispute about the absolute dating of the earliest periods. Jarmo, for instance, may be as low as *c.* 5000 B.C.

(d) Kings of Babylon and Assyria *c.* 1700–539 B.C.

1224–1219 Adadshumiddin
1218–1189 Adadshumusur
1188–1174 Melishikhu
1173–1161 Mardukapaliddina
1160 Zababashumiddina
1159–1157 Enlilnadinahhe

The Isin (4th) Dynasty
1156–1139 Mardukkabitahheshu
1138–1131 Ittimardukbalatu
1130–1125 Ninurtanadinshumi
1124–1103 Nebuchadnezzar I
1102–1099 Enlilnadinapli
1098–1081 Mardukuadinahhe
1080–1068 Mardukshappikzeri
1067–1046 Adadapaliddina
1045 Marduk ahhe-eriba ?
1044–1033 Marduk - ?
1032–1025 Nabushumilibur

The Sealand (5th) Dynasty
1024–1007 Simmashihu
1007 Eamukinshumi
1006–1004 Kashunadinahhe

The Bazi (6th) Dynasty
1003–987 Eulmashshakinshumi
986–987 Ninurtakudurusur II
984 Shiriqtushuqamuna

1207–1204 Ashurnadinapli
1203–1198 Ashurnirari III
1197–1193 Enlilkudurusur
1192–1180 Ninurta-apalekur
1179–1135 Ashurdan I

1134 Ninurtatukultiashur
1134 Mutakkilnusku
1133–1115 Ashurreshishi
1114–1076 Tiglathpileser I
1075–1074 Asharidapalekur
1073–1056 Ashurbelkala
1055–1054 Eriba-Adad II
1053–1050 Shamshiadad IV
1049–1031 Ashurnasirpal I
1030–1019 Shalmaneser II

1018–1013 Ashurnirari IV
1012–972 Ashurrabi

(e) Persian and Greek rulers of Babylon

(i) Persian kings

539–530	Cyrus
529–522	Cambyses
521–486	Darius I
485–465	Xerxes I
464–424	Artaxerxes I
424	Xerxes II
423–404	Darius II
403–359	Artaxerxes II
358–338	Artaxerxes III
337–336	Arses
335–331	Darius III

(ii) Greek King

331–323	Alexander the Great

(iii) Greek governors

323–321	Archon
321	Docimus
321–318	Seleucus
318–317	Eumenes
317–316	Seleucus
316–312	Peithon

(iv) Seleucid rulers

312–280	Seleucus I
280–261	Antiochus I
261–247	Antiochus II
247–226	Seleucus II
226–223	Seleucus III
223–187	Antiochus III
187–175	Seleucus IV
175–163	Antiochus IV
163–162	Antiochus V
162–150	Demetrius I
150–145	Alexander
145–139	Demetrius II
139–129	Antiochus VII

TIME CHART

MESOPOTAMIA		ELSEWHERE	
B.C.		B.C.	
10,000	End of Old Stone Age in Northern Mesopotamia	10,000	End of Old Stone Age in Palestine
9000– 7000	Beginnings of cultivation in Northern Mesopotamia		
7000– 5000	Earliest settled villages so far discovered in Northern Mesopotamia	7000	Jericho; earliest town settlement so far discovered
4200	Earliest settlements so far discovered in Southern Mesopotamia	4500	First farming communities in Egypt
4000	Rise of city-states		
3500	Introduction of writing	3300	Introduction of writing to Egypt
		3100	Union of Upper and Lower Egypt; Egyptian First Dynasty
2700– 2330	Early Sumerian dynasties; Uruk, Ur, Kish, etc.	2650	Step Pyramid of Djoser
		2570	The Great Pyramid
2330– 2200	Dynasty of Akkad; Sargon and Naramsin		
2200– 2120	Gutian supremacy		
2120	Sumerian revival		
2113– 2005	Third Dynasty of Ur	2000	Beginning of Palace Period in Crete
2005– 1793	Rivalry of Isin and Larsa in Southern Mesopotamia	1900	Hittites enter Anatolia; first Greek-speaking peoples enter Greece
1894	Sumuabum founds First Dynasty of Babylon		
1792– 1750	Reign of Hammurabi; First Babylonian Supremacy	1800	Emergence of Assyria; Shamshiadad I.
1742	First invasion of Kassites	1725	Hyksos conquest of Egypt

1595	Hittite invasion; fall of First Dynasty of Babylon	1567	Expulsion of Hyksos
1595–1157	Kassite rule in Babylon		
		1450	Rise of Mitanni; alliance of Egypt-Mitanni
		1400	Destruction of Cretan palaces
		1379	Heresy of Akhenaten in Egypt; collapse of Egypt-Mitanni alliance
		1370	Fall of Mitanni; Hittite conquest of N. Syria
		1350	Re-emergence of Assyria
		1300	Exodus of Israelites from Egypt
		1300	Egyptian attempt on N. Syria; Battle of Kadesh
		1200	Fall of Hittite Empire; Dorian Invasion of Greece
1156–1100	Nationalist revival in Babylonia; Nebuchadnezzar I	1175	Decline of Egypt
1100–900	Period of Aramaean pressure	1080	Decline of Assyria under Aramaean pressure
		1000	Reigns of David and Solomon in Israel
		1000	Penetration of Medes and Persians into Iran
		930	Kingdoms of Israel and Judah formed
900–626	Period of Assyrian domination	900	Revival of Assyria
		722	Assyrian capture of Samaria; fall of Israel
		675	Rise of Medes in Iran
626–539	Second Babylonian Supremacy; Nabopolassar, Nebuchadnezzar II and Nabonidus	612	Destruction of Nineveh
		597	Fall of Jerusalem to Nebuchadnezzar
		586	Destruction of Jerusalem; fall of Judah
		550	Medes overthrown by Persians
539	Fall of Babylon to Cyrus of Persia		
539–331	Period of Persian domination	490	Battle of Marathon
		480	Battles of Thermopylae, Salamis and Plataea

331–323	Alexander the Great	336	Accession of Alexander the Great
323–312	Period of disputed succession		
312–130	Seleucid Empire in Babylonia		
130	Parthian period; decline and disappearance of Babylon	150	Rise of Parthia
		A.D.	
		116	Trajan's Parthian War

N.B. Many of the above dates are approximations.

SELECT BIBLIOGRAPHY

This Bibliography is intended to be a guide both for those who wish to make a more thorough investigation of Babylonian history and civilization and for those who would like a more general picture of the development of the ancient Middle East. In a subject such as Babylonian history many important books and articles are difficult for the general reader to obtain, and only a few of the most vital have been included in this list. Many of the works cited, however, have extended bibliographies which can be used for further study. The most up-to-date information and book-lists will be found in the new edition of *The Cambridge Ancient History*, Vols I–II, now in preparation.

GENERAL

Albright, W. F. *From the Stone Age to Christianity*, New York, 1957
Andrae, W. *Babylon. Die versunkene Weltstadt und ihr Ausgräber Robert Koldewey*, Berlin, 1952
Beek, M. A. *Atlas of Mesopotamia*, London, 1962
Burrows, M. *What mean these Stones?* New Haven, 1941
Cameron, G. G. *History of Early Iran*, Chicago, 1936
Chiera, M. *They wrote on Clay*, Chicago, 1959
Finegan, J. *Light from the Ancient Past*, London, 1959
King, L. W. *A History of Babylon*, London, 1915
Moscati, S. *Ancient Semitic Civilisations*, London, 1957
Moscati, S. *The Face of the Ancient Orient*, London, 1960
Moscati, S. *The Semites in Ancient History*, Cardiff, 1959
Pallis, S. A. *The Antiquity of Iraq*, Copenhagen, 1956
Parrot, A. *Archéologie Mésopotamienne*, I–II, Paris, 1946–53
Parrot, A. *Babylon and the Old Testament*, London, 1958
Pritchard, J. B. (ed.) *Ancient Near Eastern Texts Relating to the Old Testament*, Princeton, 1955

Saggs, H. W. F. *The Greatness that was Babylon*, London, 1962
Schmökel, H. *Geschichte des alten Vorderasien*, Leiden, 1957
Thomas, D. W. (ed.) *Documents from Old Testament Times*, London, 1958

CHAPTER I

Braidwood, R. J. and others, *Prehistoric Investigations in Iraqi Kurdistan*, Chicago, 1960
Childe, V. G. *New Light on the Most Ancient East*, London, 1952
Frankfort, H. *Before Philosophy*, Harmondsworth, 1949
Frankfort, H. *The Birth of Civilisation in the Near East*, New York, 1956
Gadd, C. J. "The Cities of Babylonia", *The Cambridge Ancient History*, new Edition, Vol. I, Chapter XIII
Jacobsen, T. "Early Political Development in Mesopotamia", *Zeitschrift fur Assyriologie*, N. F. 18 (1956), 91–146
Jacobsen, T. "Primitive Democracy in Ancient Mesopotamia", *Journal of Near Eastern Studies*, 2 (1943), 159–72
Jacobsen, T. *The Sumerian King-list*, Chicago, 1939
Kramer, S. N. *History Begins at Sumer*, New York, 1959
Lees, G. M. and Falcon, N. F. "The Geographical History of the Mesopotamian Plains", *Geographical Journal*, 118, (1952), 24–39
Perkins, A. L. *The Comparative Archaeology of Ancient Mesopotamia*, Chicago, 1949
Ur in retrospect. (Iraq, vol XXII, 1960)

CHAPTER 2

Böhl, F. M. Th. *King Hammurabi of Babylon in the Setting of his Time*, Amsterdam, 1946
Dossin, G., Kupper, J. R., and Jean, C. F. *Archives Royales de Mari*, I–VI, Paris, 1950–54
Edzard, D. O. *Die 'zweite Zwischenzeit' Babyloniens*, Weisbaden, 1957
Gelb, I. J. "The Early History of the West Semitic Peoples", *Journal of Cuneiform Studies*, 15 (1961), 27–47
Jacobsen, T. "The Reign of Ibbi-Suen", *Journal of Cuneiform Studies*, 7, (1963), 36–47
Kupper, J. R. *Les Nomades en Mésopotamie au Temps des Rois de Mari*. Paris, 1957
King, L. W. *Letters and Inscriptions of Hammurabi*, London, 1898–1900

CHAPTER 3

Driver, G. R. and Miles, Sir J. C. *The Babylonian Laws*, Vols. I and II, Oxford, 1952–55
Falkenstein, A. *Die neusumerischen Gerichtsurkunden*, Munich, 1956–57
Goetze, A. *The Laws of Eshnunna*, New Haven, 1956

Kramer, S. N. and Falkenstein, A. *Urnammu Law Code*, Orientalia 23 (1954), 40–51
Steele, F. R. "The Code of Lipit-Ishtar", *American Journal of Archaeology*, 52 (1948), 425–50

CHAPTER 4
Budge, E. A. W. and King, L. W. *Annals of the Kings of Assyria*, I, London, 1902
El-Wailly, E. J. *The Political History of the Kassite Period in Mesopotamia*, unpublished dissertation, University of Chicago, 1953
Gelb, I. J., *Hurrians and Subarians*, Chicago, 1954
Goetze, A. *Kleinasien*, Munich, 1957
Gurney, O. R. *The Hittites*, Harmondsworth, 1961
Knudtzon, J. A. *Die el-Amarna-Tafeln*, Leipzig, 1915
Luckenbill, D. D. *Ancient Records of Babylonia and Assyria*, I and II, Chicago, 1926–27
Mercer, S. A. B. *The Tell El-Amarna Tablets*, Toronto, 1939
O'Callaghan, R. T. *Aram Naharaim*, Rome, 1948
Olmstead, A. T. *History of Assyria*, Chicago, 1926
Smith, S. *Early History of Assyria to 1000 B.C.*, London, 1928

CHAPTER 5
Dougherty, R. P. *Nabonidus and Belshazzar*, New Haven, 1929
Smith, S. *Babylonian Historical Texts*, London, 1924
Smith, S. *Isaiah Chapters XL–LV*, London, 1944
Wiseman, D. J. *Chronicles of the Chaldaean Kings*, London, 1956

CHAPTER 6
Koldewey, R. *The Excavations at Babylon*, London, 1914
Parrot, A. *Babylon and the Old Testament*, London, 1958
Ravn, O. E. *Herodotus' Description of Babylon*, Copenhagen, 1942
Unger, E. *Babylon: die heilige Stadt nach der Beschreibung der Babylonier*, Berlin, 1931

CHAPTER 7
Bottéro, J. *La Religion Babylonienne*, Paris, 1952
Dhorme, E. *Les Religions de Babylonie et Assyrie*, Paris, 1949
Driver, G. R. *Semitic Writing*, Oxford, 1954
Falkenstein, A. and von Soden, W. *Sumerische und akkadische Hymnen und Gebete*, Zurich/Stuttgart, 1953
Frankfort, H. *The Art and Architecture of the Ancient Orient*, Harmondsworth, 1954
Frankfort, H. and others, *Before Philosophy*, Harmondsworth, 1949
Frankfort, H. *Cylinder Seals*, London, 1939
Frankfort, H. *Kingship and the Gods*, Chicago, 1948
Gadd, C. J. *Ideas of Divine Rule in the Ancient East*, London, 1948
Heidel, A. *The Babylonian Genesis*, Chicago, 1952

Heidel, A. *The Epic of Gilgamesh and Old Testament Parallels*, Chicago, 1946

Hooke, S. H. *Babylonian and Assyrian Religion*, London, 1953

Kramer, S. N. (ed.) *Mythologies of the Ancient World*, New York, 1961

Kramer, S. N. *Sumerian Mythology*, Philadelphia, 1944

Lambert, W. G. *Babylonian Wisdom Literature*, Oxford, 1960

Langdon, S. *The Babylonian Epic of Creation*, Oxford, 1923

Lloyd, S. *The Art of the Ancient Near East*, London, 1961

Neugebauer, O. in Singer, C. and others (eds.) *A History of Technology*, Vol. I, Oxford, 1954

Pallis, S. A. *The Babylonian Akitu-festival*, Copenhagen, 1926

Parrot, A. *Sumer*, London, 1960

Parrot, A. *Nineveh and Babylon*, London, 1961

Sandars, N. K. *The Epic of Gilgamesh*, Harmondsworth, 1960

Thompson, R. C. *The Epic of Gilgamesh*, Oxford, 1930

Wooley, Sir L. *Excavations at Ur*, London, 1954

CHAPTER 8

Bevan, E. R. *The House of Seleucus*, London, 1902

Cary, M. *A History of the Greek World, 323–146 B.C.*, London, 1959

Ghirshman, R. *Iran*, Harmondsworth, 1954

Olmstead, A. T. *History of the Persian Empire*, Chicago, 1948

Rostovtzeff, M. *Social and Economic History of the Hellenistic World*, Oxford, 1941

Tarn, W. W. and Griffith, G. T. *Hellenistic Civilisation*, London, 1959

Tarn, W. W. *Alexander the Great*, Cambridge, 1948

CHRONOLOGY

Ehrich, R. W. (ed.) *Relative Chronologies in Old World Archaeology*, Chicago, 1954

Gelb, I. J. "Two Assyrian King Lists", *Journal of Near Eastern Studies*, 13 (1954), 209–30

Meer, P. Van der, *The Chronology of Ancient Western Asia and Egypt*, 2nd edn. Leiden, 1955, new edn. in prep.

Parker, R. A. and Dubberstein, W. H. *Babylonian Chronology, 626 B.C.—A.D. 75*, Chicago, 1956

Rowton, M. B. in *Cambridge Ancient History*, New Edition, Vol. I, Chapter VI

Smith, S. *Alalakh and Chronology*, London, 1940

Index

251